# DEMANDING DEMOCRACY
## AFTER
## THREE MILE ISLAND

# DEMANDING DEMOCRACY AFTER THRE

# DATE DUE

| | | | |
|---|---|---|---|
| MAY 1 6 '00 | | | |
| | | | |
| | | | |
| | | | |
| | | | |
| | | | |
| | | | |
| | | | |
| | | | |
| | | | |
| | | | |
| | | | |
| | | | |
| | | | |
| | | | |
| | | | |
| | | | |

# DEMANDING DEMOCRACY AFTER THREE MILE ISLAND

Raymond L. Goldsteen
and John K. Schorr

University of Florida Press

Gainesville

The University of Florida Press is a member of the Univer-
sity Presses of Florida, the scholarly publishing agency of the
State University System of Florida. Books are selected for
publication by faculty editorial committees at each of Flor-
ida's nine public universities: Florida A & M University
(Tallahassee), Florida Atlantic University (Boca Raton),
Florida International University (Miami), Florida State
University (Tallahassee), University of Central Florida (Or-
lando), University of Florida (Gainesville), University of
North Florida (Jacksonville), University of South Florida
(Tampa), and University of West Florida (Pensacola).

Orders for books published by all member presses should
be addressed to University Presses of Florida, 15 Northwest
15th Street, Gainesville, FL 32611.

Library of Congress Cataloging-in-Publication Data
Goldsteen, Raymond L.
Demanding democracy after Three Mile Island /
Raymond L. Goldsteen and John K. Schorr.
p.   cm.
Includes bibliographical references and index.
ISBN 0-8130-1073-X (acid-free paper). —
ISBN 0-8130-1098-5 (pbk.)
1. Community organization—Pennsylvania—Goldsboro.
2. Community organization—Pennsylvania—Newberry
(Township)   3. Environmental policy—Pennsylvania—
Goldsboro—Citizen participation.   4. Environmental
policy—Pennsylvania—Newberry (Township)—Citizen
participation.   5. Three Mile Island Nuclear Power Plant
(Pa.)   6. Radioactive pollution—Pennsylvania—
Harrisburg Region.   7. Nuclear power plants—
Accidents—Social aspects—Pennsylvania—Harrisburg
Region.   I. Schorr, John K.   II. Title.
HN80.G65G65   1991
363.17'9—dc20        91-9806
CIP

TO KAREN AND JAN

# CONTENTS

List of Illustrations     ix

Foreword, by James P. Lester     xi

Preface     xv

Acknowledgments     xviii

**ONE**: Community Rights or Private Property?     1

**TWO**: An Ordinary Community: The Old Paradigm     5

**THREE**: Loss of Trust: The Community Transformed     16

**FOUR**: They Just Can't Do This to Us:
The Words of Middle Americans     35

**FIVE**: Mistrust Confirmed     117

**SIX**: Attempting to Restore a Sense
of Community Safety     154

**SEVEN**: Trust and the Social Contract     175

**EIGHT**: NIMBY, the New Paradigm,
and Community Justice     191

Appendix: Study Methods     225

Notes     229

Bibliography     237

Index     241

# ILLUSTRATIONS

Map
Newberry Township/Goldsboro Study Area and Vicinity xxii

Figures
1. Percent who viewed living near a nuclear power plant as dangerous 119
2. Percent who viewed TMI as dangerous 119
3. Percent who would move farther away from TMI if they could 121
4. Percent who believed their chance of getting cancer was greater because of TMI 122
5. Percent who believed children's chances of getting cancer were greater because of TMI 122
6. Average psychological distress scores for men and women, 1979–1986 126
7. Percent who reported changes in their life since the TMI accident, 1986 127
8. Relationship between mistrust, perceived threat of TMI to health and safety, and distress 128
9. Percent who mistrusted utility company officials regarding the safety of nuclear energy 151
10. Percent who believed federal officials had not been truthful about radiation dangers 152
11. Percent who mistrusted the federal government concerning safety of nuclear energy 153
12. Percent opposed to reopening TMI–Unit 1, the undamaged reactor 156

13. Percent opposed to reopening TMI–Unit 2, the damaged   157
    reactor
14. Perceived chance of community groups to keep TMI closed,   166
    1982
15. Perceived chance of community groups to keep TMI–Unit   167
    2 closed, 1986
16. Percent who favored a ban on all nuclear power plants   171
17. Satisfaction with government and faith in democratic pro-   173
    cess compared to before TMI

# FOREWORD

I AM MOST PLEASED to write a foreword to this fine volume. The book will serve a variety of readers, including students of environmental politics and policy, science and technology policy, health policy, as well as courses in democratic theory and citizen participation. It will appeal to both sociology and political science students as well as philosophy students. The book is written in a manner that will interest the general reader as well; in fact, although it is a scientific study, it reads much like a good novel about the strange technological world in which we live today.

In the last thirty years, an important transformation has taken place in American politics as far as environmental and health protection are concerned. Some of these changes are discussed in the book that follows. More specifically, we seem to be moving away from the public's implicit trust in the concept of "representative democracy" to a new form of democracy called "strong, or participatory, democracy." This has become a matter of practical necessity in view of the fact that the corporate sector, often acting in concert with local governments, has all too often favored the private interest over the public interest in decisions involving risks associated with modern technologies. Citizens are now coming to realize that they must "empower themselves" in order to overcome their disenfranchisement. Quite simply, they are "demanding democracy," as the authors of this book argue.

Goldsteen and Schorr discuss this current phenomenon by describing the "old paradigm," in which the public's faith in the social contract between themselves and their elected representatives, together with private property rights, have protected corporate America from adequate community scrutiny. They do this by focusing on one of America's most famous technological accidents—Three Mile Island. The TMI accident raises questions about our most basic expectations and values of democracy. Yet, a growing number of communities across the United States and other countries are experiencing other kinds of technological hazards, such as risks associated with hazardous waste incineration plants, toxic chemical plant explosions, hazardous waste dump leaks, underground storage tank leaks that are polluting groundwater, or other such technological hazards. Incidents like Three Mile Island, Love Canal, and Times Beach are only a few examples that are contributing to the public's changing perceptions about the nature of relationships among communities, industry, and government.

The "old paradigm" was thus characterized by a basic trust in industry, industry's assurances about technological hazards, and industry's modes of decision making. However, a transformation has now taken place in which citizens involved in technological "accidents" no longer trust the information they receive from the business community. This has developed because the public was poorly informed about the accident at TMI, because TMI's reports were contradictory, because information was withheld, and because industry and government behavior contributed to a public perception that incompetence and deception characterized TMI. Feelings developed among the public that industry would choose short-term profit over consideration of long-term effects to the environment and community health, and that government, rather than being a guardian of the public interest, would choose to support industry and its growth agenda. This mistrust on the public's part at TMI affected even their basic faith in the democratic process in the United States. Over half of the community had less faith in the democratic process by 1986 than they had prior to the TMI incident in the 1970s.

The "new paradigm," according to the authors, is one in which citizens are "demanding democracy." By this, they mean that citizens are now concerned with "collective action aimed at avoiding what happened at TMI and places like it. By stopping threats *before* they begin, communities are attempting to ensure that their members never experience the powerlessness or feel the fear, distress, anger, and bitterness of victims of technological accidents." There is a feeling that science and technology will accord communities a better life if people will interject their values into the risk assessment and decision-making process. Put simply, people must take a more active role in protecting their environmental and health interests since governments and industry have priorities that are too often inconsistent with those of the community. In the 1990s and beyond, citizens must become active agents for themselves, rather than relying on elected representatives to look out for their interests. Moreover, the move to strong democracy among the public should not be looked upon as a threat to the democratic order but rather as a great democratic movement that is entirely consistent with Thomas Jefferson's version of democracy. As the authors note, "It has the potential to redemocratize the U.S. citizenry, leading to greater participation, more scrutiny, more consensus building, and more community responsibility."

In other advanced industrial democracies, such as Sweden, this version of democracy is already in place, as citizens are involved in policy formation and conflict resolution in instances involving technological risks. Such a version of strong democracy in America could, in fact, be modeled after the Swedish "study circles" or the New England town meeting approach. In any case, the arguments in this book are much ahead of their time but provide a glimpse into what will likely develop in the latter half of this decade or in the next century. Citizens, all across America, are realizing that they must become active participants in the protection and affirmation of their interests. If they do, the future is a more optimistic one, for the politics of strong democracy is a politics of hope, rather than a council of despair.

JAMES P. LESTER
Professor of Political Science
Colorado State University
Fort Collins, Colorado

# PREFACE

THIS BOOK IS ABOUT a community transformed, a community that, because of a series of events, was forced to change its view of modern American democracy, discarding the trusting complacency of its past for a new assertiveness and deep cynicism. This change in attitude is not unique to the community studied here, in fact it has come to be known generally as the NIMBY (Not in My Back Yard) Syndrome. NIMBY represents the beginning of a fundamental, grass-roots alteration in the way Americans are viewing their democracy and their communities. Many citizens are questioning the increased risks of technological "progress" and have come to see these risks, when *imposed* on them and their communities, as fundamental threats to the democratic ideals of individual and community justice.

We document in this book the story of the citizens of a community near Three Mile Island as they sought to empower themselves and to overcome their disenfranchisement, which was made so painfully obvious by the accident and its aftermath. We have transcribed the bitterness and anger we heard in the voices of the people, and we describe their frustration as their efforts failed to keep the Three Mile Island Nuclear Power Plant closed. Again and again, we heard people recount their personal transformations from faith in the system to assertiveness and cynicism.

We have been surprised at the negative press that NIMBY has received in light of what we experienced as researchers at Three Mile Island. It has been cast as selfish, self-seeking, narrow-minded, and Luddist. We have come to view it quite differently. We now understand it as people demanding a voice in what risks are taken in their own communities, demanding a fair say in the business and governmental decisions that could have a profound effect on their and their children's health and quality of life. Quite simply, we see it as people demanding democracy.

We believe that a true democracy requires that corporations not unilaterally determine the risks that communities will take. The people affected should have the ultimate right of determination, and they are beginning to demand this right. In the past, private property, ratified by our limited concept of democracy, set corporate decisions apart from public examination or input. In exchange, corporations provided communities with a small piece of prosperity. By this bargain, corporations were legitimated in conducting their affairs in private, removed from public scrutiny. As a result, private power thrived while communities remained in the dark concerning the risks in their midst.

Democracy as espoused in our country ratified the status quo. Political parties, interest groups, and suffrage were all that interested citizens were allowed. They set no agendas, nor did they determine any policy concerning the relationship between corporations and the community.

Trust allowed communities to accept this situation. They assumed that corporations would be fair, objective, and competent. They would share the common values of the community. Public affairs would be managed honorably. Citizens accepted the view that when a community had problems, the law was the best way to ensure justice. Thus, it was a faith in the social contract, without which capitalism and democracy cannot reside together and no social order would be possible, that formed the foundation of community complacency. Embedded in the views of citizens was the passionate commitment to values and to fairness, with the law as the deciding factor. Good citizens were influenced, knowingly or unknowingly, by Enlightenment thinkers. They were taught to believe in reason; they struggled for rationalism grounded in a belief in science rather than emotion. In the long run, human rights would be protected because a rational community is a tolerant one that believes in order.

However, this "rational" relationship between community and corporation has not worked for many communities. They have not shared in the rewards; they have been deceived, their rights trampled and their concerns dismissed. Communities are learning that corporations have been allowed to represent their interests without sufficient accountability and social responsibility. They have not considered community values. They have been allowed to manipulate, interpret, and subvert community knowledge concerning safety.

People vote but corporations decide, directly or through their influence in the governmental regulatory processes. Private property rights have protected corporate America from adequate community scrutiny. In an age of large-scale hazardous technologies, these property rights have shielded industry at the expense of the communities put at risk by that technology. Three Mile Island is only one, albeit a well-known, example of this community injustice.

We believe that our nation needs to develop a new paradigm to reconcile democracy and technological risk, beginning at the local level. That is what this book is about, and we hope that the reader will see that the story of this one small community clearly illustrates the need for that new paradigm.

# ACKNOWLEDGMENTS

THIS BOOK WAS MADE possible by our involvement with the citizens of Newberry Township and Goldsboro, Pennsylvania, who mobilized shortly after the accident at Three Mile Island, forming the Newberry Township–Three Mile Island Steering Committee. One concern of members of the Steering Committee was the impact of the accident on the health of Newberry Township and Goldsboro residents. Many committee members mistrusted the information they were receiving from officials about the amount and effect of the radiation to which community residents had been exposed. Many knew women who had miscarried after the accident, and they were worried.

Thus, in June 1979 the Steering Committee formed the Newberry Township Health Committee to investigate the possible health effects of the accident and to educate community residents about its findings. The Health Committee selected Linda Dominowski and Jennifer Downey to find a researcher who would assist the committee. Both were residents of Newberry Township, but neither had been politically active before the accident, nor were they opposed to nuclear energy or Three Mile Island prior to the events of March 1979.

Dominowski and Downey approached Pennsylvania Department of Health officials and asked them to undertake an epidemiological study of the possible health effects of the accident in their community. Although the department was in fact planning to survey area residents and create a registry for future epidemiological studies, Dominowski and Downey were told that the Department of Health not only had little interest in such an investigation but believed that no study was warranted. Dominowski and Downey turned elsewhere, but they were unable to interest any researchers, including those at the nearby Hershey Medical Center, to work with the committee until they approached one of the authors of this book. Raymond Goldsteen was a collaborating researcher and contractor for the Task Group on Behavioral Effects of the President's Commission on the Accident at Three Mile Island. He also happened to be living in the Three Mile Island area at the time.

By the time Dominowski and Downey reached Goldsteen, they were surprised and discouraged by the research community's lack of interest in their project. Goldsteen was sympathetic to their situation, and he agreed to attend a meeting of the Health Committee scheduled for July 1979.

At that meeting the members of the committee impressed Goldsteen. All women, mostly married and with children, they were straightforward, open, honest, and, of course, anxious. It was plain that they were not "radicals" in any sense of that word; for most, if not all, this was their first experience with political action. Their presentation of their concerns was sincere. They explained that they did not trust the information they were receiving from utility company and government officials regarding the accident. Therefore, they were concerned about the health of their children, husbands, other relatives, and friends. They felt they were being treated as lunatics, members of a fringe group, or troublemakers because of their concerns. They were appalled, surprised, frightened, and angry at the official response to their efforts. They wanted to "do something." What they proposed was an independent health study to verify official reports. They insisted that they would accept whatever answers came from a scientific inquiry. They simply wanted to know.

Their sincere concern and principled appeal were successful in obtaining a commitment from Goldsteen to help. John Schorr, who had acted as a consultant to Goldsteen in his position as contractor for the Task Group study, volunteered to assist the committee as well. However, we told the committee that, as social scientists, we could not conduct the physical health study they wanted. Rather, we could investigate whether the committee's views regarding a health monitoring study were representative of the community. Strong community support for the study might interest another researcher or group of researchers in conducting the investigation the committee desired.

The Health Committee agreed to this plan. Between 10 September and 21 September 1979, members telephoned 284 randomly selected Newberry Township and Goldsboro residents to ascertain their support for long-term health monitoring. The results of the survey indicated that 83 percent of community residents believed that an annual medical examination for members of their community for at least ten years would be worthwhile. Seventy-two percent said they would participate in such a project.

Although the Steering Committee publicized the results of this survey, they were unable to convince other researchers to conduct the health monitoring study that they wanted. However, the extent of concern among Newberry Township and Goldsboro residents did interest us in continuing to work with the committee. We volunteered to conduct a study similar to that which the Behavioral Effects Task Group had conducted for the President's Commission. Since neither the Steering Committee nor the Health Committee had the funds to pay for such an undertaking, Goldsteen trained volunteers from the community to conduct the interviews, and he supervised the data collection. We presented a final report to the Health Committee in 1980.

Between 1980 and 1986 we conducted four more surveys in the Newberry Township and Goldsboro community. Neither the Steering Committee nor the Health Committee tangibly assisted us, although their members approved of our efforts. We continued our studies because we believed it was important to record and attempt to understand a community whose reactions to an event were so strong and long-lived. This book is the result of those years of investigation and efforts to understand.

This book was inspired by the people of Newberry Township and Goldsboro whose values and concern for their community we came to admire.

We also wish to thank the following people who read our manuscript and offered helpful comments: Nancy Robinson and Karen Goldsteen, Ph.D. candidates in the Department of Health and Safety Studies, University of Illinois, and Laurna Rubinson and Warwick Armstrong, faculty members at the University of Illinois. Thanks go to Bruce Bradford of Stetson University's Geography Department for cartographic assistance and to Charles Vedder and Joel Wright of the Sociology Department at Stetson for their useful advice.

Also thanks to our editor, Phillip Martin, at the University of Florida Press and the staff at the University Presses of Florida for their unwavering support of this project throughout its development. Their professionalism was most admired and appreciated.

We would like to dedicate this book to our wives, Karen Sullinger Goldsteen and Jan Meyer Schorr, our most demanding critics but also our most steadfast supporters, and to our children, Jonathan, Benjamin, and Sune Goldsteen and Jennifer and Anne Schorr, who grew up watching us work on this book.

# NEWBERRY TOWNSHIP/GOLDSBORO STUDY AREA AND VICINITY

HARRISBURG

10 miles

MIDDLETOWN

5 miles

GOLDSBORO

THREE MILE ISLAND

NEWBERRY TOWNSHIP

Susquehanna River

Harrisburg ★

# ONE

## COMMUNITY RIGHTS OR
## PRIVATE PROPERTY?

UNTIL 28 MARCH 1979, Three Mile Island was in all respects an ordinary nuclear power plant operated by an ordinary utility company, Metropolitan Edison, a subsidiary of General Public Utilities, based in New Jersey. The plant was neither the largest nor the smallest nuclear plant, considered neither the safest nor the least safe. Metropolitan Edison was neither the richest utility company nor the poorest, neither the most progressive nor the most backward. Early that spring morning, however, a series of events within the Unit 2 reactor changed the commonplace image of the Three Mile Island power plant, Metropolitan Edison, and the nuclear power industry, perhaps forever. Equipment failure and errors in judgment led to the worst nuclear accident in the history of commercial nuclear power in the United States. Only the accident at the Chernobyl nuclear power plant in the Soviet Union exceeded the accident at Three Mile Island in amount of radioactivity released, nearness to a "meltdown," and extent of public scrutiny and concern.

From the vantage point of 1991, the story of the Three Mile Island accident might be told as a technological chronicle, the tale of a technology and its industry that unwillingly and unwittingly exchanged its image of stability and respectability for one of instability and disrepute and that then fought back, gaining the grudging tolerance it has today.

However, this book does not recount the history of the nuclear power industry since the Three Mile Island accident. Rather, it traces the drama that occurred in the hearts and minds of the people living in a community nearby. Our account tells of the accident's effect on the residents of Newberry Township and Goldsboro, Pennsylvania, adjoining towns forming a community in which most people live within seven miles of Three Mile Island (see map). For simplicity, we will refer to the community formed by Newberry Township and the Borough of Goldsboro as Newberry throughout the rest of the book.

More than ten years later, why should we care about the effects of the Three Mile Island accident on residents of a nearby community? After all, we live in a world of danger. Nuclear power plant accidents are not the most deadly of these dangers. Aircraft or automobile accidents cause more loss of life each year than all commercial nuclear power accidents combined. Floods destroy entire communities; usually no books are written about the people affected. Homelessness is increasing, and many homeless die each year from exposure and malnutrition. Poverty and drug use cause thousands of deaths every year. We are even threatened by infectious diseases today as the AIDS epidemic demonstrates. Millions of people live in conditions that could be described as disastrous.

Yet we suggest that this story about the Three Mile Island accident raises questions worthy of the attention of policy makers and the general public because they concern our most basic expectations and values. What rights does a community have with regard to risk taking? Should these rights be subordinate to corporate rights? Does progress require communities to live with risks that they do not wish to accept? Who should determine the risks a community takes? Whose risk assessments should be adopted? These are the questions that this study forces us to ask.

While our subject was a community adjacent to the Three Mile Island nuclear plant, the study's implications go beyond nuclear power plant accidents. A growing number of communities in the United States and other countries have experienced or are exposed to such technological hazards as chemical plant gas releases, hazardous waste dump leaks or infiltration, and natural gas storage tank explosions. We believe that our study of one community's response to the Three Mile Island accident raises issues common to all communities at risk.

Moreover, the experiences of these communities have touched other communities as well, resulting in a general mistrust of industry and government regarding their commitment to community health and safety. The NIMBY (Not in My Back Yard) Syndrome is the result. NIMBY actions are not isolated from each other or unrelated to events like the accident at Three Mile Island. NIMBY responses reflect a crisis in legitimacy in which both government and industry are suspect. Three Mile Island has actually had an enormous effect on society by contributing to changing public perceptions about relationships between communities, industry, and government. Our narrative links the community and industry stories.

The cornerstone of change is a belief that power must shift to the community. The end result of change, we argue, should be democratization of risk-taking and inclusion of views that will advance the quality of life for future generations as well as our own.

## COMMUNITIES

David Price has discussed communitarianism and its relationship to public policy:

> What thinkers ranging from Burke and Tocqueville to Hegel and Marx articulated was a conviction that liberalism had radically underestimated the individual's dependence on the social environments that nurtured and conditioned him for his very definition of self; that what Wolff would term a "private" value, whether "simple" or "compound," was an abstraction which at best gave a partial and distorted representation of the goods people sought in society; and that a major task confronting modern social theory was to illumine the dialectic of dependence-independence that the self experiences in relation to its social/cultural environment. The liberal idea of an autonomous individual, fully formed outside of society and voluntarily entering into, or tacitly honoring, a compact in order to secure private values, was regarded as an empirical and ethical absurdity.[1]

We take a communitarian view in this book in the sense that we believe the community is a reality and that the people living in it recognize that reality. The community is more than the sum of the individuals who make it up. As Max Weber said, "A social relationship will be called 'communal' if and so far as the orientation of social action . . . is based on a subjective feeling of the parties, whether affectual or traditional, that they belong together."[2]

We believe we observed "communitarianism" or "communality" in Newberry. Residents had a sense that they belonged together, that they were part of a group, with respect to the accident. They would speak of "us" and "we." They had a strong sense that they were "in this together."

This perception radiated from immediate family to extended family to others in the community. The bonds were strongest within a family. A resident might say, for example, "It's my child (or grandchild) I am most worried about." But residents also generalized beyond the family to the community at large and asked, "What about the children?" Irrespective of the strength of the bond, they perceived a link between themselves and others in the community.

A community is not just a place where we reside. Our private lives take place within its context, and it sets the parameters for what we have and what we can expect in our private lives. We cannot live in safety if our community is rife with drug dealers and their clients. We would not expect liberal educational practices in schools if residents of the community were predominantly fundamentalist. The community constrains or frees us depending upon the fit between individual and community values.

One role of the community is to maximize the quality of life for its residents as they define that quality. Although they may differ according to individual values, we suspect that one attribute universally desired in communities is a safe and healthy environment. This is our point of departure in the story of Newberry between 19 April 1968, when the Atomic Energy Commission issued a "non-contested" permit to Metropolitan Edison for the construction of the Unit 1 reactor on Three Mile Island, and June 1986, one year after the restart of the Unit 1 reactor, when we last surveyed residents of the community about their attitudes toward the accident and the events of the years that followed.

# TWO

## AN ORDINARY COMMUNITY: THE OLD PARADIGM

PEOPLE REACT TO EVENTS based on what they value and what they expect from the future. They dislike events that they perceive undermine or threaten what they believe is important. If events cause the loss of something valued, a host of adverse emotions may follow, including anger, sadness, and shock, and even psychological distress or physical illness. If these events are unexpected, reactions may be stronger and more long-lived than if they were anticipated. In this respect, the residents of Newberry were no different from anyone else. To understand their reactions to the Three Mile Island accident, it is necessary to know about their values, about how their life in Newberry before the accident conformed to their values, and about their expectations for community life.

### THE PHYSICAL ENVIRONMENT

Newberry is on the outskirts of the metropolitan area that has Harrisburg, Pennsylvania, as its hub. Harrisburg is located on the eastern shore of the Susquehanna River. In 1979 it was the slightly decaying seat of the state government of Pennsylvania. The downtown bustled during the day. To a large extent public money fueled this economic activity.

The state government was the largest employer, while suppliers of services to the government accounted for the employment of the next largest group. At the end of the work day, employees left the central city for their homes in the neighborhoods of the city or in the suburbs. The business district was quiet on weeknights as well as on weekends.

Harrisburg was beset on a small scale by all of the problems of older urban areas in America. Housing, schooling, and job opportunities were poor for a significantly large black population. Many elderly people had no desire or ability to leave the city where they had lived most or all of their lives. Pockets of well-to-do city dwellers in splendorous old homes dotted the riverfront and middle-class enclaves, members of the old families who never forsook the city or young people rediscovering the benefits of a life their parents had left for the suburbs. However, a large portion of the city's residents lived in poverty or near poverty, in decaying housing and with inadequate basic services—police, fire, schools, libraries, and transportation. Worst of all, perhaps, was the sense of a deteriorating social order, indicated by the city's crime and substance abuse rates.

The Susquehanna River was the area's dominant geographic feature. Following the river south from Harrisburg along its eastern shore were the run-down steel mills of Steelton and Highspire, operating at a much lower capacity than in the past. At night the mills were lit from inside by the fires of the furnaces, whose light cast eerie shadows on the rail lines, slag heaps, and old railway cars surrounding the buildings and hid the decay so evident during the day.

On the whole, however, the economic fortunes of the Harrisburg area were rising. Shopping malls and new tract housing covered many of the area's hillsides. Interstate highways 76, 81, and 83 passed and connected within ten miles of the central business district of Harrisburg and were viewed by the business community as the impetus for the area's revival as a transportation and distribution center. Residents often promoted the region by directing attention to Harrisburg's proximity to four major cities—four hours from New York, two hours from Philadelphia, two-and-one-half hours from Baltimore, and about three hours from Washington, D.C.

The road that headed west from Harrisburg crossed the Harvey Taylor Bridge and passed through the old suburbs on the way to the newly suburbanized towns of Mechanicsburg and New Cumberland. Many of the younger, more affluent people of the area lived here. They were the optimists; many of them had grown up in the area when it was declining. In 1979, they were benefiting from the prosperity brought by new businesses attracted to the area by its location and relatively low-cost labor force.

Interstate 83, which headed south along the western shore of the Susquehanna, led to Newberry Township and Goldsboro, where New-berry's two-lane roads wound through a tranquil world of rolling hills, fields, and stone or brick farmhouses sitting back off the road. Some homes were in good repair, some decrepit. Most were surrounded by a small grove of trees with a few outbuildings past which a dirt road meandered on its way to the house itself. Much of the township was fenced pasture land where dairy cows or horses grazed. Many areas were wooded, and there overhanging trees cooled the hot roads in summer.

Commerce in Newberry Township was limited to an occasional con-venience store or gas station near the interstate. In 1979 other recent building included a number of small housing developments, an inelegant golf club, an unpretentious township building, a scattering of small fire stations, an elementary school, and several trailer parks. The houses in the developments were modest ranch style or split-level homes, lovingly cared for, whose trees and shrubbery had not matured enough to soften their lines and blend them into the landscape. Still, the rural countryside dominated Newberry Township.

In the spring, this area of Central Pennsylvania was particularly beau-tiful. The farmers were preparing for spring planting, and the smell of fresh-turned earth was so rich that one did not have to be a farmer to sense that this was one of the finer places on earth to plant. Later in the year, the produce to prove it filled the farmers' markets—sweet corn, tomatoes, squashes of all varieties, peaches, potatoes, and berries.

Central Pennsylvania differed from other areas of agricultural abun-dance. While the prairies of the midwest are overwhelmingly vast, here lay a sense of intimacy with the land. Fields were smaller, and vistas broken up by hillsides, streams, and woodlands. Nothing but the river was so big that it could not be grasped.

The Borough of Goldsboro, on the shores of the Susquehanna, was left over from the time when this area was a vacation spot. Two images immediately impressed a visitor rounding the hillside on the one road leading into town. The first was the sense of Goldsboro's isolation from progress. The tiny town had only a post office, a diner, and several small retail stores. On a narrow gravel road along the river and to the south, large, old summer homes lined the shore, mostly two- and three-story frame houses with the look of summer about them—green lawns shaded by old oaks and maples. It was easy to picture vacationers playing Par-cheesi or Scrabble on the broad, woody-smelling screened porches and people in wicker rocking chairs passing a quiet summer evening with friends and family on the front porch.

It was Goldsboro's second image that kept it from seeming like a town from the past. Only one-and-one-half miles across the river was the Three Mile Island nuclear power plant, its four immense cooling towers looming over the town, dwarfing everything by comparison.

The towers were visible not just from the river but from the homes of many residents even outside of Goldsboro—no home in Newberry Township was more than ten miles from Three Mile Island and most were within five miles. Although Middletown is widely thought to be the community closest to the power plant (perhaps because the only bridge to the island is there), Newberry Township and Goldsboro are nearer (see map). And regardless of whether or not the towers were visible from one's home, they came repeatedly into sight when traveling in the township. Nearly every road at one hilltop or another afforded a clear view of them, especially after the leaves had fallen.

When the plant was operating, huge clouds of steam, visible for at least ten miles, poured out of the towers. Also, Metropolitan Edison and the Nuclear Regulatory Commission had placed warning sirens and dosimeters on various hilltops in the community. The relationship with the power plant at Three Mile Island was even more intimate for people living in Goldsboro and some parts of Newberry Township who were able to hear the immense turbines shutting down and starting up and the warning bells that signaled problems at the plant.

Mostly, Newberry was a physically beautiful community of farmland, pastures, and woods dotted with homes and a few public buildings. The nuclear power plant at Three Mile Island was the major anomaly in Newberry's landscape: four huge concrete towers rising out of the middle of the river and visible from much of the community whenever one looked east.

## THE PEOPLE

The Newberry area was first settled by Quakers in the early eighteenth century,[1] and in 1979, many residents were descendants of these early farm families. Before the opening of Interstate 83, much of the western shore of the Susquehanna, unlike the eastern shore, remained rural. However, as growth rates suggest, the area was undergoing suburbanization in 1979. In 1980 the population of the area was 10,524, according to the U.S. census.[2] The Borough of Goldsboro was the smaller of the two communities with a population of 477 in 1980, down 17 percent from its 1970 population of 576. Newberry Township, on the other hand, grew rapidly from 5,978 in 1970 to 10,047 in 1980, a growth rate of 68 percent. This growth was especially noteworthy when one considers that Pennsylvania grew at less than 1 percent in the same period and the Harrisburg metropolitan area at only 9 percent.[3] After the accident at Three Mile Island, the community continued to grow but at a slower rate; Newberry Township increased by 7 percent and Goldsboro by 10 percent between 1980 and 1984.[4]

Based on our sample of residents of Newberry, the average adult had lived in the community for almost fifteen years, giving a stable community base for the newcomers. Nine out of ten residents were married; 86 percent had children, and of these 28 percent had children under six years of age. The average age of adults was forty-four, and they tended to be housewives if they were women and blue-collar workers if they were men. Seventy-one percent had graduated from high school. The sample interviewed was similar to 1980 U.S. Census data for the area in marital status, education, age, and percentage of families with children under six, a correspondence that suggests this was a representative group (see appendix).

At the time of the accident, most newcomers lived in the new housing developments, where children provided the dominant theme with their Big Wheel toys, their tricycles and bicycles, their dogs and rabbit cages and fishing gear. One could sense people's aspirations for a good home in which to raise a family, which among these middle-class Americans meant a place removed from the city with its crime, drug use, and street influence; a place where children rode bicycles, fished, and cared for pets; a place where the air was clean and farm life still exerted its wholesome and stable influence on the community; a place where children played baseball and attended scout meetings; a place where schools emphasized discipline and a traditional curriculum; a place where family life was highly valued.

Newcomers to Newberry wanted to direct their lives, and they had chosen this semirural community as their destination. They had rejected the hustle and bustle of the city, such as it was, for the quiet of Newberry. They had foregone many of the amenities of the suburbs closer to Harrisburg. Shopping for all kinds of goods including food, clothing, and other household needs meant a trip. Fewer opportunities existed for piano, dancing, and swimming lessons for children. Sporting events, theaters, and restaurants were farther away. The new residents of Newberry had exchanged these advantages of the closer suburbs for what they perceived as a better physical and social environment for their children and themselves.

Newcomers did not differ markedly from long-time residents in the importance they placed on these values. Old-timers were models for newer residents who admired the values of rural people and aspired to pass these on to their children rather than what they perceived as the more corrupt values of urban America.

In general, then, both long-time residents and newcomers were people of traditional values who placed responsibility for their families first. The term "Middle Americans" describes Newberrians well: fairly well-educated, fairly well-off married people living in a rural suburb of a medium-sized city. They owned their own homes, had children, went to church, and voted Republican. They were not trendy: but if they did change, they were unlikely to cast off the new very easily. They were not inclined to rash or radical statements or behavior.

However, the people of Newberry neither rejected nor feared technological advances and accepted their blessings wholeheartedly. Their homes were equipped with dishwashers, washing machines, dryers, and other household appliances to the extent that the family budget allowed. It was also apparent in conversation that residents did not object, a priori, to technological advances in the home or the workplace. The key to their satisfaction with Newberry was that they perceived the community as combining that which was desirable in both the past and the present—many of the social values of the past as well as the essential modern conveniences.

Residents thought of Newberry as a safe place to live, a haven. Prior to the accident, a Newberrian might have referred to the community's lack of crime or drug problems to substantiate this view. However, the implicit vision was that this was a safe community in every way—socially and environmentally. "Nothing could happen in Newberrytown," was the half-joking, half-serious response of one resident to a question about the safety of Newberry before the accident.

Moreover, they were secure in their belief that Newberry would remain a haven. They believed they had insulated themselves and their families from the worst dangers of modern life. The presence of the nuclear power plant at Three Mile Island did not discourage this view. The building of the plant had little or no impact on Newberrians' sense of safety and well-being.

## HISTORY AND PUBLIC PERCEPTION OF THREE MILE ISLAND BEFORE THE ACCIDENT

Three Mile Island is located in the Susquehanna River in the center of the Susquehanna River basin about ten miles from Harrisburg, surrounded in 1979 by pastoral south-central Pennsylvania countryside. The foothills of the Allegheny Mountains lie to the north, the rich farmland of Lancaster and York counties to the south. The island had been owned by Metropolitan Edison (Met Ed, as it was called by the people it served) since shortly after the turn of the century. At various times, the utility leased parcels of land on the island to local farmers, and the island was the destination of picnickers, fishermen, birdwatchers, and collectors of Indian artifacts until its selection as the site of a nuclear-powered electric generating plant in 1965.[5]

By all accounts, Metropolitan Edison's decision to develop Three Mile Island as the site of its first such plant met with little resistance in the region. The Nuclear Regulatory Commission's (NRC) Special Inquiry Group reported that "preliminary hearings were virtually devoid of rancor; there were no charges of landgrabbing, no residential dislocations. Some farmers and dairymen were apprehensive about the possible effects of radioactive releases from the plant, but this seemed hardly more ominous than the potential smog and soot from a fossil fuel plant."[6] The only evidence we were able to find of an organized antinuclear action in Newberry prior to the accident was the 30 April 1977 demonstration at the riverfront landing in Goldsboro by approximately 100 protesters who released balloons to symbolize the danger of drifting radiation. We learned, however, in many of our interviews with community residents, that probably none of these demonstrators were local residents. Given the nature of the community, we have no reason to doubt that this was true.

Two nuclear reactors were built on the island. In 1966, Metropolitan Edison announced its plan to build the first reactor, Unit 1. An uncontested construction permit was issued to the utility in 1968, and operation began early in the 1970s. Unit 2 began commercial operation on 31 December 1978 although it had been operating on a precommercial basis since March 1978. Metropolitan Edison operated both reactors and jointly owned them with the Pennsylvania Electric Company and the Jersey Central Power and Light Company. Each of these three companies was a subsidiary of General Public Utilities (GPU), an electric utility holding company with headquarters in New Jersey.

Prior to the accident of March 1979, Metropolitan Edison's Communication Services Department was the region's principal source of information about the status of Three Mile Island and nuclear energy in general. The department issued two types of news releases to the media. The first, a general press release, originated in the Communication Services Department and covered such varied topics as rate hearings and retirements or promotions within the company. The second, a weekly TMI press release, described the status of operations at Three Mile Island. Written by junior-level engineers following a rigid format, each weekly release was carefully reviewed by the vice president for generation before being issued to the news media through Communications Services.[7]

Although they were issued with perfect regularity and in some detail about serious problems occurring at the plant, these weekly releases had the effect of reassuring the public regarding the plant's safety. They were written in highly technical language that was difficult for the layperson to understand. Occurrences were reported without context, making it impossible for an untrained individual to determine their significance. Finally, the format specified that each release "contain something constructive and give a positive impression."[8]

The weekly TMI press releases were sent to reporters and editors of the regional newspapers as well as to the Harrisburg bureaus of the Associated Press and United Press International. They were poorly understood by those to whom they were sent. In retrospect, reporters viewed them as unsatisfactory but lulling sources of information because of their reassurances that the events reported posed no danger to the public and that Metropolitan Edison was in control. If the papers printed these releases at all, they usually inserted them almost verbatim as fillers.[9]

In addition, the Communications Services Department administered a community relations program. The master plan for this program was first drafted in 1965, one year before Metropolitan Edison announced its intention to construct a nuclear plant at Three Mile Island. The plan, which the company followed over the years, affirmed the importance of communicating the benefits of nuclear power to young people and of reassuring the public about the cleanliness and safety of nuclear energy. To this end, the public relations staff prepared and distributed pronuclear educational materials to regional schools and civic and business organizations, scheduled speeches by Metropolitan Edison officials at community gatherings, and maintained a pronuclear slide show and display at an observation center near the island.

On the whole, the regional media offered little to counter the utility's view of nuclear energy. Newspaper coverage emphasized the kinds of events reported in the general news releases. No independent investigations were mounted of the status of the plant or the events reported in the weekly news releases. Broadcast media coverage of Three Mile Island events and nuclear energy in general was rare.

The view of nuclear energy and Three Mile Island presented by Metropolitan Edison was generally accepted by the people in the area. Antinuclear sentiment was minimal. The *Report of the Public's Right to Information Task Force to the President's Commission on the Accident at*

*Three Mile Island* stated that "few local residents supported the anti-nuclear groups operating in the Harrisburg-Middletown area. 'Most people around the area considered them a bunch of radicals,' said the Associate Editor of the *Middletown Press and Journal*." The task force concluded that, "by and large, Met Ed's intensive efforts to assure its customers of the safety and non-polluting nature of nuclear power were accepted with few questions."[10]

Our research confirms these conclusions. Nearly everyone we interviewed reported that they were unconcerned about the siting of the nuclear power plant on Three Mile Island. "It was only a name," one woman said. "We had no idea what they were doing out there or how they were doing it." By all accounts, this was precisely how most people in the community reacted. Another resident said about the building of the nuclear plant on the island:

Yeah, I never gave it a thought. I didn't know what it was. I mean, when they said atomic plant, that's what it was out there. . . . What did we know. We saw it out there, and people came and we'd visit, and we'd go past and they'd say, "What's that?" "Oh, that's the Three Mile Island, the atomic plant." That's all we knew. It was a name.

Another woman reported:

To tell you the truth, I really didn't give it a whole lot of thought before [the accident]. I didn't know the dangers. I knew it was there. But I really didn't know the dangers and everything. I felt that it was, you know, safe until the whole accident came out. I just didn't know the seriousness of nuclear [energy]. That's when I finally got educated to it, really. [I wasn't antinuclear before] because I didn't know anything about it.

As we said, many people in Newberry could see the plant from their homes. Even most of these people were unconcerned. One woman told us:

It never bothered me. I knew it was there. We can see it when we drive in our lane. All the leaves are on the trees now. But in the fall when you pull in the lane, go up the little knob there, and look down, it's quite a view. I think it's about a mile and a half. And we can look out the bedroom window and see the red light

when there are no leaves on the trees. . . . But it didn't upset me.
You know, it was just there. No, I thought these people who
fussed about them [nuclear power plants] were all kooks.

Many people in the area boated and fished in the Susquehanna, and
before the accident, they did not fear going near the island. One resident
expressed a typical view.

I didn't realize the danger. I thought it was safe. Well, we have a
place down the river, a little place where we can take our boat
over on one of the islands. And we used to go past the island
when they were building TMI, and it never gave me another
thought. We'd go past there, and they were getting up the cooling
towers at the time, and remark how large they were, you know.
And we never even gave it a second thought. I always thought
nuclear energy was safe. Really safe. . . . The way they talked
about it, it was so safe. Why it had those big thick cement walls,
you know, to contain the gases and the radioactivity, and it never
dawned on me.

Another boater made this comment.

We boated down there. We had a summer place down on Hill Island, and we used to boat all around there all summer long, right
around the power plant, like thirty feet out from shore. We used
to take the people down and show them. "Yeah, this is Three
Mile Island. Look at the lights. It looks like the Wizard of Oz,"
and all this garbage.

Before the accident, there seems to have been more awe of the plant
than hatred or fear. One man, who later became a leader in the anti-
restart movement, told us that he, like many residents, was proud of the
technological achievement that the nuclear plant represented. Prior to
the accident, he took all of his visitors to Three Mile Island. He described
leading tours past the plant and making comparisons and allusions to the
pyramids of Egypt.

## SUMMARY

Before the accident at Three Mile Island, Newberry was a community
that would have been considered a physical and social haven by many
Americans. It was within one-half hour of an urban center that provided

opportunities for shopping, cultural and sporting events, higher education, and employment. Yet it was far enough away to insulate its members from the undesirable aspects of the city and its closer suburbs: crowding, congested roads, pollution, violence, drug use, and poverty.

Newberrians were secure in their belief that Newberry would remain a good place to live. They had no fear that their community would become anything but what it was: a safe and healthy environment, physically and socially. For the most part, fear of corporate despoilment of their environment was not an issue. Rather, people were wrestling with the issues of prosperity, and they were more vigilant about social values in the community than about health and safety.

The presence of the nuclear power plant on Three Mile Island did not dissuade most people from the view that Newberry was a safe community. Both those who lived there when Metropolitan Edison announced its intention to site a nuclear power plant on Three Mile Island and those who moved to Newberry later were unconcerned. They believed the assurances of the local utility company that nuclear energy was safe and the plant was well run. They slept peacefully and went about their daily activities without fear.

The people of Newberry had accepted the old paradigm. By and large, they trusted industry, especially local industries, regarding community health and safety; they accepted industry's public assurances and private decision making. They felt reasonably confident that their valued way of life in this beautiful community was not threatened by corporate decisions regarding health and safety. Newberrians saw no reason to alter the passive relationship that had developed between communities and industry.

The people of Newberry were not so naive as to completely trust all other individuals and organizations before the accident. As many political scientists argue, a certain amount of mistrust is both natural and desirable. The important question is not whether any mistrust existed among the members of the Newberry community but whether the level of mistrust was abnormally high, especially concerning nuclear power. Although they may have been influenced by a growing societal tendency to mistrust industry,[11] we feel safe in asserting that this trend had not affected Newberrians' view of Metropolitan Edison and certainly not of the Nuclear Regulatory Commission or other proponents of nuclear power. There was no reason to suspect in early 1979 that mistrust would develop as it did after the accident at Three Mile Island.

# THREE

## LOSS OF TRUST:
## THE COMMUNITY TRANSFORMED

WHAT OCCURRED TO cause the development of mistrust of Metropolitan Edison, nuclear power proponents, and nuclear regulatory officials after the accident at Three Mile Island? In the account of the period between 28 March and 11 April 1979 that follows, we describe the accident itself, the flow of information to the public about the accident, and the community's immediate reactions to the accident. The first section documents the seriousness of the accident and the second the discrepancies between information released to the public and actual events occurring within the plant during the accident. The last section details the immediate impact of the accident on Newberrians. It was in the events of this period that mistrust had its beginnings.

### THE ACCIDENT

The accident at Three Mile Island began on Wednesday, 28 March 1979, at a few seconds after 4:00 A.M. with the failure of a Unit 2 polisher—a water-softening device designed to remove minerals from the system that supplied water to the steam generators. It was the first in a series of equipment failures that in combination with errors in judgment by plant personnel led to the most serious accident at a commercial nuclear power plant in this country.

The President's Commission stated in October 1979 that "the accident at Three Mile Island, in a very real sense, continues and will continue until the years-long cleanup of TMI-2 is completed."[1] However, the period between 28 March and 11 April 1979 might be called the initial or crisis phase of the accident. It is this period for which we will summarize both technical and public information events.

A pressurized water reactor such as Three Mile Island's Unit 2 has two fundamental systems, one that produces heat and one that generates steam. The heat-producing system is nuclear-powered. The process of generating electricity in a pressurized water reactor involves producing heat that converts water into steam that in turn powers electricity-producing turbines. The medium of heat transfer is the water that passes through two closed systems of pipes: (1) the reactor coolant system, or primary loop in which the water receives heat as it circulates past the reactor; and (2) the feedwater system, or secondary loop in which the water acquires heat as it circulates around the pipes of the primary loop.

In a normally functioning plant, nuclear fission within the reactor heats water that is pumped through the primary loop into the steam-generating system. In the steam generator, the heat of the primary loop is transferred through the walls of the pipes to the cooler water in the steam generator. The process of heat transfer within the steam generator serves two purposes. First, it converts the cooler water in the secondary loop into steam, which moves to the steam turbine; the steam turbine turns the power generator, producing electricity. Second, it cools the intensely hot water coming from the reactor so that after transferral this same water is recirculated through the reactor to begin the cycle again.

The heat transfer process in the reactor also has a dual function. It transfers heat from the reactor to the steam generator, and it removes the heat from the fuel rods undergoing nuclear fission in the reactor, thereby stabilizing the temperature in the reactor.

A loss-of-coolant accident (LOCA) is an accident in which the reactor loses its supply of cooling water. A LOCA is potentially the most serious of accidents that can occur at a nuclear power plant. If the core of a plant were to remain without coolant for an extended period of time, it would overheat and "melt" the steel container that houses it. If an accident of this sort were to occur, the barriers between the radioactivity contained in the reactor core and the atmosphere would be gone. Although the Three Mile Island accident was a LOCA, fortunately the core was not uncovered sufficiently long to destroy the reactor vessel.

"In the parlance of the electric power industry, a 'trip' means that a piece of machinery stops operating."[2] The accident at the Unit 2 reactor began with the "trip" of the feedwater pumps supplying water to the steam generators. While a backup feedwater system existed to continue the flow of water to the steam generators should such an event occur, the valves controlling these auxiliary systems were inexplicably closed on the morning of 28 March. The result was the loss of water to the steam generators resulting in their "trip," an automatic safety function of the plant.

When the steam generators stopped, so did the removal of the intense heat being generated by the reactor. Pressure built in this system as the rapidly heating water expanded. However, another automatic safety feature was designed to manage such an emergency. A pilot-operated relief valve, or PORV, opened, and steam and water began flowing out of the reactor coolant system to relieve the pressure. "Pressure continued to rise, however, and 8 seconds after the first pump tripped, TMI-2's reactor, as it was designed to do—scrammed: its control rods automatically dropped down into the reactor core to halt its nuclear fission."[3]

Although the scram ended the generation of new heat, the decaying radioactive materials left from the fission process continued to heat the water in the primary loop. But with the PORV open, pressure quickly dropped into the normal range in the reactor coolant system. Only thirteen seconds had elapsed from the first trip of the feedwater pumps to the drop of pressure in the reactor coolant system. Until that point, the reactor system had responded normally to the trip within the steam generating system. However, a subsequent event transformed what might have been a "minor inconvenience"[4] into a serious accident.

The President's Commission has determined that thirteen seconds into the accident the PORV should have closed in response to decreasing pressure within the primary loop. "A light on the control room panel indicated that the electric power that opened the PORV had gone off, leading the operators to assume the valve had shut."[5] In fact, the valve had not closed.

Subsequently, the control room panel indicators began providing information to the operators which they could not understand. Falling pressure in the reactor coolant system due to the open PORV signaled the automatic high pressure injection (HPI) pumps to pour about one thousand gallons of water a minute into the system. Water levels began to rise. But the operators assumed the PORV had closed, and therefore, indications that pressure continued to fall and that temperatures remained constant appeared inexplicable. Because they did not understand the nature of the event, the operators responded to its symptoms. They stopped the flow of water into the reactor coolant system from the HPI pumps because the rising level of water at that point indicated that the system might soon be "solid"—filled with water—a condition they had been trained to avoid. This was the final error that led to the loss-of-coolant accident.

With the PORV stuck open allowing for the release of steam and the shut-off of replacement water to the system, the water that remained was quickly turned to steam by the heat remaining in the reactor. This steam escaped through the PORV.

During the two hours and twenty-two minutes the valve remained open, the core was uncovered and the principal core damage took place. A partial meltdown had occurred.

What happens is that the hot upper parts of the core, now uncovered, are bathed in steam rising from the boiling activity around the water-covered lower core region. The steam is, of course, just water vapor, made of hydrogen and oxygen, $H_2O$. A chemical reaction takes place between the very hot zirconium alloy from which the fuel rod cladding is made, and the steam. At those temperatures, the zirconium cladding voraciously grabs the oxygen from the $H_2O$ steam, becoming zirconium oxide and liberating hydrogen gas.

This weakens the fuel cladding, which ruptures and leads to release of radioactive material from the fuel rods into the water, and will later result in serious collapse of parts of the core. For now, the reaction is making hydrogen by the bucketful. . . .

Subsequent analysis suggests that the loosened core elements, whose zirconium alloy cladding had been weakened by the earlier chemical reaction with hot steam, suddenly fell into a jumbled pile near the middle of the core, forming a solid crustlike layer at the top of the pile that seems to have blocked the upward-moving flow of coolant water. Without that flow, a steam bubble probably formed just below the hardened crust, allowing still more zirconium to heat up and oxidize, embrittling still more fuel cladding further down.[6]

Shortly after the HPI pumps were turned off, the radioactive steam that escaped through the PORV was trapped and condensed in the containment building housing the reactor core. When sufficient water had accumulated, the sump pump in the floor of the containment building activated automatically to remove the water to an auxiliary building. Here the radioactive gases began escaping into the environment through leaks in the equipment in the auxiliary building.

Meanwhile, the control room personnel, including staff from the Nuclear Regulatory Commission (NRC) regional office sent to assist, remained unaware of the true nature of the accident until much later in the day. The mind-set in the control room was that the control panel instruments were generating signals that made no sense. All signals that a LOCA was in progress were misinterpreted. Even after the discovery of the open PORV, the accident was not correctly diagnosed. The operators were even unable to determine what information to transmit to nuclear authorities outside the control room who probably would have interpreted the situation correctly.

Throughout that Wednesday, control room personnel continued to react to the alarming symptoms of the accident. Shortly before 7:00 A.M. a site emergency was declared as the result of high radiation levels in the containment and auxiliary buildings. At 7:24 A.M. the station manager declared a general emergency, a condition that publicly admits the possibility of off-site radiation. Finally, without full knowledge of what had occurred, the control room personnel closed the PORV. Several hours later they restarted the HPI pumps. At 7:50 P.M. on Wednesday they restarted the coolant pumps to circulate water in the reactor coolant system. This put the reactor into the forced-cooling mode, at high pressure, and ended the first and most serious phase of the accident.

The President's Commission states that on Thursday "a sense of betterment, if not well-being, was the spirit for much of the day. Radiation levels remained high at points within the auxiliary building, but off-site readings indicated no problems."[7] Only the problem of discharging radioactive water from the plant into the Susquehanna River disturbed the relative calm.

However, by Friday, some knowledge of the events that led to the accident and the extent of damage to the core became known. On that day, plant personnel released a large volume of radioactive gases into the atmosphere, and some Nuclear Regulatory Commission officials in Washington began to speculate that the hydrogen gas, or bubble, trapped in the reactor might explode or result in a meltdown. Nuclear Regulatory Commission officials and Metropolitan Edison personnel spent Saturday trying to manage the accident and determine the potential for such an eventuality.

By Sunday afternoon they had concluded that the hydrogen bubble was not in danger of exploding. "New measurements showed the large bubble in the reactor was diminishing. The gases still existed, but they were distributed throughout the system in smaller bubbles that made eliminating the predominantly hydrogen mixture easier. Why this occurred, no one knows. But it was not because of any intentional manipulation by Met Ed or NRC engineers."[8]

After Sunday, the crisis at the plant seemed to dissipate. By "Tuesday, April 3, General Public Utilities, Met Ed's parent company, established its TMI-2 recovery organization to oversee and direct the long process of cleaning up TMI-2."[9] The decontamination phase that continues to this day was underway.

The accident was enormously serious. The plant was out of the control of its operators for nearly a day and a half as they reacted to the accident's symptoms rather than with a full understanding of what had and was occurring. Even after Nuclear Regulatory Commission and Metropolitan Edison officials established the nature and origin of the accident, the plant could not be immediately stabilized because of the extreme damage suffered by the core. Furthermore, the President's Commission determined that a number of plausible alternative event sequences would have led to even more serious consequences. As it was, the radiation released during the accident exceeded acceptable limits for a normally functioning plant although the commission concluded that "the increment of radiation dose to persons living within a 50 mile radius due to the accident was somewhat less than one percent of the annual background level."[10]

## PUBLIC INFORMATION DURING THE ACCIDENT

The major public information events and issues of this period fall into four categories.

(1) Information released about off-site radiation levels beginning Wednesday, 28 March.

(2) Discussions on Wednesday and Thursday, 28 and 29 March, about whether the accident was caused by operator error or equipment malfunction.

(3) Confusion on Friday morning, 30 March, over evacuation precipitated by the venting of radioactive gases.

(4) Information released about the hydrogen bubble discovered on Friday morning, 30 March, leading to fear among some technical people of a meltdown or explosion.

As Rubin and members of the Public's Right to Information Task Force wrote about researching the flow of public information, "The narratives reveal which events were late in reaching the news media and the public, and which never reached them at all during the first week of the accident. They also point out the inaccurate information being passed along and the general state of confusion on the part of all participants."[11]

### (1) Information released about off-site radiation levels
### beginning Wednesday, 28 March.

Throughout the first days of the accident, radioactive gases were released to the atmosphere through the auxiliary building's venting system. The amounts released varied. The initial releases of Wednesday morning, 28 March, however, were large enough to prompt first the declaration of a site emergency and then, at 7:24 A.M., the general emergency. A general emergency is declared at a nuclear power plant when there is a possibility for "serious radiological consequences to the health and safety of the general public. . . . A general emergency represented the most serious form of emergency at Three Mile Island—a warning that radiation measurements had been found, or could be expected, off-site. The next move—whether to order an evacuation—was up to the governor. But the manner in which news of the general emergency and subsequent radiation measurements travelled from utility to state to NRC officials high-lighted serious communication problems that continued to arise throughout the accident. The first of these problems was Met Ed's reluctance to publicize the general emergency."[12]

On the first day of the accident, information concerning the seriousness of the accident and off-site radiation levels created the appearance, if not the fact, of deception by utility company officials. Utility company representatives were highly visible from Wednesday morning through Friday morning, and the information they released about off-site radiation levels on Wednesday was in turn contradictory, optimistic, and obfuscating. Early Wednesday morning, they issued two different reports concerning off-site radiation: one stated that no off-site radiation had been detected and the other that off-site radiation levels were not significant. The latter statement alluded to the general emergency but did not mention it by name. It did not connect the problems at the plant with the detection of off-site radiation.[13]

The President's Commission concluded that "the utility wished to convey the impression that there was no cause for alarm."[14] However, as a result, its officials seriously undermined the company's credibility. "Because of contradictory statements and the fact that the public information staff did not explain the general emergency, the credibility of the company, as represented by Herbein [Metropolitan Edison Vice President of Generation] in Harrisburg, and by Fabian [Metropolitan Edison Manager of Communication Services] and his staff in Reading [PA], was damaged beyond repair—at least in the eyes of several reporters and officials—by 3:00 P.M. on the first day of the 'incident' [Metropolitan Edison statements did not refer to an 'accident']."[15]

The Nuclear Regulatory Commission also issued two press releases on Wednesday. The morning release reported no radiation detected off-site while the 5:30 P.M. release reported small readings one-third of a mile from the plant. Neither mentioned high containment building readings.

Later in the day, the public became aware that utility company and Nuclear Regulatory Commission officials knew of high levels of radiation in the containment building and of off-site radiation detected as far away as Harrisburg on Wednesday morning. Lieutenant Governor William Scranton of Pennsylvania was the first to present straightforward information concerning the radiation released on Wednesday. In his 4:30 P.M. press conference on Wednesday afternoon he discredited earlier information from utility officials and reported that off-site radiation had been detected. Afterward, utility company credibility fared considerably worse than state credibility in the view of the media and the public, with the Nuclear Regulatory Commission falling somewhere in between during the first several days and subsequently.

Throughout the accident, disclosure of information by utility company and federal officials concerning radiation levels was not forthcoming or varied between reports. While the President's Commission found that this information was falling through the cracks as it passed from group to group or otherwise stagnating in one office or another,[16] to observers it looked like a cover-up.

Another prominent feature of all subsequent information releases from utility company and federal officials conceding off-site radiation was an assurance that such emissions posed no danger to the health and safety of nearby residents. However, scientists and engineers not directly involved in the management of the accident publicly contradicted these reassuring statements, indicating that radiation levels were higher and more dangerous than reported.

(2) Discussions on Wednesday and Thursday, 28 and
29 March, about whether the accident was caused by
operator error or equipment malfunction.

The part that operator error played in causing the accident is another issue that Metropolitan Edison and the Nuclear Regulatory Commission handled in a way that looked deceitful. Information released from Metropolitan Edison and Nuclear Regulatory Commission offices on Wednesday either denied or failed to mention operator error as one cause of the accident. While officials blamed equipment failure, however, a member of the Nuclear Regulatory Commission testified before a Congressional subcommittee on Wednesday evening that operator error had compounded the problem of equipment malfunction, a contradiction that added to the confusion on Wednesday and cast suspicion on previous information.

Later the public was fully informed that operator error was causally related to the escalation of the accident and had been discussed privately as early as Wednesday morning by some Nuclear Regulatory Commission officials, a disclosure that further damaged the credibility of both the utility and the Nuclear Regulatory Commission. As the Task Force reported, "The initial emphasis on equipment had important consequences for public information. By steering the press and the public toward the machine error theory, the NRC and the utility managed—deliberately or not—to at least temporarily distract attention from the real story at TMI: that confusion among the operators was significant and at various points individuals in charge did not know what was happening."[17]

### (3) Confusion on Friday morning, 30 March, over evacuation precipitated by the venting of radioactive gases.

By Friday morning, personnel directly involved in stabilizing the plant had determined that substantial amounts of radioactive gases had to be vented to maintain the measure of plant stability by then achieved. The release began at about 7:00 A.M. and lasted several hours. It was monitored by helicopters above the plant, and when readings registered 1200 mR/hr (millirems per hour) about 130 feet above the exhaust stack, control room operators notified the Pennsylvania Emergency Management Association (PEMA) of the possible need "to evacuate people downwind of the plant."[18] Thus began the disastrous communication of the venting to the public.

The Nuclear Regulatory Commission and the state reported higher levels of radioactivity detected than did the utility. The utility referred to a controlled release whereas the Nuclear Regulatory Commission called the venting uncontrolled. Confusion and misunderstanding throughout the morning in state and NRC agencies about the seriousness of the release and the condition of the plant led the governor of Pennsylvania to issue two advisories. At 11:00 A.M. he recommended that persons living within ten miles of the plant stay indoors. Later, on the advice of NRC officials, he advised the evacuation of pregnant women and preschool children living within five miles of the plant. He also ordered schools within ten miles of the plant to close. The venting Friday morning led the Nuclear Regulatory Commission to appoint Harold Denton (director, office of Nuclear Reactor Regulation) the liaison between itself and the Three Mile Island control room, state and federal agencies, President Jimmy Carter, and the media. Harold Denton's arrival substantially decreased the number of contradictory reports about the plant's status and off-site radiation levels. Denton also made the public acutely aware of the Nuclear Regulatory Commission presence at Three Mile Island.

(4) Information released about the hydrogen bubble discovered Friday morning, 30 March, leading to fear among some technical people of a meltdown or explosion.

By Friday it was clear to operators and Nuclear Regulatory Commission officials alike that hydrogen gas had been released when the core was uncovered and had formed a bubble at the top of the reactor. The first formal announcement that the gas bubble had developed in the reactor vessel came from the Nuclear Regulatory Commission in a 9:50 A.M. preliminary notification: "The volume of the bubble in the reactor vessel is *of interest* in assuring that sufficient volume remains in the upper head for collection of more noncondensable gases arising from continued operation in the present cooling mode as well as to assess the potential for movement of the bubble during a switch-over to decay heat removal operation."[19] Throughout the day, other similarly vague references were made to the gases that had accumulated in the reactor coolant system.

Some NRC staffers in Washington grew increasingly concerned that the bubble might contribute to a meltdown. At a Friday afternoon press conference, they established this connection for the first time for reporters. As one NRC engineer who spoke at the conference later testified, "In the course of the questioning, which was fast-paced and vigorous—not at all surprising—we told them that the bubble existed. I don't know who initiated the ques ion about is there a possibility of a meltdown under these conditions. . . . Brian's (Grimes, another NRC engineer) response was the first one, and it was a very candid one, and a very true one. . . . 'Yeah, there is a possibility of a meltdown.' "[20]

During the next several days, the public learned that the reactor had suffered severe fuel damage, that gases had formed in the primary loop inhibiting the natural flow of coolant water, and that some NRC officials were concerned that oxygen was being formed within the reactor coolant system, increasing the likelihood of an explosion.

Metropolitan Edison announced the dissipation of the bubble on Monday but the Nuclear Regulatory Commission was more cautious. Denton agreed only that it had decreased in size and not until Tuesday did he announce that "the bubble has been eliminated for all practical purposes"[21] and the potential for explosion was gone. Later the Nuclear Regulatory Commission would admit that it had erred in its calculations concerning the potential for explosion within the reactor. Much later the public would learn that NRC officials in Washington and Middletown were in much disagreement during these days over the possibility of a meltdown.

The explosion and meltdown scares were the final crises of this period. The plant was slowly brought to a semistabilized state and decontamination began. Schools outside the five-mile area surrounding Three Mile Island reopened 4 April. The advisories for pregnant women and preschool children living within five miles of the plant were lifted 9 April and schools in the five-mile area reopened 11 April.

## COMMUNITY REACTIONS TO THE ACCIDENT

It would take something of momentous import to shake the people of the Three Mile Island area from their tranquil existence. To quote a major employer in the community, "The men of central Pennsylvania are very solid. It takes a lot to frighten them." The occurrences at Three Mile Island between 28 March and early April 1979 constituted an event that shook the Newberry community to its foundations.

Two-thirds of the people we interviewed left Newberry during the crisis period. Most returned within four days, but some stayed away for two weeks or more. This high rate of evacuation is partly a result of Newberry's proximity to the plant. Most residents lived within five miles of the plant and the average distance from the plant was only 3.3 miles. Most of those who left relied on friends and relatives for shelter. Practically no one in our sample evacuated to a public shelter.

This evacuation behavior among a population of middle-class central Pennsylvanians is a strong indication of the disruptiveness of the event and of the fear that must have been associated with it. This mass exodus was unprecedented in Pennsylvania, if not in the United States, especially considering that there never was an evacuation order, only an evacuation advisory for mothers of preschool children and pregnant women living within five miles of the plant.

Another indication of the degree of disruption caused by the accident is our measure of how upsetting the accident was for the people we interviewed. On a scale of 1 to 10, they rated it an average of 7.86.

Perhaps more significantly, 46 percent rated it a 10—the highest possible score.

To convey a sense of the experience of people living nearby, we have included several quotations from a series of in-depth interviews that we conducted with residents and community leaders, both pro- and anti-nuclear. Looking back, it can be argued that nothing happened at TMI, and, except for the damage to the plant itself, one would be hard-pressed to find physical evidence to the contrary. However, the immediate impact of the accident on local residents was often a feeling of fear and uncertainty which would not be easily forgotten.

Discussing the accident, one woman expressed a feeling that we heard again and again.

It dawned on us that there was a possibility that we never would be able to return home again, and that's a terrible feeling because you don't know what to leave and you have a whole lifetime worth of things—things that you cherish and that you care so much about but that you have to leave.

A woman who was eight months pregnant at the time of the accident explained how she had altered her childbirth plans because of the evacuation and told how the experience had changed her:

The accident changed my life in the sense that it was such a hopeful time with new beginnings and a new baby. I don't even know how to explain it. It was so frightening those first few days not knowing what to expect. I was crushed. I just thought, "Oh, my God! This can't be happening. I can't believe it."

Another woman described the school evacuation and the general sense of uncertainty.

The schools were the worst. Everybody was running around. There was no order, with all the rumors. I just picked up my kids and took them home and closed the windows and then just waited.

Of course there were other residents who made statements such as, "The whole thing was blown out of proportion by the media." However, we believe these residents constitute a minority in the community. Between 13 and 17 percent of the people we interviewed consistently expressed the belief that the plant was safe.

Community leaders also described a town rocked by fear and confusion. One official described the township's efforts to inform the community about the advisories.

> Everything was in an uproar. It was very chaotic. The township offices were the center of activity. . . . We tried to come up with some kind of evacuation system and a way to alert people. Anything that had to be done we tried to do. Eventually people were alerted to stay indoors and later to evacuate by members of the fire company and the police who drove around the community broadcasting the news with loud speakers.

An official at the local elementary school discussed one of the most frightening incidents of the accident, the evacuation of students to a community several miles away. This evacuation occurred Friday, 30 March, at 1:30 P.M., an hour after the governor's advisory, and teachers were unable to inform the children's parents beforehand.

> Friday morning began pretty normally with attendance close to average, but fifteen to twenty minutes after school started people began to come to get their children. Many of the parents showed up packed and ready to evacuate and many were so excited that I had second thoughts about releasing their kids to them. I was worried about whether it would be safe for them to drive. Many were frantic. There is no way I can describe that day to you. No one was really informing us. By ten o'clock that morning the phone lines were absolutely jammed and there was no way to communicate with school headquarters. We were effectively isolated and in the end our only communication was through radio controlled school buses. I hope there will never be another day like it.

The same official told how students were at first confused because they saw other children being taken out of classes by their parents.

> When we had the teachers explain to them just what was happening and what we would be doing and that we would stay with them until their parents picked them up, at that time we had some tears. The kids felt that they were going somewhere with-

out their parents, and they didn't know how long it would be before they were picked up.

Two local bankers described long lines at their bank on that Friday and again on the following Monday, which they attributed to the uncertainty caused by the accident. They also told of getting calls over the weekend asking them to open the bank so that people could remove their valuables from safe deposit boxes. A doctor in a nearby community reported that Friday his telephone was very busy. Many people wanted to update their prescriptions before leaving the area.

A local minister described the scene in a rest stop along the Pennsylvania Turnpike several miles from Newberry on the Friday of the governor's evacuation advisory:

> We stopped at the second rest area on the turnpike, and it was there that we encountered some of the emotions of the people coming out of the Three Mile Island area. Some people were tremendously depressed. Ladies were crying because they were separated from their husbands. Other people were so fighting mad that they would have gone and taken care of some people if they could have. Met Ed, the governor—they were mad at everybody. One person came in with a bag of laundry, four children, and a dog. That was all they took with them; they just left.

Finally, to complete this picture of uncertainty and confusion that reigned from Wednesday, 28 March, to the end of the crisis period we include excerpts from our interview with the Emergency Management Coordinator for Newberry.

> *When did you first learn about the accident?*
> I was at work at the time of the accident. Wednesday evening I had heard rumors to the effect that there were some problems at Three Mile Island. I had called York County to check in with the Emergency Management Director of York County, Mr. Jackson, who wasn't available, and an assistant to him who wasn't available either. According to the plan that we had in effect we were under the impression that a director or an assistant would always be available at all times. I could get no information from the beginning of the situation. I ended up going to the FEMA [Federal Emergency Management Agency] people in Harrisburg to get information.

That Wednesday evening, I called a meeting of the [Goldsboro] council after finding that a problem did exist. We did not at that time know the scope of the problem as Met Ed did not know the scope of the problem. But we were in the process of planning that evening what we should do in the event that we would have to go through with an evacuation. So Wednesday evening the Goldsboro Council met in a special session, emergency session, to discuss the possibility of further action that we may have to take.

*Did you think of the possibility of a nuclear accident?*
Yes, the possibility was always there.

*Were you more concerned about floods?*
Not really. The possibility was always there. We knew the possibility was there. At the time we had a plan, and we were led to believe that it was a workable plan that the county had issued to us. It was left at that. We had no real say in the plan then, and we have no say in regard to the new plan. At this point, no local officials have been involved with regard to planning. We've voiced opinions in regard to changes in the plan, and now there is, in effect, going to be a change. We are not going to [evacuate to] Grove [Pennsylvania] but we are going to the Dillsburg area, Gettysburg area, which is a change we had in our initial plan before the county even had a plan during the incident. That Sunday right before the infamous Friday I was in the courthouse in a meeting and I said to the officials—PEMA, FEMA, county commissioners—"Show me Grove. Where the hell is Grove? Nobody here has heard of Grove." "Oh, well," someone said, "it's on the map." I said, "Good. Show me on the map where Grove is." Two commissioners and a few other people could not even show us where Grove was on the map.

*What did you do on Thursday?*
Went to work like any other day.

*Do you have any radiation monitoring devices?*
I have a civil defense meter which measures millirems per hour which I utilized Wednesday and Thursday to see if there was any readings which were more than normal background radiation readings at that time. Friday was a different story. Late Friday afternoon, we got measurable readings in Dillsburg. It was not a continuous monitoring device. It was just periodic checking. At 4:00 A.M. on Wednesday morning I was asleep. I was sound asleep, had no knowledge of the accident, was not notified by anybody including county or state [officials].

*So at the time when the worst venting could have taken place—*
What could have occurred? Nobody knows other than what
monitors were intact at that time which there is one right up
here [in Newberry]. Met Ed has a gamma ray monitor in their
parking lot right up here along the creek which under their license has been working ever since the plant, actually before the
plant was in operation. It is a continuous-type monitor.

*Did that monitor register anything at 4:00 A.M. on Wednesday?*
I have no idea.

*Why don't you have any idea?*
Well, I am going by what reports I've received from the Kemeny
Commission Report [*The Report of the President's Commission on
the Accident at Three Mile Island*]. That monitor was the one
taken into consideration for that report, and they're talking
about minimal readings at that time. That's the only information
(I have). . . . I have no access to that monitor, to check it and
see what it's reading at any time. It's locked up. I don't even
know. . . . I understand it's a gamma ray monitor. I've never seen
it. It's in an enclosed housing up there. As far as the borough, we
give them electricity to operate it.

*Have you even asked about that monitor?*
No, not really. I've just never been interested enough to check
into it.

*What did you do when you heard about the advisory?*
I got a telephone call at work that things had deteriorated to the
point where there could be a very real problem. I immediately
called York County Control [civil defense] to talk to Director
Jackson who said that things had deteriorated to the point where
an evacuation might be a real possibility. Well, I said, "Okay, I
am on my way home. I'll take some readings when I get home,
and see what we're up against. If that becomes a real possibility,
[I'll] immediately hit the tones [sirens], get the fire department
on the road, and get the state police up here. And possibly we
may have to go with evacuation."

Now when I came into town, I was met by a young woman
with a baby running out over the hill. It was a young woman and
her husband who were camping out over the hill. Apparently,
they were in town when the situation deteriorated—word of
mouth and so forth. She had grabbed her baby and was running
over the hill. I came to the fire hall. There were approximately
eight or ten state police officers that jumped me immediately,

wanting to know what the hell was going on because they had not been informed other than they were told to come here. The possibility of evacuation might exist. Just come here. That was the only information they were given at that time. So I was to co-ordinate with very little knowledge.

The first thing we did, we checked the [radiation monitor] readings to see what we were getting, and at that point, we weren't getting anything—0.02 millirems per hour, basically, which wasn't much to worry about. Later in the afternoon, we were in a situation where there was a type of drizzle and a type of a plume that had hit Goldsboro, and we were getting measurable readings. It was something we hadn't seen. That was something we hadn't seen. We were accustomed to normal background radiation readings, and all of a sudden we had something different, something other than normal background radiation. But we were in a plume-type situation at that time. Weather conditions weren't favorable for the type of radioactivity that was being released from the plant. . . . It wasn't serious at that time other than it was something more than background. Bear in mind, at all times in the past, we have seen nothing but normal background radiation levels, and all of a sudden, we're seeing something different.

*What about since that time?*
Normal background radiation. I've seen nothing but normal background radiation.

*You are convinced that from the time you had your counter out to the present that there has never been a serious emission of radiation?*
No, I can't go along with that. Wednesday, I'm only taking the word of the Kemeny Report and estimates as to what radiation was in Goldsboro at a given period up until Friday. Now from Saturday on, I know what radiation was really available. Between Wednesday through Friday, I really have no idea other than spot checks I have taken. I may have been up twenty-four hours but I wasn't watching the meter twenty-four hours [a day].

*What about the lady who was running over the hill?*
She was from another state. I really don't know her name or anything. I immediately sent a state police officer up to get her, calm her down, you know, see what he could do for her. Which he did. He took the situation from there. And everything was so hectic that, at that point, I really had no time to check back later.

*What about local residents?*
At the beginning, you could say it was panic. A lot of people really weren't sure what was going on. But I immediately sent the state police cars out as well as the fire company with the equipment and with the little cards telling people to stay inside, close your doors, turn off your air conditioners, and just remain calm, and we will get back to you with additional information. Which we did. From that point on, once we got a grasp of the situation, once we got on top of it, then we could at least make a statement to calm people down. . . . Before that, people were packing cars, trying to decide where they were going to go, what they were going to do. When I came into town, it was just chaos, basically. I could describe it as the most eerie thing I ever experienced. People were just kind of standing in the front door wondering what was going on. The state police were sent to stop any panic that might occur, but they had no information. They did not know what was going on. I did not expect the situation to deteriorate from the time I left New Cumberland to the time I got here. It was approximately nine minutes from the time I left. But it did.

*What percent of people evacuated from the community?*
At least 80 percent.

*Did you stay?*
Yes, and my wife stayed. At that time, I needed as much help as I could get. We were operating a twenty-four-hour operation, patrolling the town to make sure that looting and vandalism did not occur besides doing routine emergency operations. So I needed as much help as I could get. We were down to a handful of people.

## SUMMARY

The public was poorly informed about the accident at Three Mile Island. At various stages, the Nuclear Regulatory Commission and Metropolitan Edison withheld information from the community. Often officials' interpretations of events conflicted. Their disagreements were not explained to the public; rather, their stories, and thus news reports, simply contradicted each other. Each new incident further eroded the image of Metropolitan Edison as a publicly responsible and competent organization. The Nuclear Regulatory Commission fared a bit better, especially after the arrival of Harold Denton. However, it appeared to those living nearby that, time and again, important information about their exposure to radiation and the stability of the plant was withheld or not timely. The accident also created the baffling impression that the individuals in charge of managing the accident did not know what they were doing.

We should not forget that, although communication problems may have exacerbated fear and confusion, the accident was nearly catastrophic, and it left in its wake a severely damaged nuclear reactor that has yet to be fully decontaminated.

During the first days of the accident, the actions of Metropolitan Edison officials and to a lesser extent those of the Nuclear Regulatory Commission engendered public mistrust. While fear about the uncontrolled releases of radiation from the plant and the hydrogen "bubble" problem temporarily held the attention of observers and observed alike, it would soon be apparent that the appearance of deception and incompetence during the crisis period of the accident, especially by Metropolitan Edison officials, would have serious consequences for the people of Newberry.

# FOUR

## THEY JUST CAN'T
## DO THIS TO US:
## THE WORDS OF
## MIDDLE AMERICANS

HOW DOES IT FEEL to live within several miles of the nuclear power plant that has undergone the worst commercial nuclear power accident in U.S. history? In this chapter, we have reproduced lengthy interviews with eleven residents of Newberry to provide insight into the experience of the people who were there. As they did for us, we believe these interviews will deepen the reader's understanding of how residents reacted to the accident itself and appraised the situation afterward.

We interviewed a variety of people from the Newberry community. We talked to grandparents and to people with young children, with children in high school, with no children. Pursuit of these interviews took us to the modest and affluent suburban housing developments of Newberry Township, to ancient farms on the town's back roads, to a former summer mansion on the edge of the Susquehanna River directly across from Three Mile Island, to a cottage built on a hillside and nearly hidden from the road by trees, to some of the small ranch-style houses sitting alone on the main roads of Newberry Township, and to the older neighborhoods of Goldsboro. We conducted interviews in sight of the cooling towers and in places where they could not be seen. We talked to people who were vitally concerned about Three Mile Island and to those who were unconcerned.

We have not included in this chapter any interviews with people who were not concerned about the accident and their proximity to Three Mile Island because we found these views to be held by a minority of Newberrians. Thus, the themes that run through all the interviews we included are fear for the health and safety of families, especially children; mistrust of information from Metropolitan Edison and the Nuclear Regulatory Commission and cynicism about the motives behind their actions; and powerlessness. Many people also spoke about the first days of the accident as a period of shock and panic.

The people whose interviews we have included, reflecting the residents of Newberry, were nevertheless not a homogeneous group. Their responses to the accident and subsequent events vary in terms of what they actually feared, how much time their worry consumed, how many of their neighbors they felt were concerned about the plant, and what they believed about the future of nuclear energy in our nation.

These interviews also offer a sense of the people of Newberry. It is very well to describe them and to label them and their community—Middle Americans living in a semirural area of Pennsylvania; however, their own words best convey them as individuals. What do individual Middle Americans sound like? What do they do when a nuclear power plant three or four miles from their home experiences a serious accident, when fire engines drive through their neighborhood advising them to stay inside, close the windows, and turn off the air conditioner? How do they react afterward?

The people of Newberry are far more than stereotypes. They are neither crazed nor irrational nor inhumanly virtuous. They are decent but unique beings, each bringing his or her own eye, ear, and voice to the event. We hope that the reader will be able to identify with one of them or recognize in one or two of them a neighbor, a friend, a grandparent, a sister or brother, a mother or father, a child. We also hope that the reader will obtain a sense of the community as a whole—both the cacophony and the harmony—that is the real music of real communities created by the real people who inhabit them.

Finally, in the interests of privacy, in each of these interviews we have tried to remove any clues to the resident's identity without losing the sense of the person speaking.

## MRS. WILLIS

For many years, Mrs. Willis had lived with her husband and family in their home near Goldsboro. She was about 50 years old. Her youngest child, a boy, was in high school at the time of the accident. Her grown daughter lived in New England. She was not employed outside her home and was very involved in church activities.

*What do you remember about the day of the accident?*
Well, the day it happened I didn't really realize what was going on. I was in and out. I was outdoors almost the whole day. Well, then my friend called me, and she said about leaving, and I did not know what she was talking about. I didn't understand because we knew it [the power plant] was out there but we did not understand what it was all about until [the accident]. . . . We knew it was out there but we didn't understand what it was all about or what danger was involved. No, I had not thought about leaving. What would I leave for? She went into great detail. She got real involved. She got a lot of information—someone from State College, some man she was in contact with at the time. I did not really know what to say to her because I thought she was being a little radical.

And then by afternoon we realized what happened. We did not know the details. We started hearing more. I turned the TV on, and my husband came home, and he did not know anything about it because where he works you are out of the world. And he said, "What is going on?" And I said to him, "Something happened at TMI. Evidently something must be serious because [friend] called and said would we consider leaving?" So we kind of went along with, you know, and did not do anything until the next morning. I was on the phone to my sister. She was talking to me. Something blared out on the TV. It kind of scared me half to death. It was something serious. "Oh, my God, what's happening?" I said to my sister. "I must hang up! I must call my husband and tell him what is going on!"

So then I called him, and by then they flashed it on the TV, and I put the telephone receiver where he could hear it, and he told me, "You better pack up," and that I was to stay indoors. So, by God, I really panicked. I started to put things together. By that time the phone rang, and it was my daughter in [New England] and she was saying, "Mom, Mom! You better leave." And I said, "Why?" They were getting information we were not getting. I said, "Why should I leave?" "Mom, you should. You've got to! It's serious!" And I said, "I don't understand what's happening." Of course, none of us did. And she said, "Mom, please go! They tell us up here it is terrible!" I said, "I am getting ready right now to leave. I am packing." And of course, the ridiculous things I packed. So I called the school, for them to have the boy [her son] waiting for me.

I threw the things in the car, and I went out to school and picked him up, and I went to York to talk to my husband to find out where I should go. And he told me, he said we'll go to these friends' house up in Franklin County, and he said he would meet me there, and we'll discuss from that point on. And so we left. And my husband came that evening, and we were there, I guess it was seven days, and, of course, we were just glued to the radio and the TV, and I mean it, I really was upset. I really figured we would never come back here again the way it was going. We just figured that was it. And of course when there was no meltdown, then I hated to come back. I despised the thought of coming in here. But we came back, and my son and I cleaned the whole house the next day. It just felt like you had to clean whatever was here out, and we just got rid of all the food that was in the refrigerator and things like that that we hadn't taken along originally.

And I was so upset and nervous I couldn't stand it. I called my husband and said, "I don't know what to do. I can't stand it around here! This really has me unnerved!" And that was the following Thursday. . . . And he said, "Well, get stuff together, and we'll go away for the weekend." And we went to visit another friend of ours. . . . And we stayed there the weekend and then we came home. And of course, we just had to rectify ourselves to the fact that we lived here, and our house is here and as much as we hated it, we're stuck with it and that was it.

It was panicksville, I'll tell you. We just really thought that was it, and we would never get to be able to come back here again. We really had everything here. I didn't take anything important. I mean, what money we had was still here, you know, as far as cash and insurance policies and whatever. I mean everything was here, and I often think to this day if we wouldn't have, couldn't have come back—that would have been it. I mean, everything, here it sits.

*How do you feel now?*
I just hate it. And I think I heard yesterday . . . [that they] are going to let this gas [Krypton-85] out, and it's the best, and it's the safest. How can they say it's the safest? I mean, they haven't tried anything else really. They haven't even been able to get into the door to the darn place, and certainly you know we haven't got the right information on that. And, here we sit. We're just experi-

ments. That's what we are. We are their experiments because it's cheaper that way, and it's easier all around. What you can't see, what you can't hold in your hand, it isn't there. So we are sitting ducks here, and I just hate the thought if it ever started up again. And I know I am one against, what! And we're surrounded by it. And I just feel that until we know how to get rid of the waste and do more about it, like anyone else, we're just playing with fire. I'm scared of it. I'm desperately scared of it. I just hate the thought!

Of course, the economy is down so we can't sell our house if we wanted to. We can't get a pastor in our church! Seven have turned us down because of TMI. Our pastor left because she was pregnant, and now she just came back a week ago, last Thursday. That's the first she has come into the area. And she is just up in arms about it. Her house is up for sale, and as soon as it is sold, that will be the end of her. She will leave the area. No matter where you go, you are coming up against it.

But where are you safe? I mean really. It's so frightening, and you read in the paper there was another leak in one [a unit of the Three Mile Island plant]. It was in last night's paper. But it's nothing serious. They're never nothing serious! When is it going to be serious? I don't know. Nothing to them is serious! Certainly it's something serious! I don't know. I just feel we're stuck! And we are, because it is terrible to put your dependency on the material things, but when you have a home that's what you work for because you have to have some place to live. And if we just up and leave this, that would be it! How could we start again? My husband's almost—he will be retiring in four years not because he is going to be 65, but he was with the company for thirty years. Can we afford just to up and . . . we still have a boy to finish educating. I don't know. It is just frightening. I do feel we are not really considered because we are not the shareholders or whatever who have a big say-so in what's going to be done with that out there [the plant].

*Do you think you will have a say in the reopening?*
Well, what have you seen so far? They do exactly as they want no matter how many demonstrations, no matter how many steering committees or whatever [we have]. We can talk and talk and talk, and they do what they want to. They have all along. I mean, have they listened to anybody other than people who are worried about their money? One man, who I heard has money in Three Mile Island, and as a shareholder, he said as far as he is

concerned, he wants no part of it. Now that one man, he said he doesn't care if he realizes a cent out of his investment. But we are just small potatoes compared to big business.

I hope that there are enough people to put up a fuss, that something will be realized out of this [community's efforts], and that it will not be opened again. But so far, I don't know. I have no faith in any of that! As far as the government, there was Thornburgh [former governor of Pennsylvania and now U.S. attorney general] last night. I felt, what a rat! He did so well during the whole crisis, and we had faith in him, and now he goes along with this letting out the gas [Krypton-85 release]. I realize it's got to go somewhere but the atmosphere can only hold so much. It's got to land somewhere eventually. Is it biodegradable? You know it isn't! It has a life to get rid of. So somewhere it is going to fall on some unsuspecting soul. But it is frightening! It is just scary!

We had—last fall there was a professor from Japan, and he had a couple of young students along. Somehow we met them in Goldsboro, and we became friends with him. And we had the boys back here for supper, and they were up there [in Goldsboro] doing experiments, soil and so forth. The professor did talk with my daughter, and he said it is scary for them [Japanese] because they are so dependent [on nuclear energy], because they have so many more plants in a smaller area. . . . And what scares me is knowing that cement only has a life expectancy at the most of thirty years. It takes so many years to harden, like it takes it ten, twelve years to harden, and then from there on it's a deteriorating process. Well, what's going to be done with this? What's going to happen out there? Are they going to seal it up for eternity and for future generations to say, "Hey, what's in here? Let's open it up and find out." That may sound dumb, but you see other things that—dumps where they put chemicals and so forth. It was done, and we forgot about that. That's over and done with. And here now we're getting the results of it. This is what will happen to the future.

I get scared when I think of my grandson and the future. What are we leaving for them? Not very damn much, in plain words, because we're not leaving them any confidence in their forebears, because what we're leaving them is a mess. How can they even survive? I suppose what we will end up doing is blowing ourselves to kingdom to come . . . and that will be it. Then we will be satisfied. It is scary. One well-placed bomb could do it, to annihilate, the end of this whole area. And maybe that sounds crazy, but that is how I feel. The times we're living in—I just hate it. Before it was there [before the accident], I never saw it. Now, every time I turn that corner [toward home] I see those stacks sitting out there. I hate it! I think—monsters.

Several years ago, when my son was out of college and he was looking for a position, he would send résumés around. He would take anything to hold him over, and I had no idea he went out there to TMI and got a job as a guard. But we never gave it a thought because it was a place to work. And my son couldn't wait to get away from there. And we could not understand why. Why is he so upset? What is there to be frightened about? He said, "There is no security out there." At one point—he is a very responsible young man—a fisherman got stuck out on the river, and he just climbed the fence, and he came in there, and nothing was said, "How did you get in here?" or what. And if it was that accessible and it was that much of a danger—security-wise—somebody really goofed.

Now there are four men who work there who refuse to answer questions on what happened down there [former plant workers in testimony before the Nuclear Regulatory Commission and the Public Utility Commission]. Now they are trying to get them to answer questions. Why do they refuse to answer questions on what happened out there if it was nothing to it? They make us sound like we're radical and upset about nothing. Why not answer it? There is too much truth that has not been brought out. I just do not like it. That's how I feel! I realize in this area they do not even think about it, on all sides, retired people. They have lived around here all their lives. This is where they are going to die, and they don't even realize the danger, so that what you find here is people who have no knowledge about it. And they do not have the knowledge of what the consequences will be. When you say, "Gee, if that would have happened [meltdown], this area could never be used for anything," you know, they look at you. They really do not have a concept of what you are saying. It really is batting your head against a brick wall.

*Did you consider the plant safe before the accident?*
Yeah, I never gave it [a thought], I didn't know what it was. I mean, when they said atomic plant, that's what it was out there. But nobody wrote in the paper, had editorials in the paper before, and said, "Now, look. If they put that out there and something would happen, this is what could happen. This is the end result."

We had no idea. They made a big to-do, you know, big deal—atomic plant. But we had no idea! We are just laypeople. What did we know about what they were doing or how they were using it? There was no such thing brought up about there is a waste that we must get rid of, and, you know, it is very difficult to find a safe place, how to do it. What did we know? We saw it out there, and people came and they'd visit, and we'd go past, and they'd say, "What's that?" "Oh, that's the Three Mile Island, the atomic plant." That's all we knew. It was a name.

And what burns me up is that they bragged and said that atomic power, it will be so minimal in charge that they won't even know what to charge you. Bull! They produce it out there and send it to New Jersey. And we get stuck with the crap. We still buy ours [electricity] from York Haven, get it off of the dam, from the power plant there. That's where we get our power. . . . I guess that's where our power comes from or someplace, I don't know. Maybe they ship it in from Timbuktu. That's ridiculous! Make it out there and send it to New Jersey and so forth because they can charge more for it down there. Ridiculous! So I am telling you everything just scares me about it.

When I get to thinking about the problems of the earth, I just think we're bringing it on ourselves. And it is terrible that money is the root of it all. Because it is big money that talks. We pay the bills! Every time I read something in the paper, what provokes me, when it's something very important, I look and find an article, this big one in the back pages that said about the mortality rate, the difference between this year compared to another year back somewhere. You do not even see it unless you are looking for something. I just feel we were sold a bill of goods. They will end up doing with it what they want unless the people really revolt if they insist on opening any of them. I don't see how they can open that one [Unit 2]. They can't even get the darn door open. Those men who are willing to go in there—God, I don't know if they're courageous or just stupid!

*Why do you think some people are upset and others are not?*
Because of the knowledge and not absorbing everything that was said or reading or understanding a little bit more about it. . . . That's why people do not get themselves roused up. . . . My husband's like that. He knows the danger, but he's just very complacent and goes along with it. At the time he was panic-stricken, too, with the rest of us. But then he got used to it, you know, and

accepts it with no problem. If I would not have to worry about coming home and arguing [with him], I would probably be out carrying placards and raising hell. But you have to consider you have to live here with a husband who figures, "Well, we won't get our own way anyhow." Which I feel, in the long run, I am glad there are people who go out and do something about it. . . . It has bothered my husband. I think it gripes him that we did not sell the house before [the accident]. Now, what's the use? Nobody wants it. You see write-ups in the paper that houses are selling. That is a crock! The same For Sale signs are on the houses that were here nine to ten months ago when people decided they were getting out. No one is selling their house. I know of one house that was sold, and they are friends of mine, and it really surprised us. And even she [the seller] was surprised. And it was a young man that bought it. I don't think he realizes what is over the hill. I don't think people realize that we are so close in air miles. I don't think that young man realizes where that house is sitting, [what is] over top this hill. I do not think he would have bought it. As far as the developments such as in Valley Green, they can say as much as they want to, they're selling houses. They are lying! Because they are not. I have a friend who is a realtor with Century 21, and I told him my friend was not having too much luck. He said, "I don't promise anything because we are not moving anything in that area." I don't blame them because I would not buy in the area. I would like to go away from here myself.

*Are you worried about health effects?*
I am worried in the sense, if something has happened it already happened to us. And, of course, we are not going to know this right away. But if we are any way affected in our health, it's done! I can't get scared about something I can't do anything about. I don't like it. I just don't like it at all. It's really a nuisance. I have to laugh. You know, people who know you live in the [Three Mile Island] area, they say, "Hey, how are you doing down there? You still down there?" They make a big joke. But it really isn't.

*Are you planning to leave during the Krypton release?*
Someone said to me on Saturday, "When they let out this gas, are you staying?" I said, "Not if I don't have to, I am not." I don't know why I'm going. It's just peace of mind! If I know when they are going to let it out . . . of course now they're talking about let-

ting it out over a period of sixty days. Who can leave for sixty days? I sure can't. So I'll stay here and breathe it the same as everybody else. In twenty years—well, they say, "You're fifty years old now. You won't be here in twenty years anyhow. And if you do get sick, you'll be ready to die at that time anyhow, so forget it." But how about the young kids? How do we know how it's going to affect their reproductive organs and so forth? Like my boy! He's just graduating tomorrow night, and I suppose he's going on to college, and I think that's what my worry was—to get him out of here at the time because I've realized, you know, how they'll think. "Well, you're fifty. You've had your kids, and if anything happens, you've lived your life. There's more people to replace you." People are an easy commodity to come by. They're not really important. That's how they look at it. That's about how I feel about it.

*Has this experience changed your life?*
Well, I've certainly gained more knowledge, and I would think twice if they're going to move in something like that [Three Mile Island plant], if they should say, "Oh, well, we're gonna learn more about it." I'd make sure. I'm gonna make sure they learn more about it. And I don't think people should be so fast to say, "Yeah, go ahead. Do these things." Because they really—it was really a bill of goods [nuclear energy]. I mean, all the people who have backed this—I hate to just say Met Ed but that's the only name I can put onto it at the time—we can produce energy, we can sell electricity. But they weren't thinking at the time, "Are we going to have trouble getting rid of the waste?" As long as people are stupid, they would have no trouble, you know, because they could just put it where they want to, in these waste dumps. That's terrible! I mean, eventually, where are they going to go with it? I know I wouldn't want it, and now that the other states realize what they're getting, I don't blame them for saying, "Hey, we don't want it," and turning the trucks back or whatever.

That's what scares me—it's what we're gonna leave. When they can't even get into that place! Now it's been over a year. God, they really don't know what has been going on in there. Can you imagine what would happen if that would deteriorate to the point that the stuff would just automatically, would find its way out? I wonder what they would do? Would they tell about it? They'd just dump it out in the water or something. Oh, it just provokes me that they always say, "It is just a minimal amount, just a minimal amount, no danger." What is danger? I mean, what are they going to call dangerous? Those minimal amounts certainly together must make a large amount. Where are they going? It's changed my life. It's changed my thinking.

I was just thinking yesterday about the government. You know, are they really hunting another source of energy, working to it to the point of, working at it hard, saying this is a serious thing, do we really need it? Until we know more about this nuclear power, we better stick to maybe tried and true or find something a little bit better, just to hold us over until we know more about it and sink some money into educating, more education on nuclear power—not just what it can do for us but what we can do afterwards. I mean, can we get rid of all this? Maybe someday they will find out what to do with the waste but I do not know. I feel by that time we'll blow ourselves right out of the universe because we're not gonna be satisfied until we do.

*Did you feel that way before the accident?*
No! No, because of ignorance. I didn't know. I had no idea, you know, what was sitting over there. I just didn't know. And they [Metropolitan Edison] put it there, and they didn't tell you what could happen. And whoever heard of anything like a meltdown?

*Was your husband opposed?*
He is very complacent. He was raised here all his life, and when I say these people are set in their ways, and what they can't see, they don't understand—I know my husband. I'm involved in other things, and I guess he believes, "Oh, Lord, I've had enough of this." I guess he believes it is just another thing for me to get involved in. I am just recuperating from an accident [that] happened actually a year before Three Mile Island. And I have trouble with this leg. This is why he would not want me to be involved. . . . He has accepted it—"Well, we're stuck with it. We're going to stay." He is the kind of person who would just shove it in the back of his mind and pretend it hasn't happened perhaps. There is nothing he can do about it. He feels at this point we cannot do anything about it. But if anyone came around here for petitions, I was the first one to sign. . . . I worry myself thinking. I try to listen and read everything they have. I realize there is a lot we are not hearing. I do not care how much they say, we are not going to get the facts. No! We are not going to get the facts. They are going to tell only what they want us to

hear, and when they want us to hear it. And of course, it is going
to come out, "Oh, it is minimal. It is no problem. It's no danger."
It is bull! I want to know what is going on, and I feel we have a
right to know what is going on! I feel they must tell us. And they
cannot say it is minimal because they do not know what the dangers of low levels of radiation are. I just don't like it. . . . I wish a
good fairy would come along and say, "Hey, I will buy your
house." (laughter) It would have to be a fairy, I guess, to do it!
(laughter)

*What do you think when you see the towers?*
I just hate it. I always think in my mind—monsters. That's the
only thing—monsters—because they just loom out there and
there they sit . . . I worry. I keep thinking, there it sits and what's
gonna happen when that cement deteriorates. Oh, they say,
"That cement is so many feet thick and so many this and so
many that." But eventually, maybe I might not be here, but eventually, something's gonna give and I mean something is giving
when they find leaks here and leaks there. What happens to all
those leaks that they've been finding. We hear no more about
them. Every so often you hear they find this leak and that leak.
They don't say anything about how they repair them. That's the
thing I wanna hear about. We repaired them, taken care. We
sealed them up. All we hear is that the leaks are found. I am sure
they are doing something. I should hope so.

I really hope they are not planning on reopening. They just
can't do this to us! They just can't. They can't put the people
through the worry twenty-four hours a day once they start in
again. And you know even though it is not running, you know
we are in danger—as it sits right now. I never saw "China Syndrome" [a movie about a nuclear power plant accident]. Something like that did not even come into my mind [before the
accident]. It didn't interest me. I didn't know what it was about.

I wish they would tell us today, "Hey, we are going to close
this up. We are going to seal it up, and we are never going to use
it again. There is no danger." Then they could put your mind at
ease, in that way. But I don't think they can do that or whether
they would do it. I don't think they are going to leave a structure
like that out there and seal it up just to please the public and say
it doesn't matter that we lost millions and millions of dollars,
we're just going to close it up. When they talk about it costing

billions to clean up, I just wonder, "Why bother?" What are the alternatives? What do you do?

*How much is it on your mind?*
Every day! We all think about it! It is a big conversation point. People who come to visit—my friend, we have been friends since we were twelve years old, and she is a person who is a good Christian, and she would say to me up at the house, "Oh, Mabel, you just do not have any faith. Don't worry. It's not going to happen, not going to happen." And I would say, "Maude, I do have faith. I do have faith in God, but I do not have faith in man. He has had his hands in there, and when man has his hands in there, there is money involved. And when money is involved, friendship and ethics and everything else goes right out the window. And being right goes right out the window. Because when it is large sums, individuals mean nothing." I keep telling her this. In fact, we are very, very good friends. I would consider her my very best friend, and we really got into a hassle about it. They [friend and friend's husband] were that far away from it [Three Mile Island] that she was not afraid. It wasn't going to hurt her place. And finally her husband said, "Hey, Maude, think of it this way. That's Mabel and Bill's whole life sitting down there. They may never be able to go back with those two suitcases and that telephone book." They kidded me because I grabbed a telephone book. But I knew all my family and addresses were there. So I grabbed it because I knew I had to get in touch with everyone, to let them know where we were at. And they kid me because of it. It [the accident] was right before Easter and just that week I had made Easter eggs, and they kid me about my TMI eggs. And this year they sent me word—was I making any TMI eggs?—which I did, and I sent them up to them. I said to her, "You can sit here in your house where everything is safe and say everything is safe. But everything I own is down there. What I wanted to give my children, as little as it is, it is down there, sitting—all my mementos, everything we had, every picture we had. Everything is down there. My whole life is sitting down there." She said, "Well, you're here with your husband." And I said, "We do live with things. . . . "

Now, I'll give you an example of panic. We don't talk about this but I'll tell you something that we don't talk about. We went up there on that Thursday, and the following Tuesday my husband said would I be afraid to come back down here with him? And I said, "All right, I'll drive down with you." We came down here, and it was like no-man's-land. There wasn't a car on the road. It was terrible. It was the worst feeling in the world. There was nobody. We didn't see anyone. We came all back roads to avoid coming in the Goldsboro way. We came the other way. We pulled in here, and we got in the house. My husband went to pieces in the sense that I have never seen him do this. He took the big garbage bags, and he went upstairs, and he emptied out every drawer of my son's and took everything that boy had and just jammed it [in]. And I kept telling him, "Bill, don't do this. Don't do this." He said, "I don't care if we lose everything. He's got to have his things." He said, "It's not right." I couldn't believe it, you know. . . . I don't think he realized what he did. He just had everything, filled the car up, and he filled these bags up, and I kept telling him, "Don't do that," you know. And he took the towels and sheets. He said, "I'm taking them." And now here everything else sat, and I walked over to the mantel and I picked up what's called a rose bowl. It's carnival glass, and it was his mother's, and I had brought it from his father's, and it was something he had from his mother. And I picked it up, and I looked at it and set it back on the mantel and, you know, walked out of the kitchen. And he came back in and picked that up, and I had a couple of etched glass dishes, and he picked them up, and he said, "Here, pack these. At least we'll have something to give the kids," you know. And when he did this, I said, "Hey, you have got to stop." He went in and took the stereo, and he put it in the back of the car. He said, "I will give it away first if they are going to loot the houses"—which will always happen. He had gotten so panicked. He said, "I will give it away. I will give it all away before I see it here and there and everywhere." I said, "Bill, forget it. It doesn't matter. We will survive without these things." So about the time we got up there we could not even talk. When we got up there—she has a big back porch—I took all these bags, and I said, "You never will believe what he did." I said, "Now, do you have a Goodwill box up here?" and she said, "Yes." He had things that I had ready to go to Goodwill. And I stood on that back porch and sorted all my son's things, pile here and pile here, ending up throwing away two of the garbage bags. . . . He just went panicky. He never has talked about this. He has never brought it up. He picked up the insurance policies and his coin collections and took those things along. . . . That is when he

went to pieces. He wanted to save things for his son. He said, "We
may lose things but why should he lose everything?" I said, "It is
just clothing, his mementos, his instruments." My son is very mu-
sical, and it was all his instruments. He has an instrument collection, very odd instruments, and he [her husband] gathered all
them up. It was a flute, clarinet, and a ukelele, a dulcimer, a
mandolin, a real old mandolin, a banjo. Just any number of instruments. Bill gathered all these things up. He was trying to save
things for his son. Of course, picking up the bowl, he felt—he
knew I loved dishes. That would be one thing we would have.
But I do not think he realized what he did. I really don't. He has
never talked about it. When we got up there, I couldn't even
talk. Maude looked at me and she knew. I just shook my head,
and she looked at Bill and his face was just red and he couldn't
talk. And he went into the house and sat down. He will not even
discuss it. He just won't. It is just like a closed issue that never
happened.

And then two days later we turned around and came back. I
do not know why I came back, why I insisted that day, as good as
we had it and we work so well together [her friend and herself].
It was just not the same. It still was not home. We knew we had
to face it eventually. They were saying it was safe, safe as it could
be, so that I made the decision to come back. I think he would
have stayed as long I did not insist. . . .

Now, I read the paper, listen to the news, and I get a little angry when people say, "Are they still talking about Three Mile Island every day, every day?" And I say, "Hey, listen! That still is an
issue. Don't pooh-pooh it. I don't think they are dragging out old
stuff. Listen to it! You might just learn something."

## MRS. BROWN

Mrs. Brown was in her late twenties at the time of the accident, pregnant
with her first child and later that year had a baby boy. She held a full-
time job prior to having the baby, and at the time of the interview she
was a full-time mother and housewife. She lived in a suburban-style
home. She was not a native of Newberry Township, but her family lived
in the Harrisburg area.

*How did you feel about the accident?*
I never trusted the place in the first place and when it happened,
it just confirmed what I was afraid of. Was I panicky? I guess

somewhat—not extremely. When it happened Wednesday I didn't
hear about it until later on in the day. I was working for my boss
who works up in [a nearby town]. We heard of it on the news up
there, and then on Wednesday night on the news they said everything was under control. Then on Thursday morning they said
things were not under control, and I wanted to leave right then.
But my husband was out of town so I waited until he got home,
and I said I am going to his parents . . . so it was semi-panic. I
was pregnant at the time. I was about six months pregnant. I
wasn't concerned for myself, really, but for my baby.

*How did you feel about Three Mile Island before the accident?*
I never realized that we were that close to it. I had known that
there was a plant around Middletown, but I didn't realize this
was actually across the river. I knew it was near Middletown, but
I just didn't realize. I guess after we moved here—somehow we
never saw the stacks before, and I thought we were a lot further,
I didn't realize how close we were until one day I went down to
the post office in Goldsboro, and I then realized how close we
were to it. I remember having discussions with my boss, and once
a week he and I drove to [work], and he used to make fun of all
the people who didn't like nuclear plants. And I said, "I just
never have trusted it." There's government regulators, but they
mess up all the time. I don't trust the government. I mean, a lot
of people who work within the government could care less about
the job. And I just never trusted that it was safe. I've always felt
something could go wrong. And unfortunately, I was right. My
boss has changed his view a little bit. Our conversation wasn't
that long before it [the accident] happened, probably within a
year or less. . . . I just feel, we're not God, and anything made by
man is not always totally trustworthy because we're not God. We
just all don't know what we're doing. I did not like the idea, but
you accept it. I always had the attitude, well, it won't happen.

*How do you feel now?*
Probably a little bit more panicky now [than before the acci-
dent]. Not panicky. I guess that's kind of an extreme word. I'm
not one to get all bent out of shape and go nuts. But there's times
I just think I wish we could move. And then I think, "Where are
you going to move to that there aren't other nuclear power
plants, chemical waste dumps, and who knows what else?" I
mean, there's stuff all over the place that you don't want to live
near. And another thing is, especially now that I'm not working

and have the baby, we can't afford to sell the home and pay the higher interest rates for another home. So, practically speaking, there's no sense in moving. I would feel psychologically better by living further away but ten to twenty miles really isn't safe, any safer than here. It's just that, psychologically, you don't see it. You feel safer, you know . . . but financially it would be just too hard.

*What do you fear now?*
What I fear is—I'm panicky because I'm not one for being psychic and something happens but when this [accident] happened, when my fears of something going wrong and it did happen . . . my fears of sabotage are at this point . . . I feel that Three Mile Island has been in the news so much that everyone in the world knows Three Mile Island, and there are a lot of nuts out there. And you pick up *The Guide* [a local newspaper] and you see how lax the security is at TMI. So someone could say, "Here is my chance for me to get my name in the paper." These nuts can get into it [plant] as easily as a reporter. When I think of that, I start getting panicky because of already one thing coming true. I guess this kind of is the biggest fear at the moment. Some nut might be thinking the same as I am thinking, and that bothers me.

*Are you concerned about health effects from the accident?*
I probably—I have thought about [health effects] for my son— maybe because I was pregnant at the time, and the biggest radiation dosage we got was the night it happened. Usually the wind doesn't blow this way, but, of course, the night it happened, it did, and the only thing I fear would be maybe leukemia or something in later years, which I don't know if it's possible or not, and I'm sure in some ways the risk of what happened is—compared to some of these children who live next to chemical plants—less of a danger. But I don't know, who knows? I don't think anyone knows. I don't sit and worry about it. It's happened. You know, take one day at a time. But I really kinda think the exposure that everyone's gotten, especially since I left Thursday night, was far less than lots of other people. Sometimes you wonder about the chemical dumps in your backyard. So there is not only that risk. I won't be happy if it starts functioning again. . . . I don't know, see, I don't know if we really need it [nuclear power] or not, and I don't know if anyone knows if we really need nuclear power, if it's worth the risk. I don't know if it is. [In] my opinion, if it means—if shutting them down means that we'll have to go with-

out the luxuries we've become used to like television and air conditioning and et cetera, then I think we're going to have to learn to live without our luxuries. But if it actually means the difference between freezing in the winter and not freezing, then we're going to have to accept the risk. That's the way I feel. I know each year we are getting more and more population, but I also know the population boom is not like it used to be, that schools are closing down because we don't have enough children. People my age are having no children or one child. It's not like when my parents had children or when people had three or four or five children. So the population is not increasing as far as in the suburban areas. Maybe in some urban areas it is . . . but I don't think it's as great a need as they're trying to make you think it is. . . . If anything, we have to have it to run our televisions and the air conditioning—which is something we can learn to get along without. I mean, our parents, et cetera, have survived. I'm sure we can. It would be hard. I'm a television addict, but I would give it up. Probably I would give it up with some relief. I'm an addict to television, and there are times that I wish someone would break it for me.

*Why do you think Met Ed wants it open?*
The company just wants the money. Everyone is out to make money. I don't know. You have to separate the company from people, I guess. I don't know and I don't know if anyone could prove it that we really have to have a nuclear power plant. I don't know if I would believe anyone. If I really understood why we would have to have one, that otherwise we're going to have people freezing in the winter, all this sort of stuff, I would accept having it four miles from my home and having it run. But I still do not accept it, that we have to have it for people to live.

*Do you think the company cares about the opposition of the community?*
It depends upon if the official lives nearby, depends upon where the big shots live. . . . They care from, I think, from a public relations point of view, the picture of their company. I think if I was an official of the company, and this was my livelihood, and I was used to having some money and nice cars and a home, and maybe I was honestly convinced that it's safe, or maybe I'd made myself think that it's safe, that I'd look at all the local yokels and think, "Well, you know, what do they know? They don't know. I'm right here. This is safe. . . ." I don't know. Sometimes you

talk about companies but companies are run by individuals. I guess you have to take each individual and talk to them and find out where they live. Is the company from out of town or is it local? Do they have family and children going to school and do they really care for their family and children? You talk about companies, but companies are people. I don't know.

*Do you think the plant will reopen?*
I think they will reopen it. . . . I'm kind of pessimistic, I guess. I kind of feel that money talks louder than voices, and they [Metropolitan Edison] have the influence and money behind them, and the big shots, you know, and that they'll probably open it again. I don't know. Of course, I hope they don't. This gas [Krypton-85] they are releasing now, I don't even listen to the news, now. I don't even want to hear about it. Mom had a friend who lived . . . in Harrisburg, and she was pregnant, and every time anything happens, she leaves. And she calls me to leave, and I say no. And she doesn't understand why. I just feel I am not going to run every time something happens unless it's something like the accident.

As far as this gas is concerned, they basically say it is safe. Again, they are human, so I don't terribly trust what they say. This is just hearsay. My boss once said—I don't know anything about it, so it may not be true—he said when they first came out with x-rays, the first time that they discovered it, they thought it was completely safe. And some of these big stores, like in New York, had people stand there paying to use this x-ray machine. And, of course, now they know how dangerous that was. How much experience have they had with this gas? Fifty years is not enough. I just can say, "We're not God. No one is God." I just am a pessimistic person. It's these people, I don't trust anything they say. Sometimes I feel we try to do God's work.

*Whose information do you believe?*
I am not influenced by what antinuclear people say. I think my whole basis [for opposition] is that this is too big for us to handle. It's something beyond what we should handle, too delicate of a process. For example, if you absolutely have to use a drug for an extreme condition, you do it. But if you absolutely don't have to take the medicine, then you don't. You don't fool around with medicine if you don't have to. That is my attitude with other things such as the nuclear power plant. And in this case, it was too big for man to handle. I am not a religious person. I bring

God up a lot but I am not a fanatic. I do believe God knows what he is doing. We don't. (laughter) Except when he made us; he might have messed up. (laughter)

*Do you feel the quality of life in this area has been altered?*
If you are talking about homes, I really don't know how they have been selling. I know some have sold. I know that if I was going to buy a home, I would not want to buy one here. Yet there are people that think there is nothing to worry about, so you are probably going to sell your home to people who really don't care. I don't think I would buy one here because I would feel better a little farther away. If you had a meltdown, you are not safer ten to twenty miles away. But psychologically, I would [feel safer]. But as far as anything else, it really has not changed. It's changed only because I am home all the time. I meet my neighbors. But I don't notice any other change.

*Do you think any differently about this area?*
No, if the plant stays shut down. It is a nice place to live.

*Do you have bad dreams?*
When it happened, I had some dreams. I don't know if they were really dreams, when you are in that in-between stage of being awake and asleep. At this point, I cannot remember. I know I was frightened. Especially when my husband went back [to Newberry]. I was frightened when I was [at her parents'] home because if anything happened, we would never be able to come back to the area. When he was down here, I kept thinking of something happening and him not getting home to me. Then part of me wanted me to be with him and another part had to protect the baby. But outside of that, I might of had nightmares in the past year or so, but I don't dwell on it. Days go by and I don't think about it. One reason, when the news is on, I don't really pay any attention. When I hear about something, say the Krypton gas, then I feel panicky. But I guess that is one reason I avoid the news because I just don't want to think about it.

I guess I'm the kind of person who hides their head in the sand. (laughter) When it happens, it happens. (laughter) When they tell me the world is going to blow up in a few days, I will know about it one minute before it happens. I put it out of my mind more or less. It bothers me if I really think about it. At times, TMI is not as important as some other things. Sometimes it is important because it happened to me, but if I had not lived here, I might not have thought it was so important. I think that,

on the whole, it was one of many problems in the world including nuclear bombs, chemical warfare, and et cetera. I think what
bothers a lot of people is that you cannot see radiation but you
see a car right before you. I am not quite that bad. Wow. What
the heck. When you say, "Give me a car and you can get killed on
the way to the grocery store," I think that's kind of a silly attitude. That's really putting your head in the sand. That's really
not caring. "Oh, wow! The world is really a mess. Why care?" I
am not quite that bad. But I am not one to dwell on it [TMI] and
get bent out of shape because it is there. If you're going to worry
about it, then you might as well shoot yourself.

*Are risks all the same to you?*
If I die from cancer of the lungs, it was my fault. If I get killed in
an accident, no matter if it was my fault or someone else's, I had
the option of driving the car. I take that chance. But if I die from
radiation from TMI because some guy is making a lot of money
and says it absolutely is necessary that we have this plant and I
don't have any control over it, my death, I think that bothers
me—the fact that I don't [have control].

If there weren't so many different people, I mean if you believed government better and believed people better, and they
could convince me that it was absolutely necessary, then I would
accept it and say, "Okay, you know, it is necessary. I don't want
someone to freeze to death because I am afraid of living four
miles from TMI." It is just—I don't know if anyone will really
convince me because you don't know who to believe or if they
know what they are talking about. So I guess that is mainly the
thing, that you have some control or if you die from cancer, it
was your own dumb fault because you were smoking too many
cigarettes.

*Do you think the accident is similar to a flood or something like
that?*
Like Mt. St. Helens—I guess it's God, nature. It's terribly tragic.
The only difference is that it was a natural catastrophe where
this was because of man's stupidity. You may not understand why
there was a flood or whatever, but this is God's world. It was a
natural cause. This TMI was what man had caused. This is what
made a lot of people angry. I feel a loss. It is hard to accept this
because of some stupid mistake. It is hard to accept. I don't know
if TMI bothers me the most. When I said in the past, I had fear of
it. I don't have any more fear of that than I did of countries hav-

ing the bomb, ours included. Chemical warfare, biological warfare bothers me even more because that's something that is more scary now that more countries are getting the bomb—the more chances of something happening.

Sometimes, I think I don't know why I had a baby. Why am I bringing a child into the world? Then I think, twenty years ago my parents thought the same thing. I guess my parents thought about the hydrogen bomb. They did not stop having children. On the one hand, I am saying, "What am I doing?" On the other, "Life hasn't been bad for me, and so far the world is still going. So I guess I'll give someone else a chance."

I am not involved. I am not one for demonstrating. Maybe I should be. If I don't want it to open, then I should be, I should be involved. I don't think about it a whole lot, and I'm not involved. Sometimes I'm ashamed at my lack of involvement. Again, I'm not one for demonstrating and stuff. And I think, "Well, I should be if I don't want it to open. I should be involved." And then I get to the other part of me saying, "What good will it do anyway?" which is a terrible attitude. It's my mother. I have to fight it all the time. My mother and I have these talks all the time—how rotten our attitude is. I'm always yelling at my Mom, and I say, "Don't get mad, Mom. I'm just yelling at myself." I blame my mother. And she blames me. She came first.

*Do you think they'll consider the wishes of the community?*
Just like they took into consideration the protest of the release of the Krypton gas. So that's my answer. Take it how you want to. . . . They'll do what they want to anyway. They'll say, "Well, that's gonna cost me a few votes and that's gonna cause me a few problems here." But in the end, they'll do whatever they feel they must do.

## MRS. KELSEY

Mrs. Kelsey lived in a very new home in one of the subdivisions. At the time of the accident, she and her husband and their preschool son had lived there a little over a year. She was a young woman, about 25 years old.

*How do you feel now about Three Mile Island?*
That whole thing scares me. I don't trust that at all. I don't think

that they really know what they're doing. It's a new field. They really don't know all the things they should know about it. I think there's other sources of energy that we can use in Pennsylvania, especially coal. I think it [Three Mile Island] should be turned into coal if used at all for energy. It just really frightens me. It frightens me most about my son and all the little kids. I think, "Gee, they might have cancer by the time they're in their late twenties." And that's really upsetting. . . . I'm not so worried about myself, like most people. I still might go at an early age. I'm only twenty-five. You know, like in thirty years I'm only going to be fifty-five. Heck, I could have cancer then, and I think that's too soon to have something like that.

It's just frightening for me, really it is. I try to not think about it, you know. It's so close and everything. The best thing I guess most people try to do is put it out of their mind and try to forget about it. But every once in a while you do think about it when you hear it on the news and everything. . . . It makes me shiver sometimes when I see them [the towers].

*What do you think about the cleanup?*
They're just pulling at straws there too. They just, you know, they're trying to get things cleaned up, but they don't exactly know what they're going to do. They're just going to try things out, and we're just going to be guinea pigs in this area for whatever ends up happening. They could have leakage to exceed what we should really get, but then it's too late. We've already gotten it. I just don't trust the cleanup, as I said before, . . . I didn't trust the state or the local people. I wasn't really trusting anybody after a while because after Met Ed did what they did and everything and lied to us and everything [in the first days of the accident], I didn't trust anybody.

*Do you want to move?*
Nowadays with the way things are you just can't pack up and go and leave your job, your position, sell your home. Selling your home is a real joke out here anyhow. You know, what can you do? You're really stuck.

*What did you think about Three Mile Island before the accident?*
To tell you the truth, I really didn't give it a whole lot of thought before that. I didn't know the dangers. I knew it was there. I really didn't know the dangers and everything. I felt that it was, you know, safe and everything until the whole accident came out. I just didn't know the seriousness of nuclear. That's when I

finally got educated to it, really. I wasn't antinuclear before because I didn't know anything about it.

*Do you want to move?*
I would really like it [Three Mile Island] to be somewhere else because I like where I'm at right now, my house. All my life I've
been in this area. We floated around. We were in Dillsburg first
and then New Cumberland. Our first home we sold, and then we
came out here and built this. This is what our dream was from
before we got married. We knew we were going to purchase land,
and this was our big dream for our house forever out here in the
woods. I just can't believe what happens when you have a dream
like this and have something like this nuclear plant.

*Is it on your mind a lot?*
People try to forget a situation like this, try to put it out of your
mind.

*Who do you think will decide about the reopening?*
If it's Metropolitan Edison, they're concerned about their money,
and I think that's where the key lies. They want to get that thing
back in operation, and that seems to be all they're concerned
about—the money for money's sake. I really don't think that people's concerns matter to them much. Now, I don't know if the
Nuclear Regulatory Commission—if that matters to them or not.
I just think Met Ed is money hungry, and they just want to get it
open for their livelihood.

*Do you think it will reopen?*
Yeah, I think it probably will. . . . It upsets me, but there's
nothing you can really do. . . . They keep saying we need this nuclear. They keep pounding that into our heads with the news and
everything. We need it, we need it, we can't do without it. But I
feel certain we can do without it.

*Do you think they will consider the feelings of the community?*
I thought at least they would be concerned about the people's
health. It seems like money is always where people are most concerned and human life is, like, second. They worry about that
second.

*Are you worried about the environment in general?*
I just think it's really insane to do this to our beautiful nation—
to make areas uninhabitable and so forth from something like
that. I think that's totally crazy. I can't figure out why people

think that makes any sense. . . . I don't know what they're thinking. I just think we have such a beautiful country and everything, and everything's more industrialized as the years go on,
and I see they want to always progress and everything. But I
think we're going in the wrong direction as far as progressing
with things. They're really doin' it the wrong way because
they're really gonna end up messing up our country really bad
with this. I believe, you know, in moving on with things and im-
proving upon things but this sure isn't the right way to go about
it. . . . I don't believe in anything extra that's gonna hurt me.

## MR. CRAWFORD

Mr. Crawford lived in probably the most affluent subdivision in Newberry Township. He was a businessman who worked in Harrisburg, in his
thirties, and married. At the time of the accident, he and his wife had no
children but at the time of the interview his wife was pregnant. He had
lived in Newberry Township about three years, and both his and his
wife's parents lived in the Harrisburg area.

*Where were you at the time of the accident?*
When I first heard about it, I was [at work]. This is on Wednesday
morning, 9:30 in the morning. I had heard earlier about it on the
radio, but I had not paid any attention to it. When I was in the
building, I asked someone what was going on. He said, "Got some
problems down at TMI." I said at that point, "Well, I hope it isn't
a meltdown." And everybody just kind of looked at me. And my
wife asked me, "What's a meltdown?" And I explained it, and
that was it. Very curious, very strange time. . . . I went through
the [morning] and then just listened to it [radio reports] and
heard that everything was okay. So I went to sleep that night and
got up the next day and went about my usual activities. And that
Friday morning it all happened. . . . Well, about 9:30 in the
morning I was at my desk, and I heard that there was another
leakage, that they were going to evacuate, that things were not
right. So my wife works in the same office. So I said, "Well, I'll
tell you what. If they are evacuating everybody out there, why
don't you just go home, get the silver, get the dog and the cat,
and grab whatever else you want because you may not be able to
go back." So she said, "Okay." And I said, "I'll take care of the office here. I'm going to start letting people go," because a lot of

people lived right out here. So she came out here and everybody else was going crazy out here, trying to get out. On this block, there are thirty kids, so everybody on this block left.

So it got to be about 1:00 (P.M.) and we were back in Harrisburg, and they said, well, they definitely had to evacuate people. And then they said there were no further releases, but then there were releases at 4:00 P.M. I looked at my wife and said, "It doesn't matter." They weren't telling us what type of releases. I said, "If they're gamma rays, you got hit. Even if you go twenty miles from here, it'll go through anything, except lead, eight feet of lead." So I said, "I'll tell you what. We might as well go back home. There are only going to be idiots out on the road. Besides that, nobody's going to be on our block. There is going to be looting or whatever." So I said, "Let's just go back."

So we did. We came back. We called my parents who live in [the area]. You could hardly call. You just got busy signals or all lines are filled. We eventually got hold of her mother, and she said, "If they tell us to get out, we'll see you in Delaware." And my parents said, "Well, we'll see you in Wisconsin." And I said, "Okay, we'll end up somewhere, I guess." But my main concern was that if I didn't get my wife back over on the east side of the river, we were going to get separated because they were just going to close down the bridge. So anyway, I had figured, "Look, you've gotten hit by all this radiation. You're in duck soup anyway. You might as well come back here, and if they are looting, you might as well preserve what you've got." Maybe we could help people back here—because we didn't have any kids.

So anyway, we came back, and the neighbor down the street, same guy who helped me build this [house], said, "Well, it's all [a mess]. We might as well get [messed] up, too." So we sat out front, and we drank beer. And people come through, and we had shotguns. A strange car drove up the street. We just pointed the gun. He got the idea. So, it was myself, my wife, this guy. His wife was at the Navy Depot and they didn't want her to leave. She had a high priority security clearance, and they didn't want her to leave. She works on their computers. So she stayed at work. I guess one or two people came back, but they just came for some things, and they took off. So we sat here, and then we went to bed. And the next day we started partying again. That is basically what we did. We had a birthday party for this guy [the neighbor] that night. There was nobody for ten miles out. It was kind of like a hurricane party—waiting for disaster. It was kind of like that. It was kind of strange.

That Friday night, we went around the area on Friday night, and vigilantes would stop us. We knew the vigilantes. That's about it. Then Sunday came, and my wife said, "Well, let's go out and get some plants—might as well live a normal life." And we went out and planted them. Gave the finger to President Carter when he flew over the area in his helicopter. Basically, we took it kind of easy and by Wednesday or Thursday people started trickling back. We never left. . . . I went to work every day. In fact, that Friday when the sirens were going off in Harrisburg, they told you to stay inside, I had a conference, and we had waited a month and a half to get the conference, so I went. Everybody [was there]. It was just business as normal. All the air conditioning was off in the [building] because they didn't want to draw in the air so we all sat there and sweltered. But damnit, we just went about it like business as usual. We felt we had to do that.

We went down to the beer distributor. My God, we drove from here down almost to York Haven and got even closer [to Three Mile Island] yet to get to the beer distributor. And he has a sign up above his door that says, "Come on in out of the fallout. Fallout Shelter." Now, he's doing a bumper business. So it was more of a gallows humor type thing. What more could happen? What more could happen? Who cares?! It was totally out of our control. We didn't really have too much to say about [it]. But so what? If the thing was going to go, five miles isn't going to help you. So we partied. That's about what we did.

*Was there any source of credible information in your opinion?*
Probably CBS News because Walter Cronkite doesn't tell lies. (laughter) No, I'd say the only source was the CBS affiliate in Harrisburg. After a while you didn't even believe what the hell Met Ed was saying. So you would listen to the NRC statements. In fact, it got funny. You would kinda say, "What is Met Ed going to say after the NRC came out with their report?" I will say, at that time, when Denton [Harold Denton, NRC liaison] came on the scene, he was like a placebo. "Oh my God! Somebody's here who knows what they are doing!" He was a stabilizing force. I couldn't have given a damn what Carter was saying—that didn't make any difference to me. I mean, he worked on submarines. Rickover sold him on nuclear power. I mean, who gives a damn?

But Denton kind of—he was at least one voice you could hear, have some faith in what he was saying. Even though it was shown [later] that he was wrong!

*If he said something now would you believe him?*
No, no, probably not because I know now that he relied on the same bad information that everyone else was receiving from the plant. In fact, now it's kind of interesting that Met Ed was probably more correct. I mean, the poor bastard Jack Herbein. He was the Vice President of Press Relations [for Metropolitan Edison]. It was so bad. Jack Herbein would come on, everybody just booed. . . .

*What about local officials? Did you have any contact with local civil defense?*
They weren't even in place as far as I was concerned. They had a fire truck come out, but they added more to the hysteria than not. A good example—a contractor—he was putting a roof on the house, and a fire truck came by, and they said "Get off the roof. Don't you know there's fallout? Get inside underneath the roof." So everybody scrambles off the roof and gets inside. So they're sitting inside. What the hell's the difference? It's ⅝-inch plywood. It's [radiation] coming right through. I mean, that was the crazy stuff.

*Do you think there were dangerous levels of radiation at any time during the accident?*
I don't know. I don't know what dangerous is. That's my problem. I could say, do I think that by all the standards was it like an atomic blast? No, but I do think that there could have been radiation that was released but maybe I won't know about it for a while. It may show up later. I can hardly believe that you can factor out one or two cancers in a half a million people [in the Harrisburg area] and relate it to that. I think, I just think . . . the goddamn thing scared you so . . . that you didn't really. . . . It was apathy. What am I going to do? I've lost my house. I've lost everything that I've worked for. That occurred to me, too. It's gone! Yeah, that is why we grabbed the silver because it was one thing that if we wanted to get started again, it would be a down payment. And that's what we grabbed and the dog and the cat. You walk away from it. You say, "What if I can't sell the home? What do I do? Declare bankruptcy? Forget about the mortgage?" Take the Connollys. They left. Two hundred years (the family

had farmed on this land)! Took all their cows and beat it. They just left!

*Have there been changes in the community since the accident?*
Yeah, I'd say life hasn't been as serious, or it has not been as fun in this community. Let's put it that way. People in the community used to be fun. People were more interested in building their careers but were permanent here. More like people like myself or the builder or the guy down here who is a professional engineer. It just seems as though that the accident changed their lives. They all of a sudden thought, "Hey, I could have been wiped out. I'm here not to make a buck. I'm here to live." I think that changed their whole perspective. They party more. I've noticed it. Yeah, they do. I don't know if it's an escape, but there are parties here every weekend. It wasn't that way before. It was a very conservative, serious type of thing but I don't think they're as happy as they used to be. I don't know why. It's a curious mix. Yeah, I go to the parties. They are not cocktail parties. They're beer bashes, wild stuff! Yeah, I go to that. The flavor of the conversations, their style of interactions are different. Yeah, it's totally different. This group is different. It's been different since '78—it just—they're mad, they're upset. They don't want to talk about it. They know what's happened. And they'll look at the island and say, "F— that place." Period. They don't want to talk, but you can sense it. That's just my perception of it. . . . I'm upset but it doesn't obsess me because I really have an inner feeling, like a lot of people do, that this whole thing is going to blow over; the thing won't reopen, because it's going to cost too much. For example, the door's rusted shut. Well, if the door's rusted shut, what else is rusted in the place? How much is that going to cost? Not too many people realize that there's only one ventilation system, and they don't realize that if that doesn't work, they can't control it [the plant]. They haven't figured that out yet. It's not something they publicize. No, they don't. Very few people do not realize that it is not a cold shutdown. One pump could go, and it's back to where it was. It's in the back of everybody's mind. You can't help it. You see it every night when you come home. I see it every night I come home, and it just may be a passing thought. But it's not an obsession. It's not my whole life, like some others. . . . So, I don't know. I wouldn't say people go around and mope about it. But I think I've sensed the change. Some of the people, if they could get out, would leave.

*Of course anyone in this neighborhood you would think could
leave, but it seems that other considerations—career, school, and
other things—override. They don't move.*
Not now. Not now. Maybe a year from now or if something goes
wrong, like it will. Then it may become—

*Do you think something will go wrong?*
Oh, I'm sure there are so many things that could go wrong down
there, I'm sure something will get screwed up.

*Why do you stay?*
(A) [My business] is in this area. (B) I think I'm building a repu-
tation in the area. (C) I've got [business partners] who, if I
wanted to pull out, this would cause problems. And I like the
people out here. I like the area. Why should I have to move because of that? That's my attitude. I'd say a lot of people have that
view, especially the people who are against reopening and have
lived here for years. I think you will sense that. And I never ran
away from a fight, and I consider this a fight. And I am still en-
gaged in the fight, I still have some control. I am still there. I am
right there.

*Do you go to the demonstrations?*
People I know right in this block, nobody's going down. But there
are others in the community I am sure will go down there. Yeah,
they would be there. But if that ever happens, if they go to restart
it, Seabrook's [a much-contested nuclear power plant in New
Hampshire] going to look small because, all those people, it's just
going to be an international thing, you're going to get people
down here from all over, just swarming. And as far as Unit 2
opening again, I don't believe it will ever reopen again. Unit 1
could go on line right now, ten minutes from now. . . . So I'd say,
generally, that people are not as happy go lucky. Because I would
have to say that most people in this neighborhood don't have too
many problems. The only problems are the ones they generate on
their own. In fact, this block has been pretty stable. There hasn't
been a divorce in this block. In fact, nobody's moved onto this
block except one family. That was two years ago. But in this community that's pretty unusual. People are really mobile, transient.

*Do you think most people are against the reopening?*
Well, it's amazing. Some people who you think are going to be
pronuke are not. Some of the older people that just sit and look at

it and say, "It's not right. We never had this problem before. Why do we need it now?"

*What if the plant reopens? Do you think it would be like Seabrook?*
I don't know. This plant is totally different. It is right on the river. If you and I wanted to go over there I could have you right beside Unit 1 or 2 without any problems. We could climb the fence. I could have you there in twenty minutes. I am serious. All you need is a boat. Just go right up, park it on the island, crawl up over the fence. You would get to the reactor before anyone could get to you. Hell's bells! I know as close as two years ago a guy capsized his boat out there, drunk as a skunk, took off his clothes, swam into the shore, climbed over the fence, walked right into the control room. He is stark naked—"Hey, what's going on?" That's a true story. I don't think that quite could quite happen today. But who knows? Who knows? You still can get right up to the island. The fence isn't electrified as far as I know. But if you really wanted to get out there, it would be very simple. . . . It is totally different at Seabrook. You cannot get within a mile. But this thing, it's right up on the river. Well, if you want to get down to the basics, you just heard the 12-gauge shotgun [behind us]. There is a hill less than a mile from here that you have a total vantage point of the whole island. And with a high-powered rifle . . . unbelievable. I mean, total, just total [the view]. You come up over the hill and it's just sitting down there. What's to stop some idiot? . . . It only takes one.

*Are you against reopening the plant?*
No. I am against reopening the plant if in fact a couple of things aren't in place: (A) If an emergency plan to get us out of here is not in place. If you cannot get me out of here within a reasonable four-hour period, then don't open the damn thing next to me. If you can't give me four hours lead-way to get the hell out of here, then don't open. (B) You've got to prove to me you're going to have enough justifiable, reliable information—prove to me that that thing can be operated safely, that I'm not going to have to worry about every two days, something happening, because that's where the stress is for me and that's just starting to show now because I lost my wife for a week back in February when we knew she was three months pregnant. She left and she was gone for a week.

And she's had really strange dreams. Like last night or two nights ago I woke her up from a nightmare and she said, "I saw a casket, an infant's casket." Okay? Now she never had these types of dreams before. I said, "What the hell's it about?" She said, "I don't know. I never thought about these things before but it's that goddamn island. That has to be it." Now she has some—she has a minor in psychology. So she knows something about it. But, you know, it boiled down to, one day back in February she just said it. "If it wasn't for that thing, I wouldn't have to leave. My life wouldn't be disrupted. But I feel I've got to go. So goodbye, I'm going." And she left. She came back.

And you ask her physician a direct question. "Is the island, is what they're going to release dangerous to the fetus?" "I don't know. I don't know what to tell you. My personal belief is that no it isn't but medically I can't tell you it isn't. I don't know what the long-term effects of low radiation exposure." But what kind of solace is that? That's changed it a bit. But that's what I mean. If they can't prove, and maybe that's making them prove the negative. So maybe I'm saying, in actuality, "No, they can never open it again." But if I could have some reassurance. But I don't know how they could do that. That may be a little tough. . . . That's the other question. Nobody knows, nobody knows how much we were hit with. Nobody will ever know.

*It seems even pronuclear people in this community have these fears for their families that come out after you talk to them awhile.*
Yeah, a perfect example . . . (I know someone) at the time of the accident who was in the Air National Guard, on alert. He said, "Screw it. I am not going down there." If you get down to the nitty gritty and you can get people to go back to March 30 when they found out and were telling people to get the hell out, ask them how they felt. And then if they don't know that could be the same situation tomorrow morning if something goes wrong over there. They may not be so hep. You know, that was really a—it was like somebody belted you. Have you ever been hit in the face so hard that you don't even feel pain? You are just stunned. Well, that's just about the way it felt. When I was in college, I had two roommates who participated in intramural boxing, and they got me up one night and we started boxing. And they hit me in the face so hard—it was just, boom. It stuns you, and you sat there. And that's just the way we felt—stunned.

It was like a hollow feeling. You just sat there and you'd watch the tube, and Walter Cronkite would come on, and he'd say, "This is the most dangerous twenty-four-hour period ever in the history of the world," or the United States. And, you know, you're sitting there looking out the window. Oh, yeah, . . . well, you can see the lights on them now—there are the towers. I don't know whether you can see the aviation lights, but they're on. [So you thought,] "Yeah, that's right. Thanks a lot, Walter." (laughter)

*Do you think you should have left?*
In retrospect, yes, maybe I should have left, but, like I said, I felt the worst was over. I had that blind confidence. Maybe some of this is my . . . I think a lot of people found God in their own way in that twenty-four-hour period. Really. You don't talk about it, but there is a strong sense of it at that point. Some people absolutely went nuts. Some people weathered it pretty well. I know of a girl and a guy who came back on Friday night. They didn't know where the hell they were going. She was screaming, "Let's get the hell out of here! Let's leave!" And they left. They went down to Maryland, and they came back the next day. This person [who worked for a school] had been through the day where they took all the kids, and they evacuated them; parents didn't know where their kids were; she had just flipped out. Others hung in there. Some people got their families out, some of the guys [around here], and then came back. It's very strange. . . . I knew there was a problem, but I felt it had happened already. I felt, my family was all leaving, my sister, my in-laws. We said, "We don't care. If you go, it's your choice, but you are going out there with all the crazies. There's no place to go, and you've already been hit." I felt I had more of a duty to stabilize. Maybe that was crazy. I just felt that was the thing to do. Probably in retrospect, I'd probably do the same damn thing unless I heard them say, "It's definitely a meltdown." Then I'm gone.

*What about evacuation?*
I've been down Route 74 [the old evacuation route]. All you have to do is get behind one RV and you've had it. I knew where I was going. I was going down the dirt roads; I was going over the mountains; I was going west, and then I'll dip south. I knew all the dirt roads. Sure, I have my personal evacuation plan. Everybody does. I'm not getting on I-83 to have some idiot try to tell

me which way to go. But doesn't that show you something? It's
kind of individualistic. All these people know all these dirt roads.
(laughter)

## MRS. BOSWELL

Mrs. Boswell, about fifty, lived in a comfortable older home on one of the
main roads in Newberry Township. Her husband owned his own business, which was located next to their home. A son and daughter-in-law
who also lived in the township had a new baby at the time of the
accident. We conducted the interview on her screened porch.

*How did you hear about the accident?*
Well, in my situation, my son heard about it. He is below Washington, D.C., and he called me, and I didn't even know about the
accident at the time. He is a college graduate, and he is an engineer, and he knows a little about nuclear. He said, "Mom, you
tell Dad. Get out of there right away, as quickly as possible!" This
was on Wednesday. And I was just numb. We have a business
next to the house. I called my husband right away, and he kind of
laughed, you know. That day I didn't feel too bad about it. The
next day when the reports started coming out, I started getting
jittery. Of course, one of my sons and my daughter-in-law live
down the road and just had a baby, and that worried me. And, of
course, Friday we had the radio on. Thursday night we were up
listening to all the reports, and then Friday morning when Governor Thornburgh told that children had to be evacuated, well then
I went along, and my husband stayed here on account of the
business. So we left and went . . . about twenty-five miles away.
We stayed with relatives there. Now at that time they were all
still numb. It was like we just didn't know. In other words, if I
knew then what I know now, I would have been so terrified I
would have gone as far away as possibly I could have! I would
have gone as far away as possible. I would have gone to relatives
that live in the Midwest.

*What do you know now?*
Well, the meltdown. [And] the way some scientists talk now,
some say that we are still in a critical stage with these gases
being trapped inside the containment area. I think I learned a lot
that I never really knew. Living this close to a nuclear plant, I
mean you just sort of assume [it's okay] . . . when you go into the

area, when you see the plant day by day, I think it's a lot harder on you too. I don't see the plant every day. But my daughter-in-law does, and she has to get up every day and look at that plant. And she is a lot worse off than I am in nerves. It affects her a lot more.

*What exactly are you worried about?*
The unknown. We still—you know, as much as I've read about it in the papers, and scientists have given their opinions and everything, but still I don't think they know exactly what's going on inside that reactor right now.

*Do you think it is still dangerous?*
I just don't know. Well, this one scientist, I read his article, and he said we are still not out of the crisis. So I don't know.

*Are you worried about health effects?*
Well, not myself so much unless it, in other words, if the thing would blow, what they call blow, then I'd really be concerned. But right now I don't think of it too much. But I think of my grandchildren, what it's going to do to them because I'm in my fifties, and, well, say if I get cancer, I couldn't prove that it happened from that. It could be my genes, but the only way I would worry is if something really terrible happened. I am worried about cancer, birth defects, genetic defects for the children or for something catastrophic that could happen, like that Saturday when they came on TV, and they said there is going to be a meltdown. Well, up to that point, we were already packed to go. We had our van packed with food and clothing and what pictures and things we wanted to take along. If we would never be able to come back at least we would have a little bit of our family. . . . But then they said the danger was past.

For weeks after that everybody was talking about it, and everybody was saying, "If they are going to open that plant again, we are going to do this and we are going to do that." Everybody was so worked up. It cooled off, but now I think if they start talking about opening it up again, start cleaning it up, and start it up again, I think then that there is going to be a lot of trouble because, I think, that the people just won't stand for it. I know a lot of people who went through a lot of rough times. People over in Middletown, I guess, are more affected by it than us. I don't know why, but if you drive through Middletown, everywhere you look you see that plant. You just can't avoid it.

*What part does it play in your everyday thinking?*
I don't think about it too much as time goes by. I'd say, at first, it
was all the time. Maybe three weeks later it was less, in degrees.
But now if you hear the name TMI on the television, right away
you start thinking a little bit about it and then you think of that
article you read in the paper and then you start . . . or if you're
with friends sitting down and talking, you know, and you get on
the subject. Well, then somebody will bring something up that
you never even thought about: what if this would happen, what
if that would happen. Well, then right away you get all worked
up again. But then it passes until the next time. . . . Oh, yes, I
think subconsciously it's always there.

At first, I was very nervous, and I would take something to
sleep at night. But I can relax now. It doesn't bother me now. I
didn't have nightmares, but I'd awake at night. It would break
my sleep, you know, and I would think about it, and then I
would go back to sleep again. It would not be a nightmare. But I
am a light sleeper anyway. If I took medication, I would still
awake. So it was there because TMI was there. It's better now.
But if they would open that up, I would really be on pins and
needles again. Now I kind of feel it's stable unless they went in
there again.

*How did you cope with your intense feelings after the accident?*
Talking, I guess, going to other places, being with other people,
trying to talk. In other words, getting together and discussing it
and trying to—it didn't help, I mean, it helped to talk, but it
didn't solve the situation.

*Do you know a lot of people who are upset now?*
Yes, people around here that I come in contact with. . . . There is
a beauty parlor up in Newberry. I go there every Saturday. All
those people were quite definitely upset. I don't blame them. Yes,
everybody I know was definitely upset. I can't think of anybody
that wasn't. I don't know one person.

*Is your husband upset, too?*
Yes, but he has a business. He made me leave that Friday, but he
wouldn't leave because he said he wasn't going to leave his business. So, he felt about the same way [I did], but he is a strong person in that way. So I felt bad about that, too, and so I came back
on Saturday. I wouldn't stay. I had my son, the one from Washington, he came home that weekend. I called him up and told

him to come up to the lake and pick me up and bring me back because I couldn't stay away from my husband. If anything happened, I wanted to be here with him. Oh, my, that was terrible,
but you just can't be away and know that somebody is back there
you love. You want to be with them. . . .

Then after Saturday night, when President Carter came over,
on Sunday, that was a terrible Sunday for us. I go to church. I
think it's about seven miles away from here. It's south of here.
That's where I lived before we moved here. And we went to
church. There was hardly anyone in the church, and we have a
congregation of about five hundred people. Just everything was so
deserted. You could drive on the road, and you didn't see any
people. My sister went along with me, to church with me, and
she said, "What if they make us evacuate? How are we going to
find out where our families would be?" I sat in church and
prayed, and I said, "If they are going to evacuate, please wait until we get home." It worked out all right that way. Yes, I think
some things are fair to somebody because we were very close [to
disaster].

*What were your sources of information?*
Well, everything that I could get hold of that pertains to nuclear
power—*Time* magazine, *Harper's*, any magazine that I could get
hold of where there was a man in there who was an authority on
it [nuclear energy], not the owner of the company or the governor. He gets his information from somebody, I know, and passes it
on to us. But is that really what is going on? You have to delve a
little deeper. You have to read a little deeper and find out what
really did go wrong after they give you their version of it.

*What do you think about the information from the NRC and Met
Ed officials?*
I think—I do believe that the NRC should be the best informed
regarding nuclear plants. As far as Met Ed, because of what happened on Wednesday and Thursday of that week, from then on I
just didn't [trust them]. I thought, "Well, I'm going to have to
find out, you know, what is going on myself." I do a lot of reading. On Friday night [before the interview] there was an article in
the *York Dispatch* [local newspaper] by a psychiatrist—a woman
psychiatrist. She said TMI did not cause enough stress in this
vicinity to amount to a—stress was very little. She had done a
study. I think her name was Bromet. And I just could not under-

stand where she was from that she thought that there was no stress because everyone that I know was under stress, deep stress. When you go around and do stuff and do not even know that you are doing this and forgot you did it, and you are just walking around like a zombie for about four or five days, isn't that stress? I know a lot of people who were like that. They did stupid things that they never did before. They drank like they never did before. I drank more than under normal conditions. So, yes, I think there was a lot of stress, and I still think there is a lot because it is still unsettled over there. If it would be settled one way or another, I think it would ease people's minds a lot. But we are still living under a cloud of uncertainty. They don't know what is going to happen when they open that door [to the damaged reactor]. They don't know if they are going to start up the reactor again.

*If they clean up the plant, how would you feel about reopening it?*
I definitely say No! I say the only way that I think that's possible is if they convert to coal. Then they could open it. . . . They say it is going to cost too much [to convert to coal]. Yet it is going to cost five hundred million dollars to clean up that reactor and that containment building.

*If they did open the plant, what would you fear?*
It would be that uncertainty. Is it going to happen again? Because there have been so many things that have happened after that accident. It just seems like a jinx.

*Do you know people who had experiences that they might think were connected to the accident?*
Yes, I know somebody who had peach trees with problems. They said on that side, facing Three Mile Island, that those trees were just destroyed and that the only side that got green was on the other side. And I know a woman at the hairdresser who claims that three or four months after [the accident], she had bleached hair, and her hair had changed a different shade, and they couldn't get it straightened out for about three or four months. She wore a wiglet in her hair [before the accident], and it always matched the other part of her hair. And after that it didn't match for about three months. And they finally got it back to the right shade. My husband told me that he was out attending the gas pumps [on the Friday after the accident]. He said it was a very sultry day, and he walked out there. He felt like he could taste

metal in his mouth—he felt like he could taste it. He says he doesn't know if it was his imagination or if it really was some kind of gas that was coming out of the reactor that was doing that or what. That was Friday.

*Do you feel differently about Newberry now?*
No. I like this place—it's nice. I mean, we were living so peaceably, and then something like that happens. I mean, why do they build plants so close to—why can't they build them up in the mountains and send electricity down? I think they built it too close to a populated area in the first place.

*Are you opposed to nuclear energy?*
No, I'm not opposed to nuclear energy but, like I say, if they were built farther away. They should restrict them, I'd say, to within a twenty-mile area. They should be twenty miles out some place. At least people would be able to get out of there if something would happen. But we're only three-and-one-half or three miles from the plant. That's too close to a nuclear plant.

*Would you be concerned if you didn't have children living nearby?*
No, I don't know about that. I guess I wouldn't. I mean, I have a grandson, and I just think the world of him. I think of what his future's going to be for him. Like I say, my husband and I, we've lived a good life so far, and what's going to be is going to be. I know at the time I was very nervous, walking around like a zombie. But my chief concern was for my son and his family. I did stupid things in those days. I just wish I could remember what I had done. It was crazy. I would be walking around, and I could not get myself organized. I am an organized person. I get everything done in the morning and maybe sit down and read in the afternoon. But I couldn't concentrate on reading. All I wanted to do was have the news on, have the TV on, and find out what was happening. Lots of times they would not tell you until the next day what had happened before.

*How did you feel about the plant before the accident?*
I didn't realize the danger. I thought it was safe. Well, we have a place down on the river, a little place where we can take our boat over on one of the islands, and we used to go past the plant when they were building it, and it never gave me another thought. We'd go past there, and they were setting up the cooling towers at the time, and we remarked how large they were, you know,

and we never even gave it a second thought. I always thought nuclear energy was safe. Really safe. I was not opposed to it.

*Did you fear that you would never return to your home?*
Yes, that happened, like I say, the night that we were packed and ready to go, and we knew then from reading and talking and hearing it on the radio what could happen. Maybe we would have to evacuate fifty miles away from here. Maybe we would never be able to come back here. That's a terrible feeling because you don't know what to take, and you have to leave everything here that you bought in a lifetime, things you cherish. You get to take so much, and that's it. And my husband said positively he wouldn't leave. He said, "Even if there's a meltdown, I'm staying." And my son said, "No you're not, Dad, even if I have to drag you out and put you in the van."

All our life savings and everything is tied up in that building over there and to just give it up and leave, that's a terrible thought. A lot of people with jobs are not as affected. We own property here. We would have had to give up everything. How much would our property be worth? The government would probably give us so much money per foot or something and that would be it. We would have to move, go to a strange state and get another job. He is 53. Go get another job and start all over at that age and you wouldn't get the same as what you had here, and you'd know it was here, and you couldn't come back to it. Probably not for a hundred years would you be able to re-enter it on account of radioactivity.

*Did you realize that might happen before the accident?*
No! No! Why, the way they talked about it, it was so safe. Why, it had those big, thick cement walls, you know, to contain the gases and the radioactivity, and it never dawned on me. I don't think anyone around here thought much about it.

*Would you leave this area under any circumstances?*
Since we know more about it now, and if we knew what the conditions were—under what conditions we would have to leave—if it would be temporary, we would leave. If we could come back, if we knew, I think he'd leave then. But, to give up everything . . . oh, I guess he would go. I don't know what he would do! I have two sons, and they'd probably drag him out of here. But it would be a hard thing on him. . . . It would be a terrible decision. The only way we would go is if we could come back. Yes, I think he

would leave then. But there is no place to go. They have nuclear plants all over the United States now. I have a brother who is living in North Dakota. He is about the farthest away from any nuclear plant. He is in Fargo. So Friday morning I called him. I told him to look for an apartment for us. "If things get worse, we're leaving Saturday night, depending on this bubble. As soon as they say there is going to be a meltdown, we are leaving, and you find an apartment for us." He said, "Don't worry. I'll have everything taken care of." So we had a place to go. But it was the idea of going. We were afraid of looting. We didn't know who would stay here. Most everyone would leave except some people who thought they could take advantage of the situation because the state police or—usually they call them during riots—the National Guard, they wouldn't want to stay. They wouldn't want to watch over the buildings. They would have to leave, too. Or they would be in the same situation.

*How would you compare this event to a flood or volcanic eruption or some other natural disaster?*
This is a worse situation. If there was a meltdown, things would have been much worse. All our families are connected, we are very close. It is good to be home.

*Some people say we must live with risks, and we do every day. So what is the difference between this and other risks?*
Well, this was caused by an error. If I drive over the middle lane and hit another car, it was my fault. Or if I am going to die by being hit by a bolt of lightning, yes, I would accept that. But this is a man-made error. Somebody else did it, and I am the victim. That is the way that I feel. I think it was caused by somebody or someone pulling the wrong lever or not pulling the right lever.

*Who will decide, do you think, about reopening TMI?*
Well, I don't hope it's Met Ed. I don't hope it's the Public Utility Commission. I hope it's somebody—I hope its people who really know, have the knowledge, and think of the people who live in the area and have a human interest in us, too, not just the plant. They've got to take a human interest because we don't want to be guinea pigs. We want to live here. We like it here. And that company is run, and they have stockholders, they pay a dividend to their stockholders, I'm not going to get involved in the money situation, but I still think that we should have a say, too, in what goes on. I really do, because we're the victims.

*Do you think the community will decide?*
No, we'll go to town meetings, and we'll spout off a little bit, you
know, or maybe we'll go to the capitol building and have banners, you know, and so many thousand people will attend but in
the end what the—the little guy just does have no say. I've never
seen the little guy win yet when you come up against a big organization. Now if you have a big guy behind a little guy then that
helps. But I don't see nothing in the future for that. I don't see
anybody that is really interested in trying to keep it closed
down—except us. So I don't know what's going to become of us
or it. . . . I think monetary reasons will be the reason to get the
plant running. Oh, I think they'll advertise, be headlines in the
paper, make it look good and make you feel good, but we have to
have the electricity, they'll say. We need to have that plant in operation again. How many of those people that run that place
even live in this vicinity?

*Do you think the people who run the plant think it is safe?*
I wish I knew what they think. I just wish I knew. In the paper,
they come out and they say it doesn't hurt us, the amounts of radiation. But I know a doctor who lives down the road here, and
he said that ever since the plant has been in operation, radiation
has been escaping. They let out so much but not enough so that
it can hurt. He said your body cannot absorb that amount of radiation. Even these small amounts are not good for you. This is
since the plant has started operating. Before the accident, radiation was coming out, the doctor said. He is not my family doctor;
he is just my friend. He said that it was just small amounts of radiation, and you should only take a certain amount of it in. You
keep adding all the sources of radiation, the TV set, sun, other
background radiation, and nuclear power plants, it builds up.
And going back to the health situation, we won't even know for
maybe twenty to forty years if it had any effect either way. . . . I
don't think small amounts of radiation would show up that
quick. And they say it takes several hundred years before—What
do they say?—it decays. Thank heaven, you don't live a couple
hundred years. (laughter)

I don't know what the answer is but I know one thing: they
shouldn't build them this close to communities. I think they
should be banned from doing that. There are plenty of places up-
state that are isolated, and there are waterways right there. The

Susquehanna River starts in the northern part of Pennsylvania. But see, it's the access to get to them; it's so simple right here.

*Has the accident changed the quality of life here?*
I think for a time it did. I'd say—this happened in March of last year—I'd say until about October people were furious! People around here were very edgy, and they would go farther away on trips during the summer and try to get away from it. So I think it did have an effect, and it gradually eased off because the plant was shut down.

*Do you think there has been damage to the environment?*
I wish I knew more about radiation to answer that question. I don't know. Sometimes I believe when it happened, that day, which way the wind was blowing, that was the part that made one area more affected by the radiation. But I don't know too much about that, the aftereffects, I mean. The wind was very still, it was very sultry. My husband heard the accident around four in the morning. He didn't know what it was [but] he heard a loud hissing. He said he could not describe it. Loud hissing, like steam, then like a dull boom, not like a crack, like a dull boom. My daughter-in-law heard it, too. They have central air conditioning, had all the windows closed, and she heard it, too. It was a still night. For that time of the year, it was very sultry.

*Are you frightened now?*
No, as long as that plant is not throwing off any gases or somebody comes on the radio and says they've discovered a big leak. Then right away you start getting edgy again. Now a couple of weeks ago, they discovered radioactive water seeping out of one of the buildings. Right away, you think, "What if they can't hold it back? What if it keeps rushing out and goes in the river? What if?" You know, you are in that "if" stage, what if. I get real angry when I talk to people [around here about it]. We don't argue, you know, we don't argue pros and cons. We just get mad. . . . We just can't understand why it happened to us. My husband gets started on it. Yes, he is angry. Most people are. You mention TMI and someone picks it up from there, like a snowball, and it's going.

I have relatives living in different parts of the country. When they call, they don't even ask any more. They used to ask, "How are you are feeling about TMI?" or they would make a joke about it to cheer you up. And now they don't seem to ask anymore. It would be like if I asked someone near Mt. St. Helens how they feel. I would probably be very concerned, but I would probably forget it, too, after a while. I probably would not ask because I am not there. Everybody takes it personally. It is a personal problem. It is a personal situation. What if? What am I going to do? They're still, as far as I know, planning evacuation. They have evacuation plans all set up, ready to go.

*Do you think evacuation would work?*
No. I don't see how it possibly could work. Could you imagine hysterical people getting on the road? Did you read a book, it was about some kind of disease that hit all over the United States and everybody was trying to go everywhere. Roadblocks everywhere. Everybody died. Everybody got the disease. They didn't know what was causing it. They thought if they got out of the city they could run away from it. But they couldn't go. Everybody got hysterical. The Holland Tunnel was all jammed up. Nobody could go anywhere. That is just what would happen. There are just so many roads. It would cause mass hysteria. That is another reason my husband said he wouldn't go. What is the use of going? If they say evacuate, how far do you think we would get? We would be out in the road somewhere. It is better to stay here than being out on the road in a van and being maybe more exposed to the radiation in the van.

Most of our neighbors left on Friday; all our neighbors left. I left on Friday and came back on Saturday, but it was like living in a ghost town. Why, I could have ransacked every house up and down the street. (laughter) I hope you aren't quoting my name. (laughter) It was terrible. . . . Like I say, I wish I knew more about what is going to happen. I guess nobody knows that. They don't know what is in the building. Until then you just live on pins and needles.

*If they did reopen the plant, would the fear ever go away, do you think?*
No! No! I think that is something—if you live in a situation like that—I told you about our wall in the basement and the trouble we have with it when hurricane season comes around? I get fidgety about it . . . we are supposed to release pressure on the wall. It gets like a river down there. So it is like if this starts up over here [TMI]. My husband says, "There is nothing you can do about it. Don't worry about it." But when you live through a situation like that, it is hard to forget it. Like during the flood when

the water came in the basement. My husband saw it and was upset but he did not go through the traumatic experience. That was a traumatic experience for us just like if they try to restart it [TMI] and that is when it is really going to affect us, when they start it up.

All of these chemical plants, they have all of these dumping grounds, and they have them in barrels, and they dump them in New Jersey, and now they have found the barrels are rusting and the chemicals that were stored in the barrels are going into the ground and the water passes through there and it goes into the drinking water or the water supply that goes into the cities. And the people are getting the chemicals from these chemical waste dumps . . . and that's another thing. In years to come, what's to happen when they can't find any place to bury the nuclear waste? Now, this is just the birth of nuclear plants. In years to come, where are they going to bury all that waste? A lot of states won't even allow them to bury it. I think Georgia, North Carolina are a few states which ban nuclear waste. Now, if every state makes a law and says, "We are not going to allow you to bury that waste in our state," what are they going to do with it? What is the answer? We have got to think of alternatives. I am for nuclear energy because I think it is a good way to provide electricity for the people. But there is always a bad side, a result that is not good. Like, I say, if states make laws that ban [waste dumping], and say you can't bury the waste in our state, where are they going to take it? Do you know that they are bringing nuclear waste from Paris, France, and they are burying it over here in this country? That was on "60 Minutes." There are a lot of end results.

Well, I often say to my daughter-in-law that I really feel sorry for Michael [her grandson] because everything is going to be so polluted. The ozone layer is being broken away. We need that protective barrier. There are so many things we do not know. We have this acid rain problem now, too much carbon dioxide, sulfuric acid in the air. It's killing our wildlife, the babies, and the eggs, fish eggs. We've got to turn this around and go in the other direction.

*Are you optimistic that we are going to do that?*
No. There is too much bureaucracy. There are too many people in Washington who own these plants. There is no way of doing that. I sound like an environmentalist. I guess I am. But I have lived in the country all my life. It is just a shame to see this happen.

When I was a kid, there was nothing like this where I lived. It was all clean air, hardly any carbon monoxide, nothing to really worry about. When I think of future generations, there is going to be a lot of mutation, genes will not be like they should, because—I don't see how it is possible any other way. . . . The scale is going the other way. Nature is being destroyed. I am worried about the environment in general, the future for our children.

## MR. HAYWARD

Mr. Hayward's two-story white farmhouse was in an isolated area of Newberry Township, surrounded by little but woods and farmland. Mr. Hayward and his wife were sitting on the front porch waiting for the interviewer. He was a good-sized man who appeared to be in his late sixties or in his seventies. He had farmed in the area all his life, and his face was weatherworn.

*How do you feel about reopening TMI?*
I'm not for reopening it, myself. It's not for my own benefit. I mean all my children and grandchildren live right around, see, in this area, and that's why I wouldn't sign for it to be reopened. That's my opinion about it. I would just as soon see it to be closed . . . because I'm pretty old myself, and it don't matter too much to me anymore. But I got real small grandchildren, two years old . . . and five years old. One son lives right over there, one son lives right up there, one lives right here, another lives up the road. Eleven of them live right in this area. I give them a piece of ground to build on so they live real close. My brother, one lives there and one lives over there. Most of them [brothers and sisters] live right here in Newberry. We are a big family. There were fourteen children in our family—ten boys—and, as I said, most live in Newberry Township. That's where we were born. One brother lives in York and one lives in Harrisburg. I was born just right up, right up there about a mile and a half, straight up that way. I've lived right here for twenty-eight years. And before I moved here I lived the rest of my time at my mother's place, right down the hill about one-quarter of a mile. We [nodding to wife] got married about thirty-nine years ago.

No, I am not for it to be reopened [because] as far as a lot of questions—they are not answered. There is my health. Something struck me [the day of the accident]. I don't actually blame it on that [TMI]. I have arthritis. I guess when this accident happened last March, I planted potatoes on the twenty-ninth. Out there I planted two hundred pounds of potatoes on the twenty-ninth and hatched oats on the thirtieth. And that's when they [neighbors and friends] said they [township officials] were running around, telling everyone to get out or get in the house. I didn't hear nothing. But, by gosh! Saturday morning when I woke up I could not even walk to the barn. It was arthritis I blamed it on, I didn't blame it on that accident. I never had it that bad before, though. Not that bad! But, hell! I was doctoring and doctoring, and I even went to see a specialist at Camp Hill. I had x-rays taken and blood tests. See, my joints would swell up. I could not even walk up to the barn for about two months. I was in bad shape. I was taking all kinds of pills. And you know what? That expert put me on sixteen aspirins per day. That's what he put me on. I took them for three weeks, and they started upsetting my stomach a little. Sixteen a day is a lot of aspirin. I take four practically every day now. It does help my joints. Right now I am feeling rough, but I haven't felt right since that hit me last March. But I don't really blame it on the accident. The doctor said, "By God! I don't know what you got." He said, "You got me beat." That's what the specialist told me. So he turned me back to my family doctor over here. I go there every once awhile. The only medicine I was taking was aspirin and a few sleeping pills because of the arthritis. . . . [The accident] didn't affect the steers, though. Hell, they were all right.

*Did you leave during the accident?*
See, everybody around this area left. But, hell, I had ten steer and eight hogs. I couldn't leave and let them starve. See my boys have a hunting camp up in Tioga and that's where they went. And they wanted me to come up there bad. But, hell, I'm not going to go. I wanted to stay here and take care of my stock, so that's why I guess I didn't go. But I never been up. She's [his wife] been up every summer for a couple of days—vacation. But I never been up to the camp. The boys been up there for the last thirty, forty years, I guess.

*Were you upset by the accident?*
I really don't get upset too quick. It really didn't upset me too much, not like some people. Some people were half out of their minds around here. It didn't really seem to bother me. Maybe because I am pretty old, maybe because of my age, it didn't bother

me a lot. It didn't really bother me a lot, but I still don't want
them to open it up on account of my children.

*Do you think it would be dangerous to reopen TMI?*
I imagine it would be dangerous if they reopened it. I imagine so.
I think they lied so much about the thing; that was my opinion
about it. We never got the truth.

*Are you getting the truth now?*
Well, I can't really tell. More so than then, I would say. More so
than then. But, by God! When that happened, we didn't get the
truth at all.

*Is there anyone you believe?*
Well, not really.

*Newspapers?*
No, I don't believe in the newspapers because they make too God
damn many mistakes. I'll tell you that right straight out. Everything that I ever read in the newspaper, if we had an outing or
anything at all, when I'd read it the next day it would be wrong.
So I can't believe the newspapers no how, no siree. . . . One thing
that made me so mad. I used to do a great deal of farming away
from home. It was up the creek here right across from where I
was born. I was farming a hundred-acre farm, and I was cutting
wheat and I went to start my combine. It backfired and caught
the wheat field afire. I got it out, but I was really played out. It
was really fairly windy. I didn't let it get too far before I got it
out. I had it out before the fire companies came. Not even any
smoke before they got there. A reporter called me that evening,
and I told him the straight good about it. I read the paper the
next day, and boy, that got really under my skin—fire department outed the fire. There was not even smoke when the fire
company got there. That's the truth. So I do not believe the papers, no sir. I see in many a paper that we had an outing and it
would be all mixed up. So I don't believe the papers. We get them
every day as far as that goes. They make too many mistakes. It's
not lies. Now this fire was a lie because I told him [the reporter]
everything. . . . I just don't listen too much anymore to what
goes on at TMI. I don't really think about it too much. It never
excited me that much.

*If it reopened, would you think much about it?*
Whooh! probably would think about it some more, more than
what I do think about it now since it's closed because they just, I

don't know, I just don't know whether they know how to operate
it or . . . there is just too many lies told about stuff like that
when stuff like that happens. The public doesn't get the truth.
That's one reason I'd rather for it to be closed. In fact—maybe I
shouldn't even say this—but I heard a certain guy standing behind me one time—it was a big place—talking to another guy
about this. He said they should have never reported it, kept it
quiet, kept it hid. They should have never let it out. That was his
opinion. He had a couple hundred head of cattle, that guy
does. . . . They should have never even let it come out, should
have kept it hidden. . . . I didn't listen to him too much, but I did
hear him say that they should never let it come out; they should
have kept it hidden. No! No, siree! I don't think like that. That
should have been reported as soon as it happened, anything like
that. That's dangerous. That's my opinion. That thing's really
dangerous.

I know one farmer who had a big herd of cattle. He sold his
farm and everything and went to Franklin County. He had about
150 acres of farm. He had about fifty head of Holstein milk cattle.
His farm was about two to three miles from the plant. We are
about five from the plant. I can't see it done anything to me. I
can't tell. My cows have not had any trouble. I kill them. I do
not have any milk cows. These are beef cattle, and I buy new
ones every spring and kill them in the winter. I do not breed
them. I did buy a heifer last spring. She is all right. He is not sick
or anything.

*Do you know of people who have had trouble with their animals?*
Yeah, I know of some farmer having trouble. Yeah, I know one
guy that lost six right after one another within five miles of the
[Three Mile Island] area—beef cattle, whiteheads, they were.
Now this year they had fourteen, and they lost one, and they had
to take one out. It was too big for the heifer to have it. So he had
twelve. He raised twelve. But last year he lost six right in a row,
and he sent away to get them examined to see where it come
from. But you know he didn't get word back that it come from
Three Mile Island, you better believe that. I don't know what
they did say was wrong. . . . Yeah, I know that guy good. He lives
within five miles [of Three Mile Island]. That's about the only
ones I really know.

*Do you think most people want the plant to stay closed?*
I believe the majority of them do. [Mrs. Hayward: Yeah, the ma-

jority of them do! His brother's wife, up there, she pretty nearly went crazy. He [Mr. H.] didn't go; I didn't go either. Well, if it was going to come to kill him, it might as well kill me, too. I stayed. I didn't go no place either. I didn't like it too good. Everybody around here went. A lot of people left from around here. There was nobody here. There was nobody from around here at all left.

*Do you think the people should have a say in whether the plant reopens?*
Yes, I think it should go up to a vote. I think it should go to a vote whether it should be opened up or closed. That's within a pretty big area, not just a five-mile area. I would think that would be a good idea. Now that's only my opinion.

*Do you think people will have a say?*
Well, I don't know. Them things work funny to me. We had this new road. Which way did you come [to the house]? From Newberrytown? Well, that new piece of road that you were on, it runs, if you keep following it, takes you back up into New Cumberland. Well, that road was just built a couple years ago and it cost an awful lot of money to build it, and we had five hundred signers here in Newberry Township to rebuild the old one and not relocate that one, spend all that money. But them five hundred signers didn't amount to that much [snaps his fingers], see. So, I don't know. When you fight a big outfit, as a rule, you don't win. That's what I feel, and Met Ed's pretty big.

The way it [electric rates] went up in the last two years. Boy, well, you used to pay every two months, you know. Our bill run $32.00 to $34.00 dollars every two months. Now it's $38.00 dollars to $40.00 dollars for the one month. Just in two years! I can't see that accident would make the electric go like that. There's something wrong someplace. That is my idea about it. There is something wrong someplace. We did not get another thing [in the house] to make the electric kilowatts or anything go up, and it more than doubled just since they started collecting monthly instead of every two months. My gosh! My boy out there, sometimes for the two months his bill runs about $150.00 to $160.00 and now it's running over $100.00 a month. That's not heating the house. There's not electric heating in the house. He's got two fireplaces and an oil burner. They don't use electric to heat the house at all. It's that kind of money. That's what I am getting at.

He don't have a hot water heater. He has oil hot water. He heats it with his oil furnace. Too much, too much.

*How do you compare the TMI accident with something like the Mount St. Helens disaster?*
This would have been worse if it blew up, wouldn't it? Sure, that's what I would say. Worse! It would have destroyed everything! I compare it worse than a flood.

*Has it changed your life any?*
No, I don't think so. It's because of my age though. [Mrs. Hayward: He's awful grouchy though.] I am retired, and I don't expect to live too many more years because I had an operation in 1979. I had my gallbladder removed, and that really messed me up.

*Did you ever fear that you might not be able to come back to this area?*
I never felt that way. You never know. I know in this little bank over here everybody was withdrawing their money out of the bank. Hell, they had to send a truck to get more money. They didn't have enough money to give them. They didn't have enough because of the way they [people of Newberry/Goldsboro] were withdrawing their money. It never did bother me that much! If I would have been much younger, it would have!

*Do you worry about your children's health because of the accident?*
It could have had some effect. I think about it a little bit. That's why I would sign not to open it up anymore.

*Do you think Newberry is safe now?*
Well, as long as it's closed, I do. (laughter) Well, we got some pretty bad hoodlums around here. There's a couple of nuts. What they need is to be locked up, but they just don't lock them up. Kids!

*If the plant reopened, would you think of Newberry as safe?*
Not as safe as what I used to thought it was. I thought it [the plant at TMI] was all right then because I never heard anything, you know, about any other places or anything at all about it [nuclear energy], didn't know really how serious it was, what it could do and stuff, you know. I never give that a thought before this happened—then I realized it was dangerous. But before anything ever happened, I didn't think it was. That's the way I felt

about it . . . but maybe the accident then could have been blamed on the operators too instead of the plant itself. I believe the operators were at fault, I believe it. You got to know what you are doing.

## MRS. CASPAR

Mrs. Caspar lived in one of the suburban subdivisions in Newberry Township. In her forties and married, she had no children. She worked in the Harrisburg area at a job which she had held for many years and with which she was very satisfied. Mrs. Caspar had some health problems, which she discusses in the interview.

*How did you feel about the accident when it first happened?*
At the time of the accident, I wasn't really, I didn't really realize, I don't think, the magnitude of it because it was the first one of its kind, you know, and we didn't realize that maybe we weren't being told everything. And the Wednesday morning that the leak first occurred I was out with Katie for about a half hour, that's the dog, playing around, and we were right down here, and I knew nothing about it. So it didn't make any difference to me. So then when I got to work and they had this over the news and all this, everybody's getting panic-stricken. But since I work for [her employer], you know, they believe in being on the job, staying on the job. They said, well, you know, "Now don't get excited. Don't overreact. Just keep calm." So, of course, I stayed at work all day. Well, I got all these telephone calls. Neighbors called and said, "Will you watch our dog and cats? We're taking the kids and going to the shore." Neighbors down here called and said, "Hey, we're leaving. Will you take care of the animals? Are you guys leaving?" Well, I said, "We don't have any kids. It's probably not really that bad," because we're more or less, the company more or less teaches you not to overreact since you have to work during emergencies like the flood in '72. We went in across the bridges because we knew we had to be there.

So I didn't think too much about it, and I was the one here. Everybody else was gone. What scared me was even the garbage trucks didn't run. That's when I realized I was really alone. Now I did stay inside 'cause it was a beautiful weekend and I cleaned and everything. But I still wasn't really that concerned. But then afterwards, to find out—if it was true then, I don't know—that they were actually a half hour away from a meltdown, and I didn't leave because I figured, "Well, okay, so Wednesday morning it leaked. If I didn't get it then, I'm not going to get it," because I figured the leak was all over. There was no danger. And all this time to realize [that Metropolitan Edison officials knew it was not over] I was mad!

It isn't that I object to nuclear power plants because I realize that something's going to have to be done, you know, with the need for more power. But now, we boated down there. We had a summer place down on Hill Island, and we used to boat all around there all summer long, right around the power plant, like thirty feet out from shore. We used to take people down and show them. "Yeah, this is Three Mile Island. Look at the lights. It looks like the Wizard of Oz," and all this garbage. Now people are stuck down there. They can't sell. There are places nobody wants. We can't boat anymore, and the boating areas are limited anyway. So consequently—they haven't limited it but who wants to go down. I mean it'd be different if they'd say okay and you could trust them, and they'd say, "We're going to leak a little radiation this weekend. Stay out of the water," and so forth. But they never tell you until after the fact. How can you react after the fact? . . . I was upset with, first of all, the way we were informed and second of all the kind of people they have working there. That's too dangerous a place to have people there that don't know what the hell they're doing. I mean there's thousands of lives involved. Well, more than that if there's ever a meltdown, plus who knows what you've been exposed to, and that's what irritated [me]. I can accept the fact that they need nuclear power plants, but then I think, well, they probably don't want to spend the money for people that are qualified.

So who's paying now for the screwing that we got? We are, because now we have to pay [because of electric rate increases]. We have Met Ed now. We have to pay for their mistakes. If we're going to pay for the mistakes that are made down there, then why don't we have a say in who they hire and all that kind of stuff? It just doesn't make sense that you should pay for somebody else's stupidity. You pay for your own mistakes. That's fine. I can accept that. But to pay for somebody else's! It's just not right. You've been exposed to it. Who knows what you're going to get that you'll have to pay for later on. Plus now you have to pay for their dumb mistakes. I just can't accept that!

*Do you have any fears about the accident?*
The only thing would be health-wise because I had a thyroid
problem. I had that before I ever came here. Two people in my
family already have died of cancer. Some say it is hereditary, and
some say it isn't. But the background of all of these things, I don't
need to be exposed to anything else. I am not the kind of person
that is out to get something for nothing. In other words, if thirty
years from now I contracted cancer, I would not deliberately go
out and say I want fifty thousand dollars because I am sure I got
this from TMI. I don't really think there is really any way of
knowing whether it was caused by that or whether it wasn't.
Your chances are probably higher [because of the accident]. But
like up in Love Canal, they knew what they got was directly affiliated with that stuff because they took tests and tissue around
the nerves and the breakdown of the blood and all that kind of
stuff. But there is no test now that I could have now that could
say, "Okay, definitely, now you have more chance of getting cancer." That's my main worry!

*Do you want to move?*
I love living out here. It's beautiful out here. I wouldn't move.
Well, we couldn't move now. We wouldn't move anyway even
since TMI because I have a good job which I could never, ever,
you know, get that kind of service, that kind of money elsewhere.
I've been there almost twenty-five years. So there's no way I
could ever recoup that financially. And my husband's family has
always been within this area, and we could never sell our house
for what we have in it. I am sure—I don't think we could sell it
for what it's worth. No. Now I'm not saying, you know, we
couldn't eventually, like twenty years from now—if we wanted
to retire and go to Florida, fine,—I'm not saying we couldn't sell
it then for what it would be worth. But at the moment we
couldn't, but we were not really interested in selling; so the
health reason is my main concern because I don't think we are
going to move. We are not going to move because of TMI. If it
doesn't get any worse, we have no intentions of moving. Now if
this would keep on and keep on and keep on and things would get
worse. . . .

I just think my whole complaint is that we were uninformed
until after the fact and never given a choice of whether we
wanted to leave or not until a lot of the damage was done. I do

not think the people who left have any less chance of getting cancer because they left. They do if they are leaving now while they are leaking the other stuff [Krypton-85]. But if they were here the Wednesday that it happened and if they were exposed to it, they were exposed to it Wednesday because I believe that was the biggest leak there was.

*Is there any information you trust?*
I had pretty much faith in Denton. I really think he did his best. I felt a lot better when he came in than I did before. But everybody down there was trying to pass the buck. It didn't really matter at that time. I didn't think that they should've spent their time hassling about whose fault it was, at that time. Let them figure that out later, you know. It was a matter of keeping people informed and all they tried—they put the guy on from Metropolitan Edison. Well he said that he thought it was somebody else's fault, somebody else should come in and blah blah. We'd listen to a newscast to find out how things were going, and all we heard was who was to blame for what was going on, which, at that point, it didn't really matter. What we wanted to know was what the situation was now—Was it better? Was it worse? What they were doing about it now—which they did tell you a little bit, but mostly what they were concerned with was passing the buck, which, who cared at that time?

*Are you angry?*
Right! Because of the way it was handled, because of the type of help they had there. For the money that we're going to pay now, they could have hired help that could have not screwed up. And see, we don't even know if that's really true. Did some guy really see a red light go on and just flip the switch and turn it off and ignore it? Who knows! We don't even know that for sure. I don't think they know. You know, there are still two or three different stories about what happened.

But I do feel if the guy from the *Guide* [local newspaper] could go in there with no background and get in, and the door didn't even have a lock on it much less, I think they said, it didn't even have a doorknob on it; you just pushed on it, or they held it open—it was supposed to be a restricted area—and he could go in there and take pictures. That is another thing, you know. If a person from another country wanted to come in and sabotage the place, it would be a piece of cake. And now that is a thing to think about because the situation is not really that stable, as far as overseas, you know, détente, whatever, you know, policy. We're not just getting along [in the world]. And if that's the way it is at that one [Three Mile Island plant], you get a couple more like that, someone could come in and sabotage, and this thing would be a pushover. I'm not a radical. I would never go to demonstrations and yell and—you know. So I'm really sort of glad I was picked for this [interview] because otherwise I would have never spoken my piece.

*Are you doing anything now?*
I don't really mind conserving that much. If people can conserve gas [for cars], why can't they conserve energy? Now I don't mean that I'd like to go back to the scrubboard and all that other kind of stuff. But I don't dry my clothes in the dryer. I hang them downstairs on the line. I'd like an outside line, but that's a sore subject [with her husband]. (laughter) Anyway, so I hang them downstairs, and I do try to conserve as far as that goes. And look how they conserve gas. So if it's a threat to your life, which gas, if you want to pay the price, it's there. If they can conserve gas for that reason, why can't they conserve energy?

*Has this changed your feeling about living in Newberry?*
Oh, I think the quality of life has been changed, definitely, if it's nothing other than the attitude with which you accept different things, the way you look at different things; your perspective has changed so to speak. . . . Well, I don't know, I can't really say how, but I seem to, every time the fire siren blows, I keep wondering if it's something down at TMI . . . but I keep wondering because I know they would set off the fire sirens, supposedly, if it was an alert. They would set off the fire sirens if they knew before it was too late, I guess. But, you know, like every time I hear something now about TMI, just anything, right away your ears perk up and you turn the radio up and listen to see what they're really going to say. Is it something more about it—it's like, I don't know, I can't really say how they've changed, but you do feel more or less like you're sitting on a potential time bomb because they still haven't gotten into the reactor, have they? That's the last I heard. They can't even get in there. Now the door won't open, and all this other kind of stuff, and they had the problem with the oxygen mask, and they couldn't go in. Honestly, it just seems like the quality of everything, you know—it just scares

me. You can't leave it sit because it still could leak. It's still not over. Your hazard is still not over, so it is like sitting on a time bomb.

I couldn't really say, put your finger on how your perspective has changed, but I know . . . something sooner or later has to be—it's something that is not closed. It's not like a closed case. You couldn't even say, "Okay, we're going to shut down the whole nuclear plant. We're just going to leave it, just going to open the turbines or whatever they are down there and use the power from the river." So it doesn't still make any difference because that's still sitting down there, and I guess that radiation eats or corrodes or does something to the stuff that's in there, so sooner or later it will deteriorate. And I can't blame other people for not wanting our nuclear waste. I wouldn't want somebody else's. What do you do? You've created a monster and now you don't know what to do with it.

*Do you have dreams about it?*
I don't really dream that much. I would say every so often when things come up down there I think about it. I think about it in depth for a period of time and wonder whether it's really the smart thing to do to stay here. Then, of course, I keep weighing the odds and say, "Well, maybe it will work out all right." You know. People are very optimistic, I think, about things like this. They have to be. People say, they have jokes at work about [TMI], and they have a big long paper about it—how would you like to buy a used, corroded reactor and all this stuff. And we laugh and everything, and people say, you know, "That's really wonderful that you can still laugh, that you can still make a joke of it when you live that close." And I say, "Well, what are you going to do? You're not going to sit around and bawl and be in a blue funk until it's over with!" God, that could be years. You could be depressed for five years!

But you do go through times when your mind isn't occupied with other things, when you do think about it, and you do wonder if it is the smart thing staying here, and you once again weigh the pros and cons. And here we still are, so the pros keep winning out, but I don't know for how long. It's something that sits in the back of your mind. Yeah, yeah, it's not a closed subject. I don't dwell on it, but whenever I have problems, as you know, I had an operation, and it seemed to be clearing up. Now it is back, and I keep thinking, "If I didn't live here, would it have cleared up?" Probably not. But mostly I worry about the health hazard, because my record isn't really that good, health-wise. Mostly this is the way I feel.

*Who influences your thinking?*
I don't get influenced by my neighbors because they all left and feel very strongly about it, especially next door because she has children. But knowing what they feel about it now, I am not—I work all day, and I am not a social person with the neighbors. I know the neighbors in five or six houses. Becky is the only one I talk to at all, and it is not normally anything about TMI. The most I talk about it is at card club which I know they really feel strongly about it because they all left. We don't really delve into anything there. They say they wish they would finally make up their minds what they are doing down there, and they wish they would either shut the damn thing down or decide what is happening. You know, it gets on your nerves after it drags on for a while. It is like a toothache. It gets on your nerves even though the pain is not that bad. It is just the idea that it is there, and you know, eventually, you know you are going to have to do something about it. That is just the way this is. It is just there. But my opinions are really my own. Like I said, I do not discuss it with anybody else.

*Why do you think you feel this way?*
I think it is because of the type of person I am. You know, some people worry about every little thing, just everything, and it is a big major thing for them. If you work and you are out in the public and your mind is occupied—like I said, the only time I think about, mainly, it is here, when I am at home and happen to hear something on TV or hear something on the radio and I am by myself. And then I might think about it. But other times I am too busy. It is nothing I can do anything about. Did you ever hear the old adage, "The only time it pays to worry is if worry is going to help the situation"? And in this, what choice do you have? If you are going to live here, you are going to have to accept it. Plus, it makes a difference with your status. If you don't have a good job, have children, and you have a house that isn't worth a lot, maybe you are saying that you are putting a lot on material things, but it is just different situations that people are in and different types of people, whether you worry, and some people

crusade for any cause. It doesn't make any difference. It could be dandelions. Parade with a sign, "Down with dandelions." Some people, though, never speak their piece. Sometimes you wonder whether it really helps.

*Do you think the community will have input into the decision about reopening?*
It is really hard to tell. I don't know. Sometimes you've known of one person who stood up against impossible odds, and they got a change, just because of one person's real effort. And other times you've known of people that have protested and protested, and they've thrown themselves in front of cars, and they've done everything, and it hasn't done any good. So, like I said, it's really hard to tell if they'll be influenced by it [community opinion] or not.

It makes me mad, I don't know, that it seems like all the agencies are taken in by Met Ed to a certain extent. . . . I guess now that they ruled that we had to pay for the extra power that they [Metropolitan Edison] have to buy. I guess we don't have to pay for the damages that occurred, is that right? I haven't been listening to it lately, and I know they ruled in favor of the public in one instance and against the public in another. So, in other words, you're still—you're still getting screwed, to put it mildly. That's one of my favorite expressions, or getting the shaft. So I can't say. I hope it will influence what they do, even if it's nothing more than to see that they get qualified people in there and to see that the people [in the community] are informed.

You know, this passing the buck and telling me after the fact. Why don't they let you know how bad it really is instead of, you know, well, they don't tell anybody until, like, later. I mean, I realize that they couldn't tell you at two o'clock that this guy was going to turn this light off at four. But they certainly knew before I went to work in the morning that something had gone awry down there. And so now they say as soon as something goes wrong, they have to call and report to somebody in Washington. And so everybody said, "Boy, that makes me feel a lot better." I said, "Why? There's nothing says he's going to call you and tell you." I mean, there's nothing saying they're gonna put it on [the radio, or TV]. They just want to be sure the proper authorities are notified. But that still doesn't help the people. We could still be sitting here on a time bomb and still not know it. But I think you have the right to know what is going on and how serious it is. But they didn't want to panic everybody. Would they rather have everybody dead? I mean, which would they rather have? Of course, dead people don't sue. . . . Personally, if I would have known ahead of time, on Wednesday, I would have gotten out at least for a short time.

But the way they are doing it now [with the release of Krypton]—well, one person wants it vented all at once. But this is what I cannot understand. Is that okay? So we are going to put so many millirems in the environment now and then in a couple of weeks we are going to put so many more millirems in. But it never dissipates! If they are releasing it into the environment, and they release ten millirems today and ten millirems next week and ten the next week, at the end of a couple weeks you still have the same amount of millirems around as if you released it all at one time. What difference does it make? The people who wanted to leave said, "We want it released all at one time." I truly think my employer would frown upon me leaving three times during one month unless it was on a weekend. They would frown upon me saying, "Gee, I won't be in on Wednesday and Thursday this week. They're releasing the impurities into the air from TMI. I am going to have to leave." Of course, we could get a room somewhere, at a motel. But still, how far does it [radioactive gas] travel? Which way is the wind blowing? Of course, I think Middletown was worse off than we were because the wind blows mostly their way as opposed to this way. But it never dissipates. What difference does it make if they do it all at once or in little bits? What happens to it when it gets out there [in the atmosphere]? See, that's the problem. Even if you are informed, you're not really in a position to judge because you don't really know. I mean, you're not an engineer or anything like that. You can't even really assess what they are telling you, to a certain extent.

*Do you trust the authorities about the dangers?*
Well, the only one, I said, at that time that I had any faith in was [Harold] Denton because I felt that he was trying to get to the bottom of it. He was as well informed as was possible. But nevertheless, it was still after the fact.

*Is there anybody you trust now?*
Not really. Nobody, I could say. If they said something, the event

has sort of, it's lost its momentum for the moment. It's more or less smoldering around down there. He [Denton] was the only one we had any faith in at the time. And right now you're still back in the same boat. You still don't know who to believe about what's going on. And I still don't think they're telling you everything. They do stuff down there! They're down there fooling around every day, and they don't keep a daily report. You know, it isn't like before but . . . you get upset about it every day and nothing is changed. Why just don't they forget about it until there's something to report? Then you complain because you are not informed. They're damned if they do and damned if they don't. I don't know . . . but I can't really say there's anybody now. I would probably be in the same boat I was in before Denton came in. You'd listen to one. You'd listen to the other. And you'd try and decide who was maybe telling the truth.

*How would you decide?*
Lord only knows. You just have to, kind of have to put the pieces together. . . . You wouldn't really believe any one person in particular. You would just try to put the pieces together and decide which ones were really the truth and which ones were, not really lies, but maybe half-truths, so to speak. It would really be tough. . . . Like I said, it scares me to think we were that close to a meltdown, if that is true—a half hour, that isn't much. I don't know if we could have stayed ahead of it, if it would have melted down, with a half hour's notice. How fast does it travel? Who knows?

*Do you worry about getting cancer from the radiation exposure?*
I am sure it is a danger. My grandmother had too much when she was in the hospital—it was supposed to be controlled—when she had cancer, and it affected her in other ways, and that was from radiation. Her own doctor told her that. She had too much for her cancer, and it killed the cells in her leg. Now the cells on the inside were not affected, but the cells on the outside were, and her skin would just come off. The old cells would just fall away, the outer cells. And then she would just keep peeling all the time. It got great big like. She called it milkleg. I don't know what it was, but it was from too much radiation. It affected her one leg. It didn't incapacitate her. But why do these people who give you x-rays give you those little bibbies and all? Yeah, I worry!

## MRS. HEMINGWAY

The interview with Mrs. Hemingway took place in her home on a winding little hillside road in Newberry Township. The house was an old cottage that was almost hidden from the road by trees. In her late twenties, Mrs. Hemingway was pregnant at the time of the accident and had a little boy about a month afterward.

*How did you feel at the time of the accident?*
I felt very scared. I was about two weeks away from my due date at the time of the accident, when it happened. . . . It was just very frightening, I think primarily because of not knowing who to believe or what to believe. You know, you didn't want to believe the worst, and yet it was pretty obvious from the beginning that you couldn't rely on Met Ed, and even once the NRC got here, you weren't too sure, although they seemed a little more trustworthy.

It was very frightening for me and particularly—it would have been at any time—because the consequences were so devastating. If you think, well, if it's just a small release, you're fearful of the amount of radiation . . . for the health effects on anyone, just in general. You've always been taught that unnecessary x-rays or anything like that should be avoided just because they aren't positive about the long-range effects of low-level doses. So then you're thinking, if that's all the further it is, you could live with it. But then you're thinking, 'What if it really does melt down, and what if you have to leave your home and family and an area that you were born and raised in?' I lived in York all my life. So my roots are really here. My friends are here, and I like the area as far as a place to stay. I like the area. But just the thought, if worse came to worst, hopefully nobody would die or be sick immediately. But just even the thought if you had to leave your home forever. There's no way that you could take your things with you, sentimental things. It was very frightening.

And it was really a bad time for me. I didn't know where to go. I did go to York to stay with my mother because where she lives is about twenty miles from the plant. I was very fearful of taking a long trip at that late stage of pregnancy. And my husband and I had participated in childbirth classes, and he was going to be with me. We were afraid then. I could have gone to relatives in Western Pennsylvania, but he wanted to stay here because of our animals and what not. We were fearful of me, of taking me out there, and leaving me there when the baby might have come. What hospital would we have gone to? We were so prepared. We were so prepared to be together for the thing and then . . . and then, oh, man!

Then, of course, you really worry about their [babies'] health. You know, were the radiation levels what they said they were? Were they higher? And the bad thing about it was that the worst releases were before they told anybody about them. I mean, I was outside in the yard, so I got it, probably, whatever it was. I was exposed to it. That was long before, you know, they said stay indoors. So I was very frightened and very scared and very worried about it.

*How long were you gone?*
I went to York . . . and then I came back here on Monday when the bubble had broken. It seemed that things were at least under control. I came back in tears because that was a strain on me too, . . . being away from the house and worrying and wondering—would we be able to get up here and get the stuff, the necessities packed for him, his cradle and baby clothes and all of his things? We might really have to have them. I finally had the baby in York. He was two weeks late, so it worked out really well. The due date was the tenth of April. He was almost a month after the accident.

*How do you feel now?*
I think I still feel worried, primarily for him, not as much for my-self, because I wonder how much the dosage really was. I had a friend who had a child with leukemia, and I saw her live through that. It's bad enough when you think about it, but when you've had a personal experience with someone you know, then it's really horrible. And you just think, please, don't let that happen! . . . I feel very angry about it really, because I just feel that there was so much incompetence on the part of the utility, on the part of the NRC, on the part of the local governments—even though they don't have that much say in it—by the fact that they aren't concerned about it at all and are willing to just let it take its own course, let the utility do whatever it wants. I think that they are not living up to their responsibilities as government bodies. It just leaves the impression in your mind that the util-ities are only concerned about their profits and their money and don't really have any sense of social responsibility or social obli-gations to anybody. I think individuals may be responsible for

their acts, but as part of the company they seem to be able to say, "Oh, so what. It's the company, so therefore we don't have to be responsible." I feel anger with them because I don't think they care. . . . I wonder about their competency. I want to believe that they know what they're doing, but I don't. I can't trust them, and I can't trust the NRC.

It seems to me that it's a technology in general that has really gotten away from us. It just seemed that when the accident happened, there was so much floundering around that, at the time, I was thinking it was just a cover-up. They don't want to admit that they goofed. And the more I thought about it, the more I wondered. Well, I'm sure that was a part of it. But the more I thought about it, the more I thought, well, maybe they really didn't know what to do to correct it. And so that part of the smoke screen was the best they could do at the time—was just tell everybody, "It's okay. We're going to do this, we're going to do that, and it will be all right." That part was very scary because I think we were all very lucky, and I do feel, in retrospect, in looking back at it, probably the radiation levels weren't terribly high and maybe that was, maybe a fairly accurate thing, what they told us.

Some of the reasons that make me believe that—a friend of mine works at a hospital, in the lab, and she brought her dosimeter home from work, and we were running around here. And she never had anything more than a background radiation reading in this location. Realizing that is not the most accurate thing, but that made me feel a little better. And a woman in my La Lêche class who lives in Goldsboro, has lived here all her life, was still nursing her baby at the time of the accident. About a week after things calmed down, she had her breast milk tested. She just wondered if she should nurse by formula. And her milk didn't show anything. So that made me feel better. She is right under the plant ever since it has been operating. So that at least allayed some of my fears. I didn't feel quite so panicky about the situation. . . .

But I do worry about the future. I wonder if they're going to goof up when they get in there to clean up. Are they going to make a mess and contaminate something accidentally? Do they know how to clean it up when they get in there—if they get in, since the door's stuck? And like I said, it's very frightening to me, especially with a child, because he has his whole life ahead of him, and I figure, I'm halfway through my life, and obviously, I don't want to get cancer. I don't like to think that my risk is higher of that, but I can feel just a little more assured of taking my chances because things happen to people whether they live near a nuclear plant or not. But he has his whole life ahead of him, and if he wants to have children . . . I think the unknown is what is so frightening. And there's so many conflicting things. One group of scientists, doctors, will say, "Oh, it's no problem. People that work in labs get so much more radiation, and they're fine." And then the next group is saying, "Yes, but. . . ." We just don't know yet. I think that's what's really frightening, not just for him but for children in the whole world, because there are so many nuclear plants everywhere, and you also know that there are plenty of slipshod people and people that are in control rooms that maybe have a hangover, who knows what, and you really wonder how. . . .

I think they were taking it so much for granted. They had all these technological goodies, and it was just going to keep this safe, and the backup systems were going to work. So don't worry about it. Just push the buttons. That's it. But it just doesn't seem to be working that way. I really feel that sooner or later, maybe not necessarily at TMI, but someplace in the world, there's really going to be a bad, bad accident. And it's frightening to me, you know.

And I think, too, of other countries that have plants, and you wonder how strict their controls are. Ours are supposed to be the best in the world, and we're supposed to be such great technicians and what not, and we have certainly made enough of mistakes because there have been other accidents [at nuclear power plants]. While they were not as serious, they were containable or whatever, didn't get out of hand. It just makes you wonder. Do they have strict controls? Or in the kind of country, like India or someplace, where there is really a lot of political unrest and the government changes hands frequently, you just think, "Well, what about whatever commission or agency is in charge of keeping an eye on their nuclear reactors? How efficient are they?" I mean, how much is their political situation going to influence just the functions of a normal government bureaucracy, which we take for granted here as being solid rock. Like it doesn't matter [here]—you have an election and the bureaucracy just kind of rolls on, which is good and bad. . . . It is very frightening. . . .

It just seems to me that there are so many alternatives we could explore, you know, that I don't really think we have to go the nuclear route. We obviously need alternate energy sources, but solar could provide heating for houses and water. There's no reason we can't really get into gasohol and alcohol for vehicles. We certainly have plenty of room to grow corn and sugar-cane. . . . It just seems to me that that's not being pushed. That's not a futuristic thing. It's here; it's now. All we have to do is use it and do it.

But it's pretty obvious that the nuclear industry—which is backed by the utilities and to a certain extent big oil—they have so much money tied up in it now, and all the plants are so ex-tremely expensive to build, and they aren't going to get their money back off of them, you know. It's like, they made a mistake twenty-five, thirty years ago when they opted to go nuclear, and now instead of saying, "Hey, we goofed. This is not the way we should have gone," and just let them sit where they are. Don't build any new ones.

I understand they can't just shut them all off tomorrow be-cause a lot of areas of the country really depend on nuclear for electricity. We don't so much around here. I know places like Il-linois and the Midwest, they really need nuclear energy, unfortu-nately. It is going to take twenty to twenty-five years until they can get other electric generating capacity out there. I just can't see why they don't admit their mistake. . . . It just seems like such a pigheaded course to me. They seem to feel that they're above the law. They're above their responsibilities. They're above their responsibilities to their ratepayers and the public in general.

But I have not run into too many people that are really for them [nuclear plants]. The most I have heard anyone say is well, you know, they'll grudgingly say, "I guess we have to have them because we need the electric power." I've never once heard any-body who came out with a big defense of how great nuclear power was. I'm sure you could find somebody who works in the nuclear industry who is going to say that. But as far as just ordi-nary, common people who are not necessarily politically active or real concerned about major issues, you know, people you run into in the grocery store or someone you haven't seen for fifteen years and, you know, the subject comes up, you know, their pri-mary interest is what yours is—it's your family and your home and just getting on with your life in general. I think it would be a good idea if they had a referendum in this area and just had some questions on there—not just do you want nuclear power or don't you—but maybe five, six questions [about] how they felt about it. Would they support shutting down the plants that are here? If they'd be willing to conserve more electricity—I think people have started to do that. Obviously, as it gets more expensive, people stop and think about it a little bit, and I think we all could do with a little less than we're used to doing. It's too frightening. It's not worth it. There are alternatives.

*Has the accident changed your life?*
I think it has changed my life in the sense that it was really devastating for me at the time that it happened because it was such a hopeful time for me with new beginnings, with having the baby, and everything, and it was just like, I don't even know how to explain it—it was so frightening those first few days—not knowing what to expect. I was crushed. I just thought, "Oh, my God! How can this be happening? I can't believe it." Obviously, time heals, and time helps you get things in perspective, and we got through it physically okay and . . . but it made me think a lot more seriously about some of these things. I never was particularly pronuclear. I always felt that it was not a very safe thing to fool around with, that we really weren't ready for it. And everyone else, well, I shouldn't say everyone else, but it seemed that as far as industry and government was concerned, they took it all very lightly and kind of pooh-poohed the idea that anyone who was against it was an alarmist and going around crying doom, you know. . . . I guess it just sort of crystallized my feelings. I feel more strongly since it happened.

I do know that I would like to move from this location. We can't because of my husband's work. He is a mason. He does restoration masonry. He is working a great deal right now. He does small masonry contracts. He does not do new homes—builds fireplaces, stonework, and brick work. So his business credits are here. His ties are here to contractors that he does do work for. We don't really have enough cash to go someplace else, and we can't relocate right now. We do rent our house rather than own it because we have a lot more freedom to move. . . . Since I don't think we can go someplace where I would really feel safe, that he could possibly earn a living, I would like to move maybe ten miles or so away from the plant because we're about six here. We have been looking for a place. . . . It would make me feel safer from the small doses of radiation that come off just when a plant is operating normally and the small releases that they have every now and again. . . . Occasionally, we just have a minor release, and, sure, that one dose isn't going to hurt anybody, but if you're living close to it and you have it repeatedly year after year after year, it gets to the point that you do wonder about it, especially with a young child who has a lot less body mass and a lot more years ahead of him to absorb all that. So I know I would just feel safer with a little more distance between myself and the plant, especially if they open Unit 1 and that's back in operation. So I believe, in that sense, it has changed my life because it has put me through a lot.

*Has your outlook changed?*
I think it made me a lot less optimistic about the future. It just kind of sounded a note of like: Where is this society going? Where are our priorities?

*Did you think that way before?*
I would say I had [thought that way before] but I think I had been more equally balanced. I'm sure everybody has moments like that. Sometimes you just wonder where will it all end. There's so much violence in the world. . . . But I think it was balanced out pretty well by also being able to say, "Well, there's also a lot of good things in the world, a lot of positive things, and somehow we'll pull through and work it out." Life obviously is not a fairy tale, never has been and never will be, but after this, it just really made me wonder, "Are we going to be able to overcome this? Is our technology going to do us in before we wake up and look at it?"

It's upsetting because it just seems that the utility companies—not just Met Ed, all of them—are into nuclear, all the agencies, PUC [Public Utility Commission], they just seem to be business as usual. It was just business as usual. It seems to me that the only thing that mattered to them was that it was a monetary loss so they couldn't pay their dividends and so their stockholders are angry. It just seems that they really don't care about any of the other things involved in what they are doing. It's not like it's a company that's turning out defective sewing machines or something. Then you have a choice. You don't have to buy the sewing machine, or if you do buy it, you can at least try to take it back and get your money back. You know, it's unfortunate, but it's not the end of the world. But they're over there with a defective nuclear plant, and it's our lives here at stake. And if they mess up, they can't give you back your life or the lives of your family. It's a little different situation, but they don't seem to look at it in that way.

So I think it's made me a little more pessimistic in general, perhaps about the attitudes of the people who are in power because it just seems like the ordinary person—they pay lip service to you, but that's about it. But when it gets down to the hard decisions of, you know, the rate increases and are you allowed to do this, are you allowed to do that, are you allowed to dump this, are you allowed to dump that, it's always a big hoopla. And they let you think that you're having some say in it. But in the long run they just go ahead and do what they want to, and we're stuck with the consequences. That's how I look at it.

*Do you think the people will affect the restart decision?*
I have my doubts about it. I went to the hearing in the fall about reopening TMI 1, and the day I was there, there was only one person in favor of opening, and many, many people opposed to it. And I think in the town meetings that they had in Middletown, petitions that have been signed, letters that have been written to Congressmen and the NRC, PUC, and what not. It seems they must feel some guilt because they let you say your piece. They make a big deal about letting you say your piece, but then when push comes to shove, it's back to the same old thing of letting Met Ed do pretty much what the hell they want over there.

*Did you think about the plant before the accident?*
Yes, I had thought about it before. On certain days I could just see the steam coming, like a cloud or something. And I had thought about it, and I had not liked it particularly. But I think I had been lulled along with most other people into thinking, "Well, it's all right. It's not the best thing in the world, but it's reasonably safe, and we can live with it." But since then I just don't think we can live with it.

*Has it changed your idea of Newberry at all?*
I think probably more of a sense of community that people have because being in a scattered area like this and unless you're involved in a local organization, which I am not, you are not in such daily contact with people as you might be in a bigger city, and say it has its own newspaper or what not. You feel in the midst of that community in the sense of what is going on. This area does not have a newspaper so you get little spots from the

news in the northern end of the county. And in that sense [the accident] made you more aware of the community, more aware of how many people there were and how supportive they were toward one another, caring for each other during the accident. A lot of offers of help, friends offered to help, to move the animals because if there was an evacuation, there would have been no time. Things like that. And in that sense, it changed for me.

## MRS. CARMAN

Mrs. Carman lived in a suburban housing development very near Three Mile Island with a clear view of the cooling towers from her street. She was married and had four children living at home, the oldest in high school. Four years before the accident, she and her family had moved to Newberry Township from New England when her husband was transferred to the area. She was an active member of a township service organization.

*How did you find out about the accident?*
I [was in a meeting] Wednesday night. [One of the members] got called down to Goldsboro, and he came back and said he didn't have too much information for us. And he said, "The only information that I can tell you is that the wind was blowing in our direction." So we would have gotten more of the fallout. . . . We came home about 11:30 P.M., and I wanted to pack and leave then. But my husband thought that I was crazy. So I didn't. Thursday, I was kind of upset, but I didn't think too much about it. And then Friday I was working around the house, and I heard a siren go off. I [turned on the radio] and started monitoring. At 11:00 A.M. they said they were going to evacuate, and the schools were being closed and would be evacuated. . . . By this point I was getting panic-stricken. And I just hurried and packed. My husband came home from work, and we picked up the kids. We've got three of them here, and the other one we had to get at the tech school. But he already was put on a bus and taken down to the regional high school. Then we had to go down there. Then we just left for [home state] and stayed up there for a week. It was very nerve-racking.

I finally got over it until the whole thing started up again this year. I am really leery. I don't know from one minute until the next whether we are going to evacuate again or are you going to be here, what is going to happen, especially when they tried to go in there [the damaged reactor] the other week, and they couldn't even get in there. They said it was corroding. . . . I wonder every day what's going to go on. . . . For a long time, I wondered when I went to bed if I'd wake up the next morning, if I'd still be alive because that thing just might go, might explode or something.

I wonder, you know, not immediate health effects but in the long range, what will happen ten to fifteen years from now. You don't know, and I don't believe anyone else knows. . . . I don't believe one word they [NRC] say, and I think that Met Ed, I just think they're a bunch of mafias. I don't believe them at all, and the NRC is just as bad. . . . But I still don't believe, you know, the different doctors. You'll read articles in the paper, hear them over the radio and the TV, that this doctor says this and that and, you know, there'll be no harmful side effects. Well how do they know? There's never been anything like this before, so they can't project in the future what it will be. . . . I don't see how they can truly know because there's never been anything like this happen before, and I think it's going to take ten to twenty years, and then maybe something might show up. Who knows? But I don't feel that, you know, that they have the knowledge—well, not the knowledge—the research to predict that nothing's going to happen.

*How much a part of your life is this?*
A big part. . . . Nothing ever bothered me before. Now everything bothers me—the least little thing, you know, I get very jumpy, very nervous, especially when they say they're going to release radiation. I always have the fear that it's going to get away from them, you know, that they're going to lose control over it, something's going to go wrong. This is my fear. Not that it's going to be their fault. . . . If they couldn't get in [to the plant], what's it [corrosion] doing to the whole inside of the reactor building? You know, is it eventually going to rot out, and the radioactivity's just going to go, and they're not going to have any control over it. This is one thing that I wonder about.

*Have you thought about moving?*
We have thought about it. In fact, we were going to put our house on the market. But the houses in this area just aren't selling—this one house up the street has been on the market for over a year now and it hasn't sold yet, and the youngest boy has one more year in high school. I'd kind of like to get him through high school here rather than have him change schools.

*Do you think you will move?*
Eventually, but not for another year.

*Do you think the reason houses aren't selling is TMI?*
Partially, but also I think it is the economy and interest rates.

*What was it like for you before the accident?*
We just liked this area. When we moved in we didn't know that
was a nuclear plant. We didn't know what that was over there
until after we moved out here. It is scenic, and like out in the
country. You are not crowded like in the city. I didn't want the
atmosphere that was in the city. We have never lived in a city.
We came from a small town, and I don't think I could stand living in the city and have all the hustle and bustle. I just like to be
out.

*What information influences your decisions about TMI?*
I have my own way of thinking. I make up my own mind. No one
influences me. I'm stubborn. . . . Well, I don't really ever reach a
decision about what's going on over there, but every time they
say something, I just say, "Oh, they're lying again." I don't believe them. I don't believe them. I don't believe one thing they
say because I kept saying on the first day it happened, on Wednesday, I kept saying, "They're lying. They're lying." My husband
said, "Aw, you're full of prunes." "No, I'm not," I said, "they're
lying." It took a long time for the truth to come out. . . . I think
the state at the same time was rather lax in not having a
monitoring system of their own. I, you know, I not only blame
TMI officials, I blame the state plus the federal government. I feel
that they were all lacking, and there is no one [organization] that
can be put at fault. But right now, in the long run, we're the ones
that are paying for it.

*Are you against it reopening?*
If they can prove that it will be safe. But I think there's going to
have to be a good many changes made in the system for it to be
safe. . . . But as far as reopening it the way it is now, I don't
think that that's right. I don't feel that they should be allowed to
open it the way it is now.

*Do you think the people will be considered?*
No, they're going to do what they want.

*Do you think they care what the people think?*
No, I don't think it would bother them at all. Because I feel they

have one aim in mind and that is to raise money, to earn money. And I don't think they have any feelings as far as other people go—I don't think it bothers them. It makes me wonder if they have a conscience, because I know if I was in that position I would be very upset, and you know the things that have been written and have been publicized. It's just like they don't even care. . . . Well, if they cared, they wouldn't have lied in the beginning. . . . In fact, I'll tell you, there was more printed up north in the papers than there was down here. The articles up there were much larger and more informative because I know when I came home [to Newberry] different ones said different things . . . because I think they were told to cool it. They didn't want to panic the area.

*How would you compare this to say a hurricane?*
It's something that's constantly there. A hurricane comes and goes, and there's the cleanup afterwards. Well, once you've cleaned up, you know, it's gone away. It's not going to come back for a few years. And it's the same with a tornado. It comes, it goes. It's not going to say it can't come again but, you know, that it wouldn't be like the next day or possibly that night. Where this, anything could happen at any time. You don't know. And I think it's just one constant fear. . . . Different ones will say, "How close do you live to it?" And I'll say, "Well, I can look out and see it from my house everyday." "Really?" they'll say. And I'll say, "Uh, huh." I think if anything happened again, I don't believe I would ever come back. I would just go and stay. I told my husband he can stay. I am going.

## MR. CROWN

Mr. Crown lived in a new suburban home in one of the subdivisions of Newberry Township with his wife and their two preschool children, one born since the accident. He was a young man with a good job, which he enjoyed. He commuted every day to his work just outside of Harrisburg. He was not a native of the Harrisburg area, but he and his wife liked the area and were content with their life there.

*How did you feel about the accident?*
In general, it was a unique experience, something I would not want to repeat. And because of that I am against the plant opening up again.

*What upset you the most?*
I did not get very upset when it was happening, to tell you the truth. We got her [his wife] and the child out, and I just went to work normally because a lot of the people at the place I work, they just took off; half of the crew just left. So obviously someone needed to get work done because the company I work for just can't shut down. What we do is for places all around the country, not just locally. We just can't close down because of a storm or something or even something like this. Once we got them [the family] out, I just went about my normal business. It [the accident] probably had less effect on me at that time than it does now simply because of the thoughts that come into my mind since that time.

*How do you feel now?*
I really don't want to see it open up again. The location of it is such that it shouldn't have been built in the first place. We didn't live here at that time. When we moved out here, I was conscious of it, and I was one of the few that was. I knew it was out there. I knew how far away it was, and I had a lot of things I would do if there was an emergency. It seems that in my conversations, lots of people never gave it much thought. They just figured it was a power plant. But I really resent the fact that somebody can run a utility, a reactor like that, in such a shoddy way, in a slipshod manner, when it is such a potentially dangerous way of operating, the whole operating system. And it could deprive me of everything that I've worked for. In other words, had something happened at that time, and I had gotten out—of course, my family was already gone—I would imagine had it melted down the whole area would, to a certain extent, be a waste. In other words, you would have radioactivity in the water supply and radioactivity in the air, and I am not sure that a lot of people even think of that. How many hours were we away from a meltdown? And it doesn't matter to many of the people around here anymore.

*Do you know people who it does matter to?*
Yeah, yeah, I feel I know both. The ones it does matter to at work generally get . . . there is one guy, in particular. He is active in the antinuclear movement, but he smokes about four packs of cigarettes per day. So everybody just says, "You're going to die anyway." I know both sides, but I believe a great number of people have not given it a great amount of thought. I am not into

the movement, okay, as far as closing it down. So I cannot really make a statement and say, "No one cares about it." But it seems the great majority of people are going about their business. And as far as I can see, every step has been to open it up. Every step the Public Utility Commissioner and anybody has taken has led me to believe that we are going to get to a point that they are going to want to open it again. Whether or not that happens, it will be interesting.

*Are you concerned about health effects of the accident?*
What happened already? Not necessarily so. But what is still possible, what is still in there, all the radioactive water, all the Krypton gas, and all that. Yeah, I think to a certain extent. I know what they are going to try to do with it. They have no alternative. They've got to go somewhere with it. They are going to try and blow it out the door and dump it out in the river. I fully expected that as soon as I heard that they had it all in there. So I wasn't really surprised by it. And I am not sure if there is a safe alternative now that we've gotten to this point. Again, what irks me is that they can run nuclear power in the hole. There is no way of disposing of nuclear waste and nobody seems to care about it. The utility companies, in the need for a type of energy that they can sell to people, that they can control, have gone ahead with nuclear power regardless of the fact that there is nothing to do with the nuclear waste. Put it in some container, and put it in the ground, and hope the container doesn't rust or an earthquake doesn't occur or something. They are not disposing of it. They are just hiding it temporarily. I don't see it as a good source of power. I am not sure there is another source of power. It is easy for me to sit here with my lights on and say, you know, we shouldn't have nuclear power. But if it is absolutely necessary, then they should put it in places, in nonpopulated areas.

*Why do you think some people are upset and others aren't?*
I don't know. People don't have the concerns, in my opinion. A lot of the people who don't have concerns left the area. I guess it is just human nature. Some people just don't get down about it or anything. Some people give things more thought. I just attribute that to human nature more than anything else. Some people just don't get hyper about things, and they take them as they come.

*Is there any information you trust?*
Well, the NRC, during the crisis, was up-front as far as I was concerned, because there was too much at stake for them not to be.

In other words, this is going to be the big black mark that if they can't get Three Mile Island operating again, get it going again, it is going to be a situation where they failed, where nuclear power failed. And I don't think they want it on their record. So I am convinced anything they do from here on out is going toward opening up. They are going to be careful to a certain extent because they can't get caught red-handed, do something completely against their own regulations, as far as safety goes. I think they, and of course Met Ed, are pushing to open it back up. And as far as I am concerned, PUC has cooperated in it all. There was a lot of talk about Met Ed losing their license and stuff like that. That was just talk. They will slap their wrist a few times, but they will sign the license.

*Have the antinuclear groups been truthful, do you think?*
I really have not got into that because immediately you have the connotations of Jane Fonda and all of the old antiwar radicals and a few Commies in there. We were overseas—we were in West Berlin—and the Communists come to mind because they always have a way of catering to the cause at that particular time, okay. And that is the way I see a lot of the antinuclear types—their activities are catering to the cause at the time. I should not knock them because I am glad they're around. Hopefully, people are hearing things that they are saying. Maybe they are thinking a little more about it instead of presuming it is not going to happen again. I shouldn't really knock them. But I am not really active in them, either.

*Do you think the newspapers did a good job or not?*
No, I think they, I shouldn't talk about it because I only get the Sunday paper. I thought the news media, in general, covered it well. In other words, they sensationalized to a certain extent, but as far as I am concerned it was a sensational occurrence. It was that close to whatever they wanted to make it out to be because it was a first-time situation. Nobody knew what was going to happen. Nobody knew what was coming off, did not know whether their little bubble was going to go away or if it was just going to get bigger. They were acting on reason, and a lot of unreasonable things happened. And they didn't have any kind of precedent for it. I don't think it could have been sensationalized out of the realm of being somewhat credible, being close to being credible. We got a lot of coverage. It was kind of strange to see coverage of something right around where it happened. I've never

been in that kind of situation before. But I don't think they [newspapers] said anything that wasn't true.

*Do you want to leave this area?*
No, no, I don't really feel that I can let them drive me away. No matter what. If they should open the thing back up again, then I don't think that even though, that I don't feel entirely safe—I may do something like get a second car or something just because the strangest thing about it all was when she [his wife] was still here. We were thinking she would stay. She would stay, and I went to work and when I got to work, I was totally uneasy about the fact that they [his family] were twelve miles away from where I was and anything could happen. We talked a couple of hours into my work shift, and we said, "Call home [to his wife's parents] and tell them you are coming tomorrow." The first thing in the morning, we put her on the bus. I just don't want her and the kids sitting down here when something would happen and I am somewhere else. I don't want to move out, though, just because I don't think it is entirely safe. I just don't think it is right for them to drive me away. There is no other reason that I would move. [I like] my job. I would not move at the present time. Some things have come up when we have had occasion to do it. And we turned it down. So I am not going to move for Met Ed either. It is just not going to happen.

*Is there anything you would like to do now?*
Sabotage. (laughter) I often wondered what I would do when it comes to opening. I know I am going to go up the wall if I just have to sit and watch it happen. I don't know to what extent I would go to at the present time. I think I could go to some extremes (laughter) if it were to come to us, be in some danger or if the plant opened up. It is a strange situation. I have never been in it before. I have never been driven to do something. I really do not want to see it open up again.

*Is Newberry as safe as before?*
Besides the nuclear plant this was a safe area. Most people did not have an awareness of it [the plant]. A lot of people did not know it was there. I knew it was there even before we moved out here. In fact it was in my mind. It really was because we used to see the vapor coming up and also because I knew there was a nuclear power plant. We are not from this area. We are from Erie [Pennsylvania]. We were in Texas before we moved in here. When we moved here, I remember, I don't remember how, but I found out

there was a nuclear power plant, and I saw where it was. When it was time for us to locate a house, it was in my mind. I actually thought of things like normal wind direction and ways I wanted to go and things like that, which would be the quickest way out before the accident occurred, just because I had some familiarity with nuclear power before that time. I read a fair amount, and I retain a lot, and, you know, and I am pretty comfortable with my knowledge of nuclear power. I knew there was danger in it, and in fact, dangers in anything. So it was in my mind before. Besides the nuclear power plant, I'd say this is an exceptionally safe place to live.

*What about now?*
Except for the radioactive waste sitting inside the building. The plant is powered down. It is not dangerous now just because it is not active. Normal operations—the amount of radiation would not be dangerous particularly because I do not live next door to it. This is a good five miles from it. For the most part, the wind goes the other way. It's more from the catastrophic situation that it could occur. Although I have not been impressed with the day-to-day operation that Met Ed has, so far as their honesty and acts. It is always that someone catches them at something first. Then they have to tell that something occurred—you know, a release of radioactivity. Someone would catch it. Then Met Ed would acknowledge it. You know, they are just not up-front. They realize what they are up against. Heck! If they show themselves to be fools, they are going to lose their license. They can't openly admit they screw up time and time again. That is not good business.

*Has the event changed your life?*
To a certain extent. In other words, it is on my mind to a much greater degree than it was before. Also the awareness of what my own situation might have been if it continued to get out of hand, had they not gotten it under control. At the time, it didn't bother me. What with working the second shift—I was on second shift, and I was pretty busy. Like I said, half the crew took off. It was a really busy weekend for us the whole weekend when it happened. There was significantly more work to be done where I work. So I really was busy. I was working twelve-hour days, whatever was needed. And I came home fairly tired, and I would just go to bed. I don't like it with all the silence—no wife, no kids—so I would go to bed with the radio on. I probably would have slept right

through the siren or anything if there were any problems. The fact that my children would have been deprived of a father, husband, whatever, just because of someone's profiteering—as far as I am concerned—that doesn't sit very well with me. Also, in fact, this entire area could be a radioactive wasteland. That bothers me at times. You know how the Carlisle Pike is really packed? Well, we were just sitting at a light, and all of a sudden I said, "Could you imagine what this would be like if TMI melted down? There would be no cars, just be empty." It was just a strange thought at a strange time. But thoughts like that come to my mind. Like over in West Berlin, a particular part of the city used to be thriving, and now it's the Berlin Wall. Now there are three blocks cleared on the east side so no one can be hiding in there, trying to escape. It is a cleared, bulldozed area when at one time it used to be the heart of the city. I have seen things that would make things like that come into my mind, a situation where it is now a wasteland because of something that has occurred. TMI to me makes the same kind of situation come to mind.

*How would you compare this event to a natural disaster?*
I imagine there are a lot of similarities because people are saying their life can never be the same, making that kind of statement on TV. And I can see where it wouldn't be [the same] because of what occurred out there [at Mt. St. Helens]. [There is] a little bit of difference because that one is natural and this one was promulgated by errors or whatever you want to call them, the snowball of errors that has occurred. Because as far as I am concerned, Met Ed is out to make a dollar on the going type of power, which is nuclear. I am sure, at one point in time, they thought nuclear power was going to be cheap. Now as far as I am concerned, it just prevents us from importing oil which is a good cause, but it is not cheap by any means, particularly when you have a situation like TMI.

*Are you concerned about chemical dumping?*
There are a lot of similarities there, too. What I feel toward Met Ed, I am sure the people at Niagara Falls [Love Canal] must feel toward Hooker Chemical, probably more on their side because their children are affected. We have had a healthy baby since this occurred. I prefer to think, feel, that we did not have any health effects. She [his wife] was only two months pregnant when it occurred, where up there [Love Canal] they have got children with

birth defects and illnesses that they just can't account for except for that stuff [chemical waste]. I guess that I am lucky that I live near Three Mile Island when there are places like Hooker Chemical to live near. I guess we are lucky.

*Do you worry?*
I don't think the things that are being done are the right things. Sometimes I think of a higher morality as far as how a person lives. It is not necessarily whether you can afford the gas or whatever. It's which you use versus which you could be using. I think there is a lot of thoughtless waste and just abuse of nature in general. That bothers me. It bothers me. I have a personal vendetta against that sort of thing. I am not going to come up with a solution to the world's problems. All I will try to do is whatever I can do personally to recycle or conserve gas or whatever the situation.

*Would you say you fear living near TMI?*
I do not fear it. I resent it. The fear I had was before my family left. And I had very real fear, and I could not concentrate on my work very well. Once they were taken care of, I had no real fear. I did come back and forth even though I was offered a place to stay by my work because they said I lived in The Zone. But I turned that down because I felt that the more the people evacuated, the more the danger of someone coming into, breaking into the house. I came home on purpose every night. . . . More and more people left. We set up a command post at work to kind of keep track of all our people as far as where they were going, whether they were going to leave. You were supposed to call in and tell them you were leaving and tell them where you were going. And I got two calls in a row which said, "West on the turnpike." And I just said something is up. But if I was to say any fear at any time it was then. I completed my normal shift and spent an extra four hours because things were pretty bad [at work] and then I went home. Once the family situation was taken care of, it didn't bother me as much. But again, as I said, I didn't want to move, I don't want to move out of this area. I don't want to leave this house, and that is the big reason why I would resent them reopening this up again. It is just because that potential is there. I don't think any of the cleanup operations, in themselves, that could be foolhardy or get themselves out of control, would pose a danger to me, being five miles from the thing.

But firing it up again would certainly [be a threat]. That is why I'm against it.

*Do you think they know what they are doing?*
I really don't think they know what they are doing. I just haven't seen anything to convince me of that. Time and time again, in the newspaper and on the news, you hear of something that they botched, something else that wasn't thought of in advance. I just don't think so. I don't know if any electric company has extensive experience in nuclear power. I think the industry, in general, was pushed by the federal government by such things as the Price-Anderson Act. My gosh, the federal government is going to subsidize a nuclear disaster! No insurance company in its right mind would do it. They would be broke. The first one that occurred, they would be out of business! So the federal government says they are going to foot the bill. Obviously, the federal government has supported it through its development. I think they continue to support it today, like I said, partially because it is an alternative energy source to Arab oil. But I still don't think that their experience overall is good enough, and particularly with Met Ed. I don't think they know about it as much as they should. I'm not sure about their level of technical expertise.

*Do you think it matters to the people who want to open this plant how the community feels?*
I would like to think that it did, but I think that it's going to be a financial thing. I think that, I feel that business in the United States carries enough sway to get to a situation where someone could walk in and say with absolute confidence that he was going to be forewarned about an evacuation at TMI so that we could have gotten our people out. . . . See, we would have been in a world of hurt if we had to evacuate our building, okay? Our customers would be in a world of hurt. All the data processing that we had accumulated for them over a period of time would be left in a building. So we need a little bit of advance warning if that building is going to blow up or whatever, which we obviously can get. But in a situation like this, where there would be a chance of us getting out, selected information that would save our business and would save the business of our customers, that is the consideration that we had—for getting out earlier. So I believe that American business is what runs this country, the almighty dollar, whatever way you want to put it, and that

financial considerations are going to dictate the TMI outcome. So I am kind of pessimistic about that. I think it is going to open. Whatever happens at that particular time, we will just sit back and watch. But I don't doubt that it is going to reopen. Financially, Met Ed wants it to and I think financially they're going to make it happen. And we're all paying for it. I resent that less. I would pay for it to stay shut. Obviously I do when I pay for the replacement cost.

If you are familiar with rock, pop, whatever, music, at the time that TMI occurred a song came out by John Hall called "Power." It was a song against nuclear power. I first heard it a day or two after you [his wife] left, and I wrote her and told her about it. Ever since that time, any kind of a song, I wouldn't say any kind of a song, any kind of well written—I like music, I like what I consider rock—but there have been some artists since that time who came out with distinctive antinuclear songs that did carry a good message besides just "close them down" or whatever. There were songs which had a good story line. They were well built, well written, whatever. And those types of songs—I can't listen to them without feeling an emotional reaction which, when you talk about crying, I will get to that point very easily while I am listening to these songs. It is strange! It doesn't happen otherwise. I attribute that directly to TMI. I can't think of any other explanation for it . . . more or less that I might have lost everything—not necessarily lost my life, but everything that I had that I am so comfortable with. I'm very comfortable with my life and my family and everything. They'd take that away from me. That's, I guess, why it affects me the way it does.

This chapter has allowed the reader to hear Newberrians express, in their own words, how it feels to live within a few miles of the Three Mile Island Nuclear Power Station. We hope that, by including these long, essentially unedited, interviews, the reader now has a better sense of the complexity of the reactions in Newberry to the nuclear accident.

The themes of fear, mistrust, cynicism, and powerlessness are clear in the words of these Newberrians. Their dreams, hopes and concerns are much like those of most Americans. The difference between "them" and "us" is their transformation after the accident at Three Mile Island.

# FIVE

## MISTRUST CONFIRMED

A SERIOUS ACCIDENT had occurred at the Three Mile Island nuclear power plant. Immediately after the accident, there was fear and even panic among many residents of Newberry. A substantial portion of them evacuated at least for several days. But within two weeks the reactor had been stabilized, and residents were assured that Newberry was safe; people could return to their homes, they were told, and resume their former lives. Was that the end of the story?

According to previous research, that should have been the end of the story. Many sociologists who study the effects of disasters on communities have found that disasters do not usually have long-term effects. When disaster strikes, community equilibrium is temporarily upset, while disaster response mechanisms strive to restore balance. The magnitude and intensity of the response to disaster may even bring a community closer together. However, regardless of whether people are drawn closer as the result of a disaster, balance is eventually restored with few if any enduring effects.[1] Moreover, by the usual measures of disaster researchers, the Newberry community was no exception. People who remained in the area went back to work, to school, and to the routines of daily life. We learned of no one for whom this was not true.

However, we interviewed people in the Newberry community six times between 1979 and 1986, six months after the undamaged Unit 1 reactor was put back into operation. We found that the story did not end two weeks or even two years after the accident first occurred. Instead, throughout this seven-year period, a large portion of residents perceived their community as dangerous because of its proximity to Three Mile Island. They would have moved from the community if they could. Many believed their health and the health of children in the community had been threatened by exposure to radiation during the accident. A number thought that many aspects of their lives had changed for the worse, a decline they attributed to the accident. Finally, as a group, residents were more psychologically distressed than would be expected in a similar community.


## PERCEIVED DANGER

The majority of Newberry residents felt that it was dangerous to live near a nuclear power plant. The portion of the population who perceived living near any nuclear power plant as dangerous varied between 1979 and 1986, with a high of 72 percent in 1979 to a low of 60 percent in 1982. At the time of our last survey, 65 percent believed it was dangerous (fig. 1). A consistent proportion, over 80 percent, perceived the Three Mile Island nuclear power plant as dangerous both before and after the restart in 1986 (fig. 2).

We also found the theme of danger expressed in personal interviews and in comments added to questionnaires. In 1986, we received only 15 comments like the following, which views Newberry as restored to its pre-accident state. "Three Mile Island created a situation we are not likely to forget, but I feel that life in Newberry Township has fairly well returned to the way it was before the accident." Instead, we received many more that focused on continued fear. Of the 155 open-ended comments added to questionnaires received in 1986, 63 dealt with fear. Another 77 expressed negative attitudes toward Three Mile Island. A sample of these comments follows.

"Since the nuclear accident in Russia, I strongly feel our fears are renewed and again dominate our thoughts."

"The 'feelings' have been renewed with the [Chernobyl] meltdown in [the] USSR. I'm scared, but can't do anything about it. So life goes on. I'd probably be worse if my husband didn't calm me down."

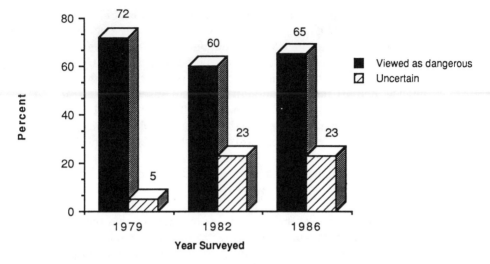

Fig. 1. Percent who viewed living near a nuclear power plant as dangerous

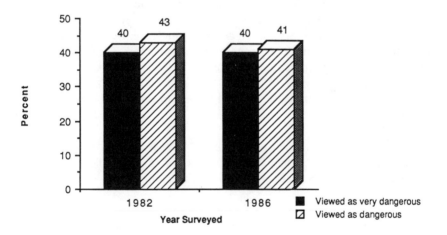

Fig. 2. Percent who viewed TMI as dangerous

"The effects of Three Mile Island have still caused a lot of fear in the community, the same as March '79. People outside the community cannot understand why we feel the way we do. Let's just hope they don't have to experience what we did. Let's remember what happened a few weeks ago [Chernobyl]. It most likely could have happened here."

"We live with Three Mile Island tension. Most fear is of a meltdown. I've had cancer twice—two different kinds—one before the incident at Three Mile Island, one after. I'm not saying the cancer is related to Three Mile Island but I do think if an official had a taste of the disease and also had a fear, they might change their attitudes. It is no fun to hear an unscheduled alarm going off, not knowing if it is false or not. If it is so safe, why must we have an alarm system? I don't think people who don't live around a nuclear power plant realize the terror that one feels when an unscheduled alarm goes off. I have heard several unscheduled alarms that stop after one or two minutes. Then no explanation is given of why they went off."

By 1982, nearly half of the residents we interviewed said they would move if they could, this in a community which had been, and still is, a net gainer of residents. [We have not investigated the views of people who arrived after 1979.] The portion of the community that expressed a desire to move was about 39 percent immediately after the accident and about 46 percent by 1982 and thereafter. The portion of people who were uncertain also rose and remained constant at about 30 percent (fig. 3).

Of course, as the interviews in chapter 4 indicate, residents varied in the amount of time and energy their worry consumed. The comments of these four residents indicate the variation in overt concern.

"I think it's dangerous, but I don't lose sleep about it. I can cope with life."

"I'm probably a little bit more panicky now. Not panicky. I guess that's kind of an extreme word. I'm not one to get all bent out of shape and go nuts. But there's times I just think I wish we could move."

"It's just frightening for me, really it is. I try to not think about it; you know, it's so close and everything. The best thing I guess most people try to do is put it out of their minds and try to forget about it. But every once in a while you do think about it when you hear it on the news and everything. . . . It makes me shiver sometimes when I see [the cooling towers]."

"It worries me a great deal. . . . I wonder every day what's going to go on. . . . For a long time I wondered when I went to bed if

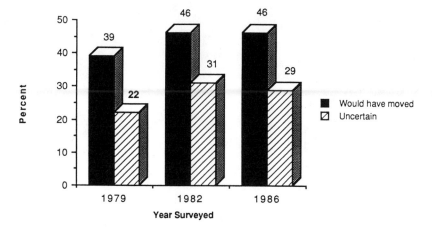

Fig. 3. Percent who would move farther away from TMI if they could

I'd wake up the next morning, if I'd still be alive because that thing just might go, might explode or something."

## PERCEIVED HARM TO HEALTH

There was also worry about the health effects of the accident. In 1979, 35 percent of Newberry residents believed their chances of getting cancer had increased because of the accident. In 1982, that portion had risen to 47 percent. A great number of people were uncertain at both times (37 and 35 percent, respectively) (fig. 4).

People who were worried about health effects were especially concerned about their children and grandchildren. In 1979, 53 percent believed that for children living in Newberry chances of getting cancer had increased, and in 1982 that portion was 49 percent. The amount of uncertainty remained constant at about 35 percent of the community (fig. 5).

The following excerpts typify the views of many Newberry residents in 1980.

Mrs. Hemingway: Then, of course, you really worry about their [babies'] health. You know, were the radiation levels what they said they were? Were they higher? And the bad thing about it was that the worst releases were before they told anybody about them. I mean, I was outside in the yard, so I got it, probably,

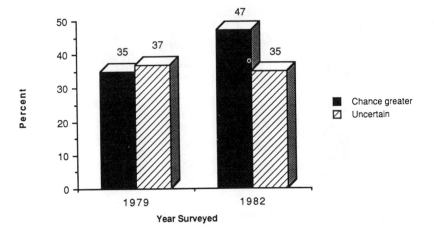

Fig. 4. Percent who believed their chance of getting cancer was greater because of TMI

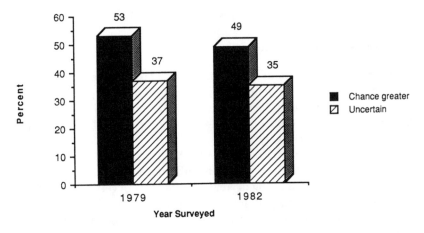

Fig. 5. Percent who believed children's chances of getting cancer were greater because of TMI

whatever it was. I was exposed to it. That was long before they said stay indoors. So I was very frightened and very scared and very worried about it. . . . I think I still feel worried, primarily for him [her baby], not as much for myself, because I wonder how much the dosage really was. I had a friend who had a child with leukemia, and I saw her live through that. It's bad enough when you think about it, but when you've had a personal experience with someone you know, then it's really horrible. And you just think, please, don't let that happen.

Mrs. Brown: I probably, I have thought about [health effects] for my son—maybe because I was pregnant at the time, and the biggest radiation dosage we got was the night it happened. Usually, the wind doesn't blow this way, but, of course, the night it happened, it did, and the only thing I fear would be maybe leukemia or something in later years, which I don't know if it's possible or not. And I'm sure in some ways the risk of what happened is—compared to some of these children who live next to chemical plants—less of a danger. But I don't know. Who knows?

A woman with a teenage daughter and a grandson by another daughter said:

I am concerned about the younger children. We have a teenage daughter which I feel might possibly be over the age, I hope, to be affected by it [the accident]. . . . I have a little grandson right up here [in the house next door]. Now, I'm concerned about him. Of course, his mother's concerned, too. He's just a year old, I guess, next week. . . . So, I think, this is in the back part of her mind, not in the back part, but she does think about it.

Mrs. Boswell: I mean, I have a grandson, and I just think the world of him. I think of what his future's going to be for him. Like I say, my husband and I, we've lived a good life so far, and what's going to be is going to be.

The previously quoted resident further stated: I wasn't terribly upset about the accident [when it first occurred]. I wasn't happy but I wasn't really upset about it. . . . We stayed home and planted fruit trees. . . . As time goes on, I'm more concerned because I feel with letting out this gas and with different things, I think it's worse than I thought it was. . . . Well, I feel there's been a lot of miscarriages since then. I had a daughter who had a miscarriage that August and there's been other problems.

A local businessman who had lived in the community all his life was not concerned for himself but for his many young relatives in Newberry.

We try to worry about things we can control. That is my philosophy. Live moment by moment, to the fullest, and enjoy life. This thing of worrying about what happened fifty years ago or what will happen fifty years from now, it is things you have no control over. That's the way I think about TMI. Live for today. The day is over; we start over. Enjoy today. Thank the Lord for another good day! I don't think about me. I am worried about the children and when they get married. Are they going to be sterile? My wife, we don't expect to have any more children but you [the interviewer], a young man, I hope you have a half dozen. But here is a boy who is seven years old. We waited eighteen years until he was born, and he is our pride and joy. It is a little hard on the old man to go out and play ball, go out fishing, but we get along. I worry about him. This fellow's daughter is getting married, and she wants children. Is she going to be able to have normal children? You know I have four grandnieces who are pregnant in our family. It concerns me. One of my nephews is expecting, lives two doors from me. It is their third child. I really hope they have a normal child, and there is not any defect from this TMI. You just don't know.

A Newberry Township official reported his grandchildren's views of their own health.

We have been able to deal with it in our family. I have grandchildren—twelve years old, twin grandsons—and they were concerned because of what different things were said in school and about their future and health. I was surprised that children discuss this. They do. They get it from their parents, schoolteachers. I would not say they were frightened, but they talked about it. They wondered what the future would hold for them.

Health concerns did not fade. The following comments were added to questionnaires in 1985 and 1986:

"My wife is 37 years old and now has cancer with no cancer in her family background. I don't know if this is because of TMI, but it seems from the local statistics that our area has a higher rate of cancers. TMI has changed our lives forever."

"I think it is inhuman to subject a community to a potential disaster and pretend all is well. Property values are a lot less due to Three Mile Island. People dying all around you with cancer from Three Mile Island."

"As I noted on the other page, my wife has incurable leukemia. My life and hers have been altered forever. I feel Three Mile Island is to blame. But who really cares anymore?"

"Harold G. died October 21, 1985, of cancer of the stomach. He first had cancer of the stomach June 1983. He was operated on, had three-quarters stomach removed and some taken off the esophagus, took chemo-treatments, was good for two years. You will never change my mind about all the people with cancer in this one place that it isn't from Three Mile Island. Thank you."

"After getting lymphoma, which I think was related to Three Mile Island, it has spoiled my living in the community, and I cannot afford to move as I am also retired and on Social Security."

"Many of my friends have had or died of cancer. Many are complaining of different skin conditions. I think all are related to Three Mile Island."

"We, as a family, are concerned about the effects of Three Mile Island on our health, but we do not let our concerns affect our everyday living. Property values have dropped considerably because we see Three Mile Island from our development. Oddly enough, people are still buying in the same area but where Three Mile Island is not visible. Out of sight, out of mind, I suppose. [Our] son, 17, has had problems with his hands and sometimes feet for the last five years or so. It has been diagnosed as Raynaud's Syndrome. He was among the students waiting for the school bus during the escape of radiation from Three Mile Island with [the] wind blowing in our direction. No wonder we're concerned."

## PSYCHOLOGICAL DISTRESS

Worry about Three Mile Island was not confined to direct concerns about health and safety. We also found that psychological distress after the accident was higher in Newberry than would be expected in a community such as this. Distress was elevated when we first measured it in fall 1979 and through our last survey in 1986, after the restart of Unit 1, the undamaged reactor. Typically, distress is defined as anxiety, depression, and psychophysiologic symptoms such as sweating palms, diarrhea, and stomach upset.[2] In 1979, the community mean on our measure of distress was almost as high as the mean for a sample of mental health center

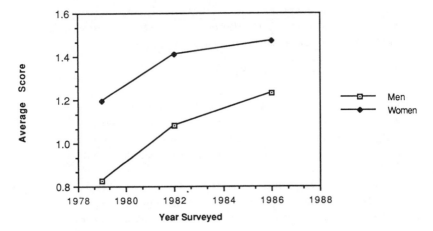

Fig. 6. Average psychological distress scores for men and women, 1979–1986

clients. This high level of distress did not change over all the years we surveyed people in Newberry, and the restart in 1986 did not substantially alter it (fig. 6). Although distress was higher than would be expected, most residents displayed distress that was in the subclinical range. That is, it approached the levels reported by mental health center clients but did not surpass them. Therefore, we can say that most residents were not impaired.

Since we have no measures of distress before the accident, we cannot say with certainty that distress was caused by the Three Mile Island accident. However, it is highly unlikely that, prior to the accident, distress would have been elevated in a community such as Newberry. Other research evidence that corroborates our assumption that distress was related to the accident includes a study that found that the people living near Three Mile Island were more distressed than people in communities with a coal-fired electric plant or no power plant.[3]

## OTHER EFFECTS

In 1986, after the restart of Unit 1, we asked people, "How has your life changed since the accident at Three Mile Island in March of 1979?" The majority reported no change in the areas of family life, general outlook on life, and personal health. But fewer people reported improvement than reported decline. Furthermore, the majority of people who perceived their situation as worse in 1986 than in 1979 attributed decline to the Three Mile Island accident, all or in part (fig. 7).

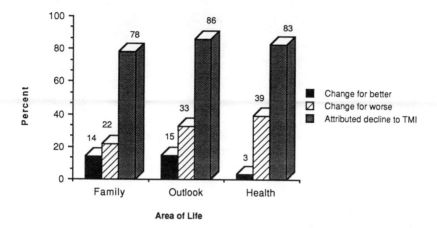

Fig. 7. Percent who reported changes in their life since the TMI accident, 1986

In summary, the appearance of normalcy was deceptive. The outward calm, the evidence of people leading ordinary lives that was so apparent to any visitor to Newberry after the accident at Three Mile Island, concealed a great deal of insecurity with respect to community safety and health. Furthermore, a substantial portion of residents reestablished outwardly normal lives in Newberry not because they wanted to stay in the area but because they believed they could not leave. Moreover, psychological distress was higher than would be expected in a community such as Newberry. Finally, many people felt a general sense of decline in quality of life that rightly or wrongly they attributed all or in part to the Three Mile Island accident. Therefore, the positive effects of a disaster—for example, in family cohesiveness and general outlook on life—were absent. The community underwent a profound and enduring change as a result of the accident.

## LOSS OF TRUST

Why did fear for health and safety, distress, and desire to move from the area develop after the accident and remain for so many years afterward? During this seven-year period, Metropolitan Edison and Nuclear Regulatory Commission officials continually assured nearby residents that the Three Mile Island nuclear power plant was safe. Furthermore, they consistently asserted that the amounts of radioactive gases released during the accident were so small that exposure would result in no deaths among people living in the vicinity of Three Mile Island. They expressed

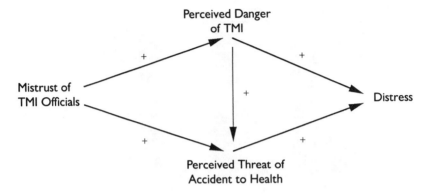

Fig. 8. Relationship between mistrust, perceived threat to health and safety, and distress

certainty that no cases of cancer or other illnesses were linked to radiation exposure resulting from the accident. Why, then, did the people of Newberry continue to worry?

We believe that the fear and distress in Newberry originated in the low credibility of authorities associated with the accident and their perception of the danger created by the reactor. People in the community did not trust those responsible for the operation and oversight of Three Mile Island; therefore, their assurances about its safety were meaningless. In fact, we have demonstrated statistically that mistrust was causally related to perceived threat and distress.[4] Mistrust of Three Mile Island officials led to perceiving Three Mile Island as a threat to health and safety. These perceptions, in turn, were associated with high levels of distress among the people of Newberry after the accident. Thus, comforting statements by officials about the insignificance of radiation exposure were heard but not believed (see fig. 8).

## THE ACCIDENT

Before the accident most people living in Newberry, if they were concerned at all, thought it highly unlikely that a serious accident would happen at this or any nuclear plant. By and large, residents believed the assurances of Metropolitan Edison officials that Three Mile Island and nuclear energy, in general, were safe. However, the events of March 28 and the days immediately following changed these perceptions for the majority of Newberrians.

First, the impossible had actually occurred: a serious accident had taken place at the local nuclear power plant. Residents asked, "How could this have happened? A nuclear power plant is a run-of-the-mill producer of electricity; it is nothing to be concerned about, is it?" Unfortunately for Metropolitan Edison's credibility, that was how its officials had presented nuclear energy to the community when they proposed to build Three Mile Island; afterward they fostered this view through public relations efforts. Nuclear power plants were sources of safe, clean, and cheap electricity. They were not a danger to people living nearby. The probability of a serious accident at a nuclear plant was so remote as to be ridiculous.

Furthermore, the consequences of a serious accident astounded the residents of Newberry. They learned that the effects of the most serious nuclear power accidents would include the immediate death of many nearby residents from radiation exposure, death from radiation-induced cancer for many more, and contamination of the area surrounding the plant so that it could not be reentered probably in the lifetimes of the people affected. The accident, especially the bubble incident, made this scenario real to residents of the Three Mile Island area. This image of devastation juxtaposed against the reassuring words of Metropolitan Edison officials before the accident hurt official credibility.

> Mrs. Hemingway: It's not like it's a company that's turning out defective sewing machines or something. Then you have a choice. You don't have to buy the sewing machine, or if you do buy it, you can at least try to take it back and get your money back. You know, it's unfortunate, but it's not the end of the world. But they're over there with a defective nuclear plant, and it's our lives here at stake. And if they mess up, they can't give you back your life or the lives of your family. It's a little different situation, but they don't seem to look at it in that way.

The actions of Metropolitan Edison officials during the first few days of the accident were not conducive to the development of trust. When the public learned that, while Metropolitan Edison officials had been issuing comforting reports about the accident, workers at the plant were desperately trying to determine what was happening and how to stop the alarming events occurring within the reactor, mistrust was fostered. When residents learned that company officials had known that radiation was leaking uncontrollably from the plant but did not inform the public or explain the risk, trust was seriously undermined. Newberrians found it difficult to believe members of an organization that had displayed, from the very first, a pattern of concealment when these officials assured them that the radiation released in March 1979 was not harmful.

Many people believed that Metropolitan Edison officials knowingly lied during the first days of the accident. Statements by some of the residents we interviewed testify to this:

"I wasn't really trusting anybody after a while because after Met Ed did what they did and everything and lied to us, I didn't trust anybody."

"As far as Met Ed, because of what happened on Wednesday and Thursday of that week [crisis period], from then on I just didn't trust anyone."

"I don't believe them [Metropolitan Edison and Nuclear Regulatory Commission officials]. . . . I don't believe one thing they say because I kept saying on the first day it happened, on Wednesday, I kept saying, 'They're lying! They're lying!' My husband said, 'Aw, you're full of prunes!' 'No, I'm not,' I said. 'They're lying.' It took a long time for the truth to come out but I was right, wasn't I?"

Some people believed that the utility was doing its best but that its best was simply not good enough. The issue of competence was raised. The remarks of Mrs. Hemingway typify this view:

It just seemed that when the accident happened, there was so much floundering around that, at the time, I was thinking it was just cover-up. They don't want to admit that they goofed. And the more I thought about it, the more I wondered. Well, I'm sure that was a part of it. But the more I thought about it, the more I thought, well, maybe they really didn't know what to do to correct it. And so that part of the smoke screen was the best they could do at the time—was just tell everybody, "It's okay. We're going to do this, we're going to do that, and it will be all right."

Bernard Barber argues that trust is "the expectation of the persistence of the moral social order." It has two dimensions that are of particular importance for understanding social relationships and social systems: "The first of these two specific definitions is the meaning of trust as the expectation of technically competent role performance. . . . The competent performance expected may involve expert knowledge, technical facility, or everyday routine performance. The second meaning of trust . . . concerns expectations of fiduciary obligation and responsibility, that is, the expectation that some others in our social relationships have moral obligations and responsibility to demonstrate a special concern for others' interests above their own. . . . Trust as fiduciary obligation goes beyond technically competent performance to the moral dimension of interaction."[5]

At Three Mile Island we see that, from the outset, people lost trust in their local utility company based on one or the other or both of these appraisals. It appeared to those who mistrusted Metropolitan Edison that its officials were either lying to the people for the company's benefit or bungling the job of managing the accident and communicating to the people because of incompetence. Some probably believed that there was a little of both incompetence and lack of fiduciary responsibility behind the actions of Metropolitan Edison. Irrespective of attribution, however, Metropolitan Edison lost its image of trustworthiness in the first several days of the accident.

## AFTER THE ACCIDENT

Could trust in Metropolitan Edison officials have been restored? Could further erosion of trust have been prevented? While no definitive answer to these questions exists, we believe Metropolitan Edison officials and those of their government collaborators at the Nuclear Regulatory Commission never made a credible attempt, although circumstances beyond their control did not help. Five major issues during the period between the end of the crisis in April 1979 and our last survey in April 1986 had an impact on Newberrians' trust in officials related to the Three Mile Island accident: (1) the process of decontaminating Three Mile Island's Unit 2; (2) the efforts to reopen Three Mile Island's Unit 1; (3) the debate over the health effects of low-level radiation exposure; (4) the increase in electric rates in the Three Mile Island area; and (5) the inability of other public officials to allay fears about health and safety. The events surrounding these issues confirmed residents' mistrust of Metropolitan Edison officials and led to their distrust of the Nuclear Regulatory Commission. Immediately after the accident, especially once Harold Denton had arrived in Harrisburg, the Nuclear Regulatory Commission was viewed as more credible than the utility company. However, the commission members' support of Metropolitan Edison's goals and their association with apparently bungled decontamination operations quickly put the Nuclear Regulatory Commission in the same camp as the local utility company.

### (1) The process of decontaminating Three Mile Island's Unit 2

The control room crew (at Three Mile Island) watches over a control panel and what is now essentially inert rubble on the floor of the reactor vessel. The pile is the debris of fuel rods that generated the unit's uncontrolled heat four years ago.

The pile is kept inert by a bath of boron dissolved in water. The solution prevents bombardment of the unspent fuel by neutrons that, unchecked, could set off chain reactions and a new buildup of heat inside the reactor.

The pile remains the principal unsolved technological problem, according to Robert C. Arnold, present of the General Public Utilities Nuclear Corporation, the division that runs the parent company's nuclear plants. As the billion-dollar cleanup proceeds, Mr. Arnold said in a telephone interview, the division's experts must find a way to remove and contain the radioactive debris.

"We will be pretty much breaking new ground," he said.[6]

The decontamination process involved the continued release of radioactive gases into the atmosphere as well as instances in which radiation-contaminated water was released into the Susquehanna River. These controlled, or planned, releases of radioactive materials infuriated nearby residents. First, people were concerned about additional radiation exposure. Second, it invariably appeared that Metropolitan Edison had selected the cheapest way to address the problem at hand. One instance involved the venting of radioactive water into the Susquehanna River. The following story, published in March 1980, describes a citizens group's failed attempts to force the utility to choose another method to dispose of radioactive water held in the plant.

The Third Circuit Court of Appeals, in an opinion received in Harrisburg Tuesday, has reversed a U.S. Middle District Court order dismissing a request for an injunction against dumping wastewater at Three Mile Island.

On Oct. 12, Judge Sylvia H. Rambo dismissed the Susquehanna Valley Alliance's (SVA) request that TMI be enjoined from dumping the wastewater until an environmental impact statement could be made. She ruled that only the Nuclear Regulatory Commission could make that decision. . . .

The Lancaster-based organization (SVA) filed suit in federal court May 25 against the NRC, Chairman Joseph A. Hendrie, General Public Utilities Corp. and several of its subsidiaries. . . .

In part, SVA wanted to halt Metropolitan Edison's plans to build and operate a wastewater treatment system, Epicor II, for the contaminated water. However, Met Ed went ahead with those plans after Rambo's ruling.[7]

The release of Krypton-85 into the atmosphere between 28 June and 11 July 1980 was another well-publicized, planned release, and hearings solicited public reaction to it. But in the end, the people living nearby felt that Metropolitan Edison and NRC officials had selected this method on the basis of cost rather than safety. An editorial in the *Philadelphia Inquirer* expressed the view of many.

There are alternatives to venting into the atmosphere the radioactive krypton gas trapped inside the TMI facility. They are expensive and would require time. They involve known and proven techniques, although none has ever been applied to a clean-up operation as large as that at TMI. The gas can be compressed. It can be pumped over charcoal beds to trap the radioactive particles. . . . The temperature of the gas can be reduced, liquefying it. Any one of those processes would make containment and safe storage possible.

The alternative to using one of those procedures is to vent the gas, subjecting the people living downwind of the plant to low doses of radiation with potential health damage and genetic effects which science today has no responsible basis for estimating. Venting is by far the cheapest and easiest method. . . .

To do so, with alternatives available, would be irresponsible— and unnecessary.[8]

Some radiation releases were uncontrolled, or at least unanticipated. At these times, the issue of notification was an additional problem since, necessarily, information was relayed to the public after releases had occurred. These events further exacerbated residents' mistrust of those managing the decontamination of Unit 1. They especially affected perceptions of competence. One such occurrence was reported on 21 March 1980 on the front page of the Harrisburg *Evening News*.

Radiation levels inside the auxiliary building at Three Mile Island returned to normal after a slight but puzzling increase that lasted about twelve hours, officials said. . . .

The plant has been troubled by various contamination problems since it was hit last March by the worst accident in the history of U.S. commercial nuclear power. . . .

Thursday's increase in radioactivity at the plant was at first believed to be due to a small water leak in a pump system that adds water to the plant's primary reactor cooling system.

But technicians inspected the building and could find no visual evidence of a leak.

"There was a type of decontamination activity that uses a jet spray, and that could cause additional airborne activity," said spokesman David Klucsik. . . .

Plant operators said an extremely low amount of radioactivity escaped into the air. They said it could not be detected on sensitive monitors in the building's ventilation system.

Officials said it posed no health threat.[9]

Another example of uncontrolled venting was reported on the front page of the *Wall Street Journal*.

Last July, the company repeatedly assured the public that vents in the Unit 2 reactor building would be kept closed while it lifted off the reactor's 170 ton steel cover as part of its cleanup program. But technical problems during the lift forced workers to open the vents anyway [allowing the escape of radioactive gases into the atmosphere].[10]

Other events related to the decontamination process contributed to residents' mistrust of Three Mile Island officials. After the accident, Metropolitan Edison routinely assured residents of the Three Mile Island area that it was pledged to a safe cleanup and recovery of the plant.[11] However, many reports of mismanagement both before and after the accident belied this pledge.

Investigations after the accident led to public knowledge about Metropolitan Edison's poor management prior to March 1979. For example, during Public Utility Commission hearings in 1980, the President's Commission on the Accident at Three Mile Island management task force report was introduced. The following account, given in the Harrisburg

*Evening News*, fostered the perception that Metropolitan Edison was incompetent and socially irresponsible even before the accident:

> The findings were based on interviews with 35 employees of General Public Utilities, ranging from plant operators to the president. . . .
> The Kemeny Commission, headed by Dartmouth College President John Kemeny, was appointed by President Carter to look into the TMI accident. [Joan] Goldfrank, a lawyer, was on the task force that investigated TMI management.
> Based on its interviews, Goldfrank said the task force found that the three companies (which co-owned the Three Mile Island plant) didn't have enough information about safety and didn't act on the information they did have.
> In addition, she said the task force found that Met Ed operators were not well trained, and the company "did not require attention to detail as a way of life at TMI."[12]

The decontamination process itself continued to raise the issue of Metropolitan Edison's competence and commitment to the safe cleanup of Unit 2. For example, a series of incidents reported in *The Guide*, a local newspaper, raised these issues. Accompanied by a television camera crew, a reporter for *The Guide* walked across the dry riverbed to Three Mile Island and roamed about the grounds. Ninety minutes passed before security guards noticed them. According to the reporter, a member of Metropolitan Edison's public relations department convinced the television station to withdraw the story. However, *The Guide* printed it.

> Three Mile "Island" is not an island. Several times I have walked across a dried-up Susquehanna River bed to the site of the atomic generating facility unnoticed by guards stationed at the plant's main security gates. . . .
> This was at least the third time in two years that the utility intervened in attempts to prevent Harrisburg area media from reporting problems at the troubled nuclear reactors. . . .
> I was one of the three journalists who walked into the nuclear generating station on July 7. With me were WHTM reporter Cher Wilson and cameraman Mike Reiber. Ms. Wilson and Reiber accompanied me to document a news article I was researching concerning plant security and sabotage possibilities.
> Three days before, on July 4, I had walked unnoticed onto Three

Mile Island to prove that the nuclear facility is not as secure as Met Ed has led the public to believe.[13]

Another story published in *The Guide* told of the ease with which someone could have sabotaged the Three Mile Island plant.

> Yet Met Ed is doing little to protect its vital areas from potentially hazardous inside forces—like saboteurs, a month-long *Guide* undercover investigation has revealed. A *Guide* reporter was hired on the spot as a security guard and spent four weeks in TMI. . . .
>
> But a month-long *Guide* look by a reporter who got a job on TMI as a security guard shows glaring gaps in its security defenses, gaps that would permit a terrorist or saboteur to sneak through and destroy the plant from within.[14]

Continuing incompetence was documented in a report in the *New York Times* on an incident that occurred in 1983.

> Four engineers who have participated in salvage efforts at the Three Mile Island nuclear plant here have asserted that mismanagement of the $1 billion recovery program has wasted millions of dollars, posed new threats to safety and delayed cleanup operations for years.
>
> In public statements and private interviews the engineers, who include the former site operations manager for the plant's operation, have complained that leadership and direction have been lacking, that protests about safety problems and violations have been ignored, and that federal funds have been spent out of all proportion to the results achieved. . . .
>
> "The cleanup operation has become an enormous boondoggle and is stretching on and on with no end in sight," said Lawrence P. King, former site operations manager for General Public Utilities Nuclear Corporation. Mr. King was discharged from his $60,000 a year position a month ago after complaining about a lack of safety and mismanagement for almost a year.
>
> Richard D. Park, an engineer with the Bechtel Corporation, the prime contractor for the cleanup efforts, also was ousted from his position last week and placed on leave after making similar charges. . . .
>
> "The operation is disorganized and at times irresponsible," said Mr. Park. "There is a serious lack of coordination between Bechtel,

G.P.U.N., the subcontractors, and the Federal agencies involved here, the Nuclear Regulatory Commission and the Department of Energy."

Two high-level engineers who also were interviewed reiterated the complaints of Mr. King and Mr. Park, adding that they were on the verge of quitting because of the frustrations they were having trying to push forward with cleanup operations.

To buttress their complaints, the engineers have amassed thousands of pages of memos, statements, letters, reports and other written materials that they said document their assertions.

Their complaints again call into question the safety and competence of the nuclear power industry at a time when new questions are being posed about its hazards and costs.[15]

In the view of many Newberry residents, these events raised again the issue of competence. Did the utility company, the Nuclear Regulatory Commission, and other experts who were responsible for the stabilization and decontamination of Three Mile Island really have things under control? Many Newberrians could not be sure they did.

Mrs. Kelsey: They're just pulling at straws there too. . . . They're trying to get things cleaned up, but they don't exactly know what they're going to do.

Mrs. Caspar: For the money that we're going to pay now, they could have hired help that could have not screwed up. . . . I do feel if the guy [a reporter] from the *Guide* could go in there with no background and get in, and the door didn't even have a lock on it, much less . . . a doorknob on it; you just pushed on it, or they held it open—it was supposed to be a restricted area—and he could go in there and take pictures.

Mrs. Boswell: As much as I've read about it in the paper and scientists have given their opinions on everything, but still I don't think they know exactly what's going on inside that reactor right now.

A resident gave this statement regarding the utility: They do not have the people who know what they are doing down there. When my brother-in-law went down there, he went down there cold turkey. He learned on the job. Just from the things he says and the people I have met that work down there, there are too few people who know how to run the place. They do not keep people down there long enough who know anything. The smart guys with NRC leave. They get bought out by one of the big companies.

In addition to the issue of competence, many residents continued to believe that the truth was simply not being told, that officials at Metropolitan Edison and the Nuclear Regulatory Commission were deceiving the people in the area about the safety of the plant during the cleanup. Mrs. Caspar's view is typical of many residents' beliefs about the period after the accident. "And right now you're still back in the same boat. You still don't know who to believe about what's going on. And I still don't think they're telling you everything." A local businesswoman said in reference to the Krypton-85 release being discussed at the time, "I don't know what they're going to do about it. I mean, I think they're just going to release it, and we're not going to know about it until it's too late. That's what I think."

## (2) The efforts to reopen Three Mile Island's Unit 1

After the accident, Metropolitan Edison wanted to reopen Unit 1, the undamaged reactor, as soon as possible, and its officials vigorously pursued NRC approval of this plan. However, as the approval process progressed, the issues of Metropolitan Edison's competence and social responsibility were continually raised. The proceedings strengthened many residents' mistrust of Metropolitan Edison officials. What came out in the proceedings contributed to loss of trust in the Nuclear Regulatory Commission. The residents believed that the rush to reopen Unit 1 demonstrated Metropolitan Edison's self-interest. They perceived the Nuclear Regulatory Commission's continual support of Metropolitan Edison's efforts to restart Unit 1, regardless of the competence and integrity of the utility, as evidence that this government agency had little regard for the community.

The Nuclear Regulatory Commission restart hearings began in Harrisburg on 15 October 1980. The major issues were plant design and hardware, emergency planning, financial capability, and management integrity. Before the hearings were even over, Metropolitan Edison had requested restart approval. The Nuclear Regulatory Commission rejected this request, and the main restart hearings ended on 9 July 1981. However, six weeks later, the licensing board reported that General Public Utilities Nuclear (GPUN), the organization newly created by General Public Utilities to operate its nuclear plants, had the managerial ability to restart Unit 1 safely. NRC credibility was damaged, however, in October 1981, less than two months later, when charges surfaced that some Metropolitan Edison reactor operators had cheated on their licensing exams. This caused the reopening of the hearings on 10 November of the same year.

By July 1982, the Nuclear Regulatory Commission and the Atomic Safety Licensing Board had recommended the restart of Unit 1. However, the issue of Metropolitan Edison's integrity was still unresolved. On 7 November 1983, the utility company was indicted on eleven charges of criminally falsifying test data on coolant leaks and destroying documents before the accident. Later in November, GPUN president Robert Arnold was implicated in management integrity issues. Before the accident, Arnold had been vice president for generation at General Public Utilities Service Corporation, an off-site staff technical group for General Public Utilities. He resigned from General Public Utilities Nuclear over the integrity issue, and six months later the Nuclear Regulatory Commission found that he had made inaccurate statements about the pilot-operated relief valve (PORV) that played such an important role in the accident of March 1979. Nevertheless, in December 1983 the NRC staff recommended the separation of the integrity issue from the restart decision. In January 1984, the Nuclear Regulatory Commission voted three to two to accept this recommendation.

On 28 February 1984, in a plea-bargain agreement, Metropolitan Edison pled guilty to one count and no contest to six others of falsifying test data on coolant leaks and destroying documents before the accident. Later in the year, James Floyd, a former supervisor of operations at Three Mile Island, was convicted in federal court of cheating on licensing exams in 1979. In February 1985, Mick Rood reported on the state of the restart petition in the Harrisburg *Evening News*.

Another public meeting to discuss issues affecting the potential restart of Three Mile Island Unit 1 . . . by the Nuclear Regulatory Commission. . . .

The NRC is legally bound to lift the 1979 shutdown order and allow generation of power at Unit 1, the utility has argued.

Under the Atomic Energy Act, the NRC also is charged to consider the integrity and character of a nuclear plant licensee. NRC licensing boards have held hearings on and off since 1981 on those and other issues. . . .

The board still has before it hearings on falsification of coolant water leak rates at Unit 2 in 1978–79 and on the involvement of record-rigging, if any, of current Unit 1 management.

The pivotal choice for the NRC is whether to wait for completion of those hearings and for the board recommendations on all three issues before addressing the restart of Unit 1.[16]

Despite the unresolved issue of integrity, the Nuclear Regulatory Commission voted that no further safety hearings were needed before a restart decision. The decision was made on 13 February 1985, and the vote was three to two. Ron Winslow of the *Wall Street Journal* presented a view of the Nuclear Regulatory Commission held by many people in the Three Mile Island area at that time:

> Meanwhile, the NRC's handling of Three Mile Island is also coming under fire. The agency has been setting deadlines for a restart vote since 1981. Each time it has retreated, often because more evidence against the company has surfaced. Ellyn Weiss of the Union of Concerned Scientists charges that instead of denying GPU's request each time, the NRC has allowed GPU "another opportunity to win."
>
> In February, the commission decided to cancel hearings into some issues it had previously considered vital to a restart vote. That angered several critics, including Pennsylvania. In an NRC filing, the state termed further hearings "essential" to the restart decision and to "how this commission regulates the nuclear industry." . . .
>
> In addition, a federal grand jury in Washington, D.C., is looking into the NRC's investigation of the Three Mile Island accident. Last November, David Gamble, one of the NRC's Three Mile Island investigators, testified before Mr. Smith's (licensing board) panel that the NRC investigation deliberately "precluded a full development of the facts and reached conclusions (favorable to GPU) that were not supported by the facts."
>
> In the end, though, none of these developments are likely to persuade the NRC to keep Three Mile Island closed.[17]

In the end, Ron Winslow was right. The Nuclear Regulatory Commission was not persuaded to keep Three Mile Island closed. On 29 May 1985 the Nuclear Regulatory Commission voted four to one to allow its restart.

In June, at the request of the Commonwealth of Pennsylvania and Three Mile Island-Alert and other antinuclear groups, the Third U.S. Circuit Court of Appeals in Philadelphia stayed the Nuclear Regulatory Commission restart order for the purpose of allowing further safety hearings. In August, the Thirty-fourth Circuit Court ruled against the appeal and upheld the Nuclear Regulatory Commission's restart order. On 24 September Supreme Court Justice William Brennan, Jr., continued a stay on the restart but on 2 October the Supreme Court ruled eight to one not to hear the Three Mile Island case. The stay was lifted, allowing General Public Utilities Nuclear to restart Unit 1.

Problems at the plant continued. For example, on 15 June 1985, Metropolitan Edison heated Unit 1 to operating temperatures without running the reactor. This condition is known as "hot standby." On 9 September 1985, an electrical fire at Unit 1 damaged switches used to operate the nuclear reactor control rods while the reactor was on "hot standby."

The Unit 1 reactor began operating again on 3 October 1985. But the restart process had contributed to the continuation of mistrust. Again, it showed Metropolitan Edison to be a corporation which lied for its own benefit. Furthermore, it portrayed the Nuclear Regulatory Commission as an agency interested in allowing Metropolitan Edison to restart Three Mile Island irrespective of the utility company's capability for safe operation of a nuclear power plant or concern for community safety. Many people came to perceive the federal government as an unquestioning supporter of nuclear energy, and, therefore, not an impartial regulator of Metropolitan Edison. Mr. Crown stated an opinion with which many Newberry residents would have agreed:

I think the [nuclear power] industry in general was pushed by the federal government with such things as the Price-Anderson Act [a federal insurance program for the nuclear power industry]. My gosh, the federal government is going to subsidize a nuclear disaster! No insurance company in their right mind would do it. They would be broke. So the federal government says they are going to foot the bill. Obviously, the federal government has supported it through its development and continues to support it now.

### (3) The debate over the effects of low level radiation

Between 1979 and 1986, Newberry residents were continually exposed to the controversy about the effects on human health of low level radiation exposure. For instance, soon after the accident, a group in Middletown, Pennsylvania, was addressed by Dr. Ernest Sternglass, a professor at the University of Pittsburgh, who told them that their children did not have a future as a result of the accident. Other seemingly equally qualified scientists argued that the radiation exposure of any individual living near Three Mile Island had not exceeded the equivalent of several chest x-rays and would have no effect on the health of area residents.

The following two examples from the *New York Times* are representative of the conflicting information obtained from the print media.

Scientific findings that have been emerging in recent months are forcing the experts to take a new look at the potential health hazards of radiation. Indeed, various authorities now suggest that ionizing radiation—the kind that has traditionally been considered most worrisome—should probably be judged four to twenty times more likely to produce cancer than previously believed. However, these new risk estimates remain tentative and their significance for human health is still uncertain.[18]

The other side of the issue is illustrated in this statement by Alvin M. Weinberg, director of the Institute for Energy Analysis in Oak Ridge, Tennessee.

Indeed the whole question of low level radiation is so critical to the acceptance of nuclear energy that I would judge this to be a leading, if not the leading, scientific issue underlying the nuclear controversy.

Governor Thornburgh's decision to evacuate pregnant women was, I presume, based on the retrospective study of Stewart and Kneale who claimed to have found significant correlation between childhood cancer and fetal X-irradiation. But this finding is contradicted by the experience at Nagasaki: Slight irradiation of fetuses there did not increase the risk of cancer. The matter is, to say the least, moot. I would hope that eventually the risk of low level radiation would be sorted out. If, as I believe, low level radiation is nowhere near as dangerous as, for example, Tom Brokaw of NBC seems to think, then the public's, and perhaps more important, the media's reaction to the possibility of such irradiation may be far more restrained.[19]

In addition, dispute over the methods selected by Metropolitan Edison and the Nuclear Regulatory Commission to decontaminate Unit 2 centered on the low level radiation exposure debate. The Krypton-85 release was an especially volatile issue. Although the Union of Concerned Scientists approved the utility company's plan to release Krypton-85 into the atmosphere, it was opposed by others. For example, two scientists from the Institute for Energy and Environmental Research in Heidelberg, West Germany, issued a statement regarding the Krypton-85 release.

1. Previous discussion of the venting of radioactive gases from TMI-2 has concerned only the noble gas Krypton-85. Besides Kryp-

ton-85, the atmosphere of the reactor building includes a great number of other radionuclides, some of which would be released into the environment during the blow-off of the gases. This could lead to radiation exposures significantly higher than those caused by Krypton-85. . . . Even allowing for high filter efficiency, a model calculation for only three of these nuclides showed that population doses would be high enough to cause about three additional cancer cases and an equivalent amount of genetical damage.

2. Uncertainties inherent in the meteorological models and dose calculations mean that . . . in the proposed purge program individual skin doses due to Krypton-85 could exceed the 10 mrem limit.

. . . . . . . . . . . . . . . . . . . . . . . . . . . . . . . . . . . . . . . . . . . . . . . . . . . .

4. The environmental monitoring program cannot ensure that all significant radiation doses to the community as a result of decontamination of the atmosphere of the TMI-2 reactor building will be detected. Most measurements are not frequent enough and are not made at all in some important localities. Important pathways and radionuclides are neglected.

5. As considerable health damage could be caused by venting the atmosphere of the TMI-2 reactor building, we strongly advise against this procedure. The report of the Union of Concerned Scientists (UCS) concludes that decontamination is not as urgent as stated by Met Ed and NRC. Therefore, we strongly recommend that the alternative methods for decontamination proposed by UCS . . . be used.[20]

Of course, within the scientific community, these uncertainties are well known and accepted. For instance, the classic public health text, Edward P. Radford's *Maxcy-Rosenau Public Health and Preventive Medicine*, includes a section on ionizing radiation that summarizes current knowledge on the risks of radiation exposure. "Evidence supports the view that any extra exposure to radiation carries a finite public health risk (the "no threshold" concept), with important implications for control of this risk as a result."[21] Furthermore, Radford states, there is evidence that certain subgroups are at higher risk than others: children (for leukemia), girls and women (for thyroid gland and breast cancer), and perhaps people with hereditary conditions leading to abnormalities in DNA repair mechanisms.

However, the uncertainty about the health effects of radiation exposure remains. "Taken all together, these unresolved questions indicate that the current life-time cancer risk estimates above could be too low or too high by perhaps a factor of two, with about equal reasons for thinking that underestimation or overestimation applies. The genetic risks show a similar degree of uncertainty."[22]

Unfortunately, these uncertainties were not well communicated to the public before the accident. Afterward, when the debate about the effects of low level radiation exposure became known to Three Mile Island area residents, it fueled their mistrust. Residents asked, "If scientists cannot agree among themselves about the health effects of radiation exposure, how can their assurances be trusted? Isn't the truth that no one really knows?"

Residents viewed the uncertainty within the scientific community about the effects of low level radiation and the methods selected for the cleanup as the incompetence of omission rather than of commission. Scientists, they felt, really did not know enough about the long-term effects of nuclear energy. "If scientists cannot agree on these issues which affect our health and safety, why should we accept the assurances of some, especially when the most adamant supporters of nuclear energy have so much to gain by giving these assurances?"

Mrs. Willis expressed frustration about this uncertainty and the view that people in the area should accept expert opinions despite a lack of surety:

> I realize that there's a lot we're not hearing, and I don't care how much they say, we're not going to get the facts. You *know* we're not going to get the facts. I mean, they're only going to tell us what they want us to hear when they want us to hear it. And, of course, it's always going to come out—oh, it's minimal, it's no problem, it's no danger. It's bull! . . . And they can't say it's minimal because they don't know what the dangers of low level radiation are.

> Mrs. Hemingway said: I think the unknown is what is so frightening. And there's so many conflicting things. One group of scientists, doctors, will say, "Oh, it's no problem. People that work in labs get so much more radiation, and they're fine." And then the next group is saying, "Yes, but. . . ." We just don't know yet.

## (4) The increase in electric rates in the Three Mile Island area

On 13 May 1980, the Public Utilities Commission awarded Jersey Central Power and Light, one of the three subsidiaries of General Public Utilities, a sixty million dollar rate increase to avoid bankruptcy. By 27 June 1980, the *York Dispatch* reported:

> Metropolitan Edison company customers are paying about 42 percent more for a typical month's use of electricity than residents of nearby areas served by Pennsylvania Power and Light Co. . . . In the past six months, according to the chart, the Met Ed bill has jumped 22 percent as compared to nine percent for PP&L.[23]

The people of Newberry organized a ratepayers' strike in 1981 in response to the enormous increases in the electric rate in their area. The following passage is from a brochure called *Project David*, which explained the purpose of the strike.

> "My electric bills are too high!" "I'm paying two hundred dollars a month!" "I'm paying two-fifty a month!" These people were among ninety citizens of Newberry Township who crowded into a local elementary school's auditorium on Wednesday night, January 14, 1981. . . . Before the meeting ended, one percent of Newberry Township's entire population voted not to pay the Met Ed electric bill which is due in March 1981. . . . The citizens of Newberry Township decided they will keep their electricity payments in their bank accounts. This March, the electric bills which are normally mailed with the payments to Met Ed will be collected by Newberry Township neighborhood groups. The electric bills then will be burned on the steps of the state capitol building on March 27, 1981. . . . In this bold fashion the residents of Newberry Township will protest the high cost of Met Ed's electricity. The citizens of Newberry Township proudly challenge neighboring communities to stand up against the tyranny of high cost electricity. "We must show the electric company that it can no longer double or triple our electricity rates without a fight from us!" said one Newberry Township homeowner. . . . The citizens of Newberry Township have named their ratepayers' strike "Project David."[24]

Project David did not succeed in affecting electric rates in the community. However, it indicates how serious a problem electric costs were for the people of Newberry after the accident. It also can be seen that increases in electric rates would have contributed to the mistrust that residents already felt for Metropolitan Edison. The decision to seek rate increases was confirmation to many Newberry residents that the utility company had no interest in the welfare of the community but only in its own survival.

## (5) The inability of other public officials to allay health and safety fears

Finally, mistrust was fostered in some people by occurrences that they actually observed after the accident and that they had difficulty explaining. The way in which these occurrences were handled by government officials, both state and federal, also led to perceptions of cover-up.

Because it was a semirural area, quite a number of Newberry Township residents had farm animals. Therefore, many of their observations about the period after the accident were associated with their animals. Following are two stories that were related to us. A woman whose daughter owned a horse gave one account:

> We had a horse that just died of respiratory problems, a seven-year-old, healthy horse. My daughter has a girlfriend whose horse died four months ago. She has a schoolteacher whose horse just died from respiratory problems. We went to see a horse in Elizabethtown two weeks ago, and the horse had respiratory problems. And I'm beginning to wonder. I was raised in the country. We never had sick horses, you know. It's very unusual to me, and, you know, all of a sudden I think, "Is there a connection?" In fact, I thought people were radical to think that this TMI was affecting their animals when this happened. I hate to admit it but I sort of laughed at them. . . . And the vet that was here, we asked him, and he didn't want to answer us. We asked if this had any effect. He wouldn't answer us. But he says there are problems with the breeding and offspring of animals now. So, I really can't say it has a connection but it does seem odd.

An older woman who owned a small farm gave a second account:

> We had sick animals about one month after [the accident]. We kept them in for two or three weeks, day and night. We only gave them water. We gave only fresh water. . . . Their feed came from the barn. . . . The milk cows looked like they lost a hundred pounds. They looked like their flesh was going to fall off them. They would not eat or drink. They laid down. We got the vet, and he got this one up and in two days we had another one down. So he gave them shots. We had three [sick] inside of four days. So

when he came the second time, I said to him, "What's going on?" He told me to get vitamins and minerals to all of them. So we did that, had to give them double what was called for. So eventually, they got up, and I tell you they looked a wreck all last summer [the summer of the accident]. They did not get back on their feet right. We have one now that looks awful but I don't know if that was due to [Three Mile Island]. It was really scary to see those cows because you could not believe anything could lose weight so fast. They would lay there. They would not eat or drink. They would not get up. The vet said, "That's how it is everywhere." He did not tell us where they [the other sick animals] were but it is in this area. I never had this happen before. I never saw anything lose weight that fast. You could not put your finger on anything different. The only thing they could have gotten was off the grass. They were all right as long as we left them in the barn. We did not have a lot of rain at that time. We had a lot of haze or fog. I don't know what it was. They [state officials] never came around and tested the cows. I think I called to see if they were going to test, and I was told even where they made the milk they didn't expect to get testing for it. I don't think they were interested. I think it should have been [tested]. We had the same vet who went in front of the Public Utility and testified. He said the same thing [there]. He said to me he was looking into it and that there had to be something going on. Too many had the same thing at the same time.

Although accounts such as these have been dismissed at Public Utility Commission hearings and by state officials, they cannot be ignored in any description of the people's perception of the event. Furthermore, such occurrences were not well explained to the residents of the Three Mile Island area. If they were able, bureaucrats who handled such matters should have been more willing to demonstrate convincingly that there was no connection between these events and the Three Mile Island accident. Instead, they projected disdain for members of the community who raised such issues by not taking them seriously.

It is difficult to ignore these accounts when their sources are considered. None of the people we spoke to was radical or deranged. The connection drawn between these occurrences and Three Mile Island may appear illogical and without basis to anyone physically, emotionally, and intellectually distant from the realities of rural people. But they were reported, and we believe they must be included if all of the causes of mistrust are to be understood.

The Pennsylvania Department of Health (DOH) also played a major role in the development of mistrust. The department was in a position to allay or substantiate residents' health fears. Unfortunately, its officials also became objects of community mistrust.

In June 1979 the Department of Health developed a registry of residents living within five miles of Three Mile Island. In addition to providing this list, the enumeration survey had also provided other pertinent information that could be used in epidemiological studies regarding the health effects of Three Mile Island. Of course, the department also had access to other important health data files. However, it never presented itself as the zealous investigator of Three Mile Island health effects. Rather, to the people of Newberry, its officials appeared to be interested in explaining away any unusual health reports. To many, the Department of Health appeared to hold preexisting beliefs that the accident would have no health effects.

For example, the six cases of hypothyroidism in infants born in Lancaster County (near Three Mile Island) between June and November 1979 were investigated by Department of Health officials. About this investigation, Dr. George Tokuhata, director of the Department of Health Division of Epidemiological Research, said, "I don't think there's a connection between the Three Mile Island accident and the infant hypothyroidism but we feel an obligation to investigate and explain it to the public." He went on to say that he was confident that he could explain, at that time, all but two of the cases and these would be studied further. The implication of his statements was that these two would also be found unrelated to the event.[25]

To people who were worried about the health of their children, Dr. Tokuhata's words were not reassuring. Although he said he wanted to investigate these events and communicate to the public, he preceded these thoughts with his opinion that there was no connection between them and the Three Mile Island accident. In the eyes of residents, he was biased. It was no surprise to them that the Department of Health later reported no relationship between any case of infant hypothyroidism and Three Mile Island.

Later, Dr. Tokuhata refused to release Department of Health data about the outcome of pregnancies following the accident and the cases of hypothyroidism to residents who contended that the Department of Health studies were unscientific. The couple had filed a request for the data under the Freedom of Information Act, and their request had been denied. The newspaper account of this incident included the sentence, "He [Dr. Tokuhata] could not be reached for comment."[26]

Finally, the Department of Health never successfully addressed the fears of many residents about high rates of miscarriage and cancer in their community after the accident. As we have discussed previously, concern about cancer among family and neighbors was a consistent theme in the comments of the people who participated in our surveys. The following are a sample of comments added to the 1985 and 1986 questionnaires expressing these concerns.

"On a one mile stretch of road on York Haven Road, there are thirty houses, fifteen deaths (most of cancer) plus three have had heart attacks all within 3–4 years of the accident. But we are told there has been no increase in cancer deaths in the area. This is in the five mile area."

"I think the health study was a cover-up."

"We live close to TMI, approximately 1½ miles. Since the accident I got cancer. I never had anything wrong with me before the accident, so I blame the TMI accident as the cause. We did not evacuate, because there just wasn't any place we could afford to go. My cancer seems too acute as I never had any indication of it before the accident."

"I was wondering what the statistics were on cancer victims before TMI and now. It seems that's all I seem to hear these days are neighbors, friends and family finding they have cancer. Also, I was six months pregnant with my daughter at the time of the accident."

"Since TMI I have had a pregnancy [1981] which resulted in the premature birth of my son, who is multiply handicapped due to complications of an early birth. I don't know if TMI had an effect on this event, but I have never been included in a statistic so I therefore question much of the statistical results."

A woman sent us the names of people she knew who had cancer or had died of it. She wrote:

"These 33 names my sister-in-law and I got in about 15 minutes and they are just the ones we could think of quick. There are probably a lot more we didn't remember, and a lot more we didn't know of. These people all live within one mile (approximately) of my home, and I live 2.5 miles from TMI. This area is

rural. How many people within a mile of your home have cancer? . . . My neighbor's family has had four cases in this past year;
her aunt died; her mother is very sick and terminal."

Data were available to the Department of Health to study the inci-
dence and prevalence of cancer in Newberry and, in fact, department
officials did. In 1985, they released a report stating that a study of residents living near Three Mile Island showed no evidence of increased
cancer following the accident. However, what they did not do was
communicate with the people of Newberry successfully. They were unable or unwilling to demonstrate to Newberrians' satisfaction that cancer rates were normal in their community. This was not an impossible
task. Open discussion of the data, their methods, and their findings and,
at that point, replication by outside health researchers should have done
it.

To people who were already suspicious about the truthfulness of authorities concerning the dangers of the accident, these kinds of occurrences were seen as evidence that the Department of Health should be
placed in the same camp as nuclear power proponents. The department
did not appear to be a vigilant guardian of community health but an
apologist for the nuclear power industry. Just as at Love Canal, Department of Health officials behaved as if they were obligated to Metropolitan Edison and the Nuclear Regulatory Commission. As described by
Adeline Levine, the relationship between the Love Canal community
and the New York State Department of Health is similar to that which
developed between Newberry residents and the Pennsylvania Department of Health:

They (Department of Health [DOH] physicians and scientists) did
not seem to view themselves as having clinical responsibilities for
the affected population. . . . Because the DOH officials did not pay
serious attention to the task of providing to them and working
through the implications of the information, the residents felt that
they were being treated not as rational, respected individuals but
rather as though they had somehow lost their mature good sense
when they became victims of a disaster they had no way of preventing. . . . It seemed that the general ethos of the state's effort was to
mitigate the Love Canal situation almost solely by imposing technological and other practical solutions on the area and the people,
without considering the people's reactions. . . . The state public
health officials became alienated from the very people whom they
were, after all, supposed to serve and protect.[27]

In summary, the events of the period between April 1979 and 1986, when we last surveyed the people of Newberry, contributed to the perpetuation of the negative image that Metropolitan Edison authorities had gained immediately after the accident. After the crisis period, the utility company did little to restore the confidence of area residents either in its competence or in its fiduciary responsibility to the people of the area. The Nuclear Regulatory Commission, which sent Harold Denton to the site of the accident, had originally been viewed as more competent and concerned about the community. However, residents viewed its actions after the crisis period as designed to support Metropolitan Edison at all costs, and, before long, they saw the Nuclear Regulatory Commission as untrustworthy as the utility company. The actions of other public officials did not allay residents' fears that the accident was more serious than they were being told.

## EXTENT OF MISTRUST

Our survey findings corroborate our assertion that mistrust of Three Mile Island authorities was widespread in the Newberry community. In 1982 and 1986, the portion of people who reported mistrusting Metropolitan Edison regarding the safety of nuclear energy was well over 70 percent. Most of those remaining were uncertain; less than 10 percent believed

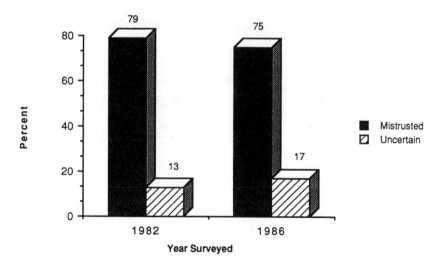

Fig. 9. Percent who mistrusted utility company officials regarding the safety of nuclear energy

that Metropolitan Edison was trustworthy regarding the safety of nuclear energy (fig. 9).

Mistrust of federal officials was also high. At every period we surveyed, a clear majority of community members did not believe federal
officials had been truthful about the radiation dangers (57, 73, and 61
percent, respectively). By 1986, some who mistrusted federal officials in
1982 had become uncertain, but the portion who remained mistrustful
remained high (fig. 10).

A clear majority of Newberry residents also mistrusted federal officials
concerning the safety of nuclear energy in general (57, 69, and 60 percent, respectively) over the period of our survey (fig. 11).

## SUMMARY

In Newberry, utility company and federal officials were highly likely to
be mistrusted on the grounds of either fiduciary irresponsibility, incompetence, or both. The accident itself and the actions of Metropolitan
Edison in the first several weeks after the accident laid the foundation for
the development of mistrust. Later, the utility company's absorption
with reopening the plant despite the opposition of the community, its
announcements of radiation leaks after the fact, its release of Krypton-85
into the atmosphere over community objections, and continual findings

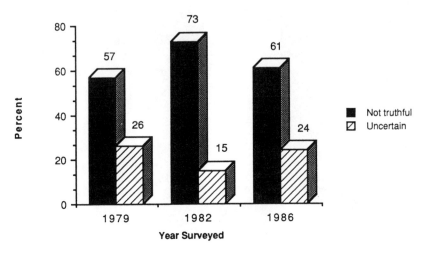

Fig. 10. Percent who believed federal officials had not been truthful about radiation
dangers

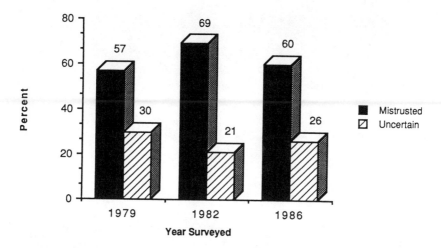

Fig. 11. Percent who mistrusted the federal government concerning safety of nuclear energy

about criminal wrongdoing and mismanagement within the company kept mistrust from subsiding.

The failure of the Nuclear Regulatory Commission to appear impartial with respect to the utility's plans for decontaminating Unit 2 and restarting Unit 1 led to its being considered untrustworthy as well. Contributing to community mistrust were uncertainty within the scientific community about the health effects of radiation and the best methods of decontaminating Three Mile Island, unusual occurrences among animals, and seemingly high miscarriage and cancer rates in the community, poorly explained by government officials. This was not a monolithic community in its attitudes toward Three Mile Island or the officials responsible for its management. However, based on our survey findings, the large majority of people mistrusted Three Mile Island authorities.

The mistrust that originated in the crisis period of March 28 to early April 1979 was confirmed in the years that followed. Its symptoms were fear for health and safety and distress among community residents.

# SIX

## ATTEMPTING TO RESTORE
## A SENSE OF
## COMMUNITY SAFETY

MISTRUST HAD DIRE consequences for many Newberrians. Despite the assurances of utility company, government, and other officials for at least seven years after the accident, residents of Newberry viewed their proximity to Three Mile Island as dangerous, and they worried that the radiation to which they had been exposed might result in cancer or other health problems. As a group, they were more distressed than people in similar communities, and a substantial portion perceived a decline in family life, outlook on life, and health, which they attributed to the Three Mile Island accident. They felt that their beautiful community had been spoiled. These were the symptoms of mistrust. The inability of Metropolitan Edison, Nuclear Regulatory Commission (NRC), and other officials to convince residents of their competence and fiduciary responsibility made this response inevitable.

Could the anxiety and distress of Newberry residents have been relieved? The answer to this question is Yes—if authorities had been able to restore residents' trust. But trust was not restored. However one judges the efforts of Metropolitan Edison, the Nuclear Regulatory Commission, and other government officials to convince community residents of their competence and fiduciary responsibility, one must conclude that they were unsuccessful.

Another way in which anxiety might have been alleviated was to address the fear about health and safety directly. Perhaps the mistrust itself could not be gotten rid of, but the people of Newberry could have obtained relief from their anxiety about their future safety.

One way in which fear might have been treated was for residents to move from the area, and in fact, many people did move. Nineteen percent of our original sample had moved by the time we conducted our 1986 survey, although all of these relocations were not motivated by attitudes toward Three Mile Island. Moreover, many people expressed the view that they wanted to move or might move if they perceived the situation as getting worse.

However, most people did not move. They were too attached to Newberry, financially unable to move, or convinced that other places would be no better since hazards exist everywhere. Three excerpts from personal interviews illustrate these points of view.

Mrs. Brown: And then I think, Where are you going to move to that there aren't other nuclear power plants, chemical waste dumps, and who knows what else? I mean, there's stuff all over the place that you don't want to live near. And another thing is, especially now that I'm not working and have the baby, we can't afford to sell the home and pay the higher interest rates for another home. So, practically speaking, there's no sense in moving.

Another longtime resident: No, I wouldn't want to leave the area. I like it here. And it would be an awful lot to make me leave. I think that was one of the big problems when they had the accident because, you know, thinking it might blow up and you couldn't go back to the area and so forth. This was a terrible thought because we like it here. So I would not leave the area unless I was told I had to.

Mrs. Caspar: I love living out here. It's beautiful out here. I wouldn't move. Well, we couldn't move now. We wouldn't move anyway even since TMI because I have a good job. . . . I've been there almost twenty-five years. So there's no way I could ever recoup that financially. And my husband's family has always been within this area, and we could never sell our house for what we have in it.

## MOBILIZATION

Another alternative for the people of Newberry would have been to mobilize to achieve a sense of safety in their community. Most people believed that if the Three Mile Island plant remained closed, the community would be safer, perhaps safe enough. Although decontamination of

Unit 2 would still be a problem, at least there would be no fear of a similar accident, or a worse one. While it would not relieve their anxiety about their chances of getting cancer due to the accident itself, at least it would reduce their future exposure to radiation.

Our survey results indicate that the number of Newberry residents opposed to reopening Unit 1, the undamaged reactor at Three Mile Island, was around 70 percent during the years between 1979 and 1985. Those who were uncertain comprised between 11 and 16 percent of the community (fig. 12). The number of residents opposed to restarting Unit 2, the damaged reactor, was even higher. The percent opposed to reopening Unit 2 went from 74 to 81 percent between 1979 and 1985. The portion who were uncertain was consistently around 12 percent (fig. 13).

Two statements illustrate the role of mistrust in residents' opposition. The first indicates that Metropolitan Edison's fiduciary responsibility and competence were suspect. The second statement suggests a suspicion that the siting of the plant was an incompetent decision.

"I'd rather they didn't open Three Mile Island because I don't think they're [Metropolitan Edison] very trustworthy. I don't think they're honest. And I think they're rather sloppy."

"I'm not opposed to nuclear energy but, like I say, if they were built farther away. They should restrict them, I'd say, to within a twenty-mile area. They should be twenty miles out someplace. At

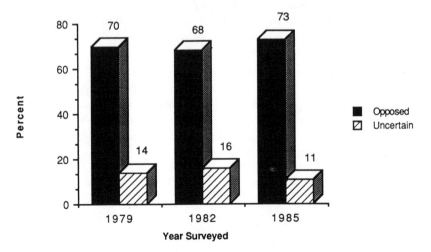

Fig. 12. Percent opposed to reopening TMI–Unit 1, the undamaged reactor

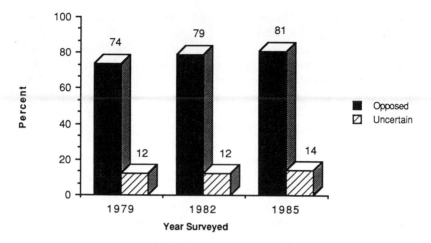

Fig. 13. Percent opposed to reopening TMI–Unit 2, the damaged reactor

least people would be able to get out of there if something would happen. But we're only three or three-and-one-half miles from the plant. That's too close to a nuclear plant."

Many residents did mobilize. They joined Three Mile Island Alert (TMIA), People Against Nuclear Energy (PANE), or the Newberry Township–Three Mile Island Steering Committee. Some were involved in the Project David initiative. These people circulated petitions, organized meetings, rallies, and marches, and made appearances before the Public Utilities Commission and the Nuclear Regulatory Commission. Most efforts were directed toward preventing the restart of Unit 1 but sometimes the rallying issue was Metropolitan Edison's decontamination methods for Unit 2.

Concerned residents established the Newberry Township–Three Mile Island Steering Committee which then formed the Newberry Township Health Committee (see the preface). These organizations sponsored two of the six surveys that we conducted—one indicating people's willingness to participate in a health monitoring project and the other people's psychological distress and attitudes toward the accident and the possible restart (1979). The efforts of the Steering Committee and the Health Committee were mainly directed toward opposing the restart through legal means. Along with other opposition groups, they hoped, by introducing the issue of psychological stress into the restart deliberations, to prevent Metropolitan Edison from reopening the plant. (See Walsh for another description of the mobilization activities of the Newberry Township/Goldsboro community.)[1]

Jordan Cunningham, an attorney and a resident of Newberry Township, represented the Newberry Township–Three Mile Island Steering Committee. Excerpts from an interview he gave in April 1980 explain the group's plan to prevent the restart through an agency intervention, its efforts to that date, his hope for success, and the difficulties of the group in maintaining mobilization activities.

*What is an agency intervention?*
An agency intervention is simply a representation of a class of recognized interested individuals before the NRC or before any agency, and instead of filing a complaint with an issue, you file a statement of interest and a series of contentions, which are your issues, which are then either accepted or not accepted and then eventually litigated. The litigation is pursuant to the agency rule, which is somewhat different than a trial.

*If you win, could Met Ed appeal the ruling of the agency?*
They could appeal the agency ruling to the Third Circuit Court of Appeals. It would go to court to determine whether there was a basis in fact for the agency decision. In other words, the court would not rehear the testimony because they do not have the expertise. They would review the agency ruling and determine whether the decision they made, the final decision, had basis in fact from the evidence presented. Their ruling would simply be a legal ruling as to whether there had been an error made at the lower level.

*What if Met Ed lost at that level?*
It would go to the U.S. Supreme Court.

*Does the Newberry Township Steering Committee have plans to go further if they lose at the agency level?*
No, we don't have the money to go further. To go further would cost you thousands, just literally thousands. First of all, you would have to buy transcripts of the whole proceedings which would cost about $3,000.00, I would assume, at about the rate they're charging so far just in the pretrial conference hearings. There are about 2,300 pages of testimony, and I think the cost per copy page is about a dollar. So you are at $2,000.00 even before you start the hearings, and that's only for six days of meetings. So the hearings are projected to go on about a month or so. It would be quite expensive.

And that's another problem. As you know, we are financially strapped. The total remuneration I have received for services to date has been $200.00. The total number of hours put in, my last calculation has been 220 to 225 hours, which if you turn that into the hourly going rate [for lawyers] in Harrisburg, you would be close to $12,000.00. Just time, just time spent. And when you go to meetings, you are asked legal opinions, and you're there for your input but also for your legal opinions. That's total time, probably. And there are other people who have spent a hell of a lot more time, like Linda Dominowski. She couldn't even begin to calculate the hours. It's probably up in the thousands. You know, it causes problems. It causes problems in my office. They say, "Hey, we really like you doing public service work but we've got a payroll to meet." So every Friday you think about that. How am I going to make that payroll and keep things rolling and be involved in what I am doing? We've got some funding from outside sources, being a legal fund, but the rate they are willing to pay is $12.50 for each hour up-front and then at a later date maybe another $12.50. Therefore, every hour that I put into it, I'm about $25.00, $30.00 in the hole. That isn't so bad. At least I'm getting paid for it. A lot of people are doing it for nothing.

But there comes a point when you say, "I'd love to do it but I've got a family to feed." . . . And people around here . . . didn't really think about it that way. But as they became more and more involved, and they found out that they were ending up doing everything, then they started, it clicked with them: "Hey, this is even interfering with my nine-to-five job."

I think they have a true perspective of it now. They understand it, and I understand it. And I knew that getting into it last August when I entered my appearance. But it's kinda hellish when they say, "Well, how much do you think this will cost if you get involved?" and I sit there with a deadpan face and say, "$25,000.00 if you want to do it half decent." And their jaws drop to the ground. "$25,000.00 just on one thing?!" So I've made my own compromise. I figure I owe something to society. They put me through a state college, and I went to a private law school but it was state funded in a way. They got a grant every year for $100,000.00. But, you know, it's a little bit of a trade-off. I get full exposure. My name gets known.

*What about environmental law? Is that one of your areas?*
No, not at all. Not that I'm not concerned [about the environment] but I'm not even interested [in environmental law]. I am

doing it because it is my community. It [TMI] is next door. People
needed help and I was there. So, I felt, okay, here is something I
could do, and I did it. So, I'm involved now. That is one of the
problems. . . . There are very few people who have any expertise
in the area, a handful of law firms in Washington and that is
about it. So everybody is kind of in the same boat. Met Ed has got
their experts because they've been through it before. They have
been involved in NRC proceedings before. They know what to expect. They know when to pull the punches. They know when to
complain. They know when to lay off. But some of the intervenors, PANE and the Union of Concerned Scientists [UCS] have
people who have been there before too. So it's a pretty equal
fight.

There are quite a few intervenors. For example, CEA which is
Chesapeake Energy Alliance, I believe. They are out of Bal-
timore. There is a group out of State College (Pennsylvania).
There is a guy my age or a year younger from Mechanicsburg, Mr.
S. He's representing himself. He is just an individual intervenor.
There is a couple from Coatesville. They own a farm in
Coatesville. There is a [man] . . . out of Philadelphia. Commonwealth of Pennsylvania is an intervenor, also Susquehanna Alliance and TMI Alert. Now they [TMIA] are represented by the
firm in which the former consumer advocate is now associated. I
don't know how much of an edge that gives them but of all the
groups, TMIA has already paid legal counsel about $20,000.00.
Probably the most experienced legal counsel is with PANE or the
Union of Concerned Scientists, probably UCS. There are also
eleven other intervenors but they have conveniently been
dropped. It was everybody else who signed the petition down in
Newberry but we just consolidated it to Newberry. Met Ed is the
licensee, and it's everyone versus Met Ed.

I'd say of all those people who are involved, the person who
seems to know the most about what he is doing is Mr. S. No experience before. He has a reason, and I found out why. He works at
a sewage disposal plant. Right after the accident he had a son or
daughter who suffered from a thyroid condition, and so I think
the reason is that he connects that to the accident. It is personal.
He really does a lot of work. Of all the people, he always seems to
know where everybody should be going. In fact, it is so bad that
at times the board chairman of the Atomic Safety and Licensing
will say, "Mr. S., you kind of know this area. What is your sugges-
tion? What should we do here? You always come up with good

ideas." I told him quite candidly after this, "After this is over, someone from Met Ed or the NRC will approach you and offer you a job"—just because he knows so much. He said, "Well, I would never go to work for Met Ed." But I didn't know, at that time, the circumstances. He is the guy who raised some very serious contentions. He is the guy who raised the security problem.

*Why do you think some of the people in Newberry who really, really feel frightened don't move?*
For two reasons. One, they have a sense of, they have intervened. They've got someone representing them. They're taking action. That is the way we directed them. We said to them, "You are not going to make any headway just by going out and demonstrating. You are going to get a headline or two but that is it." And you need some of that but the real way you are going to get at it is go to the power, go to the source. We formed a nonprofit corporation. We went out, and we intervened. We filed a contention. We had people spend hours reviewing the contentions, not only myself but others. We have had these meetings. We are involved. How many pronuclear meetings have there been?

*What are the chances that you'll lose the intervention, do you think?*
Fifty-fifty. I think the odds are good, not on the technical issues because the technical issues can be corrected. The issues that everybody's been pooh-poohing are the ones that Met Ed is most concerned about. How can they not prove or how can they prove? They're almost set into the negative to prove that psychological stress shouldn't be considered. And who's to say? If our studies [of psychological stress] are right, and from all indications they are, how can they say that shouldn't be a consideration when the National Environmental Policy Act says that all factors that enter into the quality of human life should be considered. So I think they're going to have a tough time overcoming that. All the studies are showing that there is acute—I don't know whether it's stress, it's sensitivity to the issue. And I think they're going to have to deal with that. And they're going to have to come up with some way of [dealing with it]. I don't know what it's going to be, because I think it's pretty hard to alleviate the fear.

Number two, they're going to have to show, that is, if they stick with the issue of emergency planning, take for example, the issue down in Florida. When you go along the Florida highway, the evacuation route. Do you see that around here? Do you see anything like that around here? Have you spoken to anybody who knew what the evacuation plan was? That's the problem. There is a new evacuation plan [now]. Nobody knows about it. It has already been designed. It's there, if I can believe what Met Ed has to tell me. It will be out. Met Ed's going to issue it June 1. Nobody knows about it. And worse yet, nobody knows, I don't know, where we are supposed to go even under the new plan. We were supposed to originally go down toward Peachbottom—Grove, Pa.

I know the people that are controlling the issues and will eventually argue them. If I saw a bunch of idiots, then maybe I would be a little more concerned. But of everybody that is in the restart hearing, then I would say they've [Metropolitan Edison] got some real competition. And I know some real money is being poured in by [others], I know it can't be strictly Met Ed. They couldn't afford [it]. I'm sure the nuclear industry is involved. This is big time.

This period had its special difficulties for the active members of the community. They were giving so much time, and they felt the brunt of the pronuclear community's anger. They felt as if they were treated like traitors. Pat Smith, who chaired the Newberry Township–Three Mile Island Steering Committee, tells this story:

I did like Dick Arnold [General Public Utilities Vice President of Generation] up to the time we were at one of the [public meetings]. There was this guy taking all these pictures [of the audience], and I said to Linda [Dominowski, of the Health Committee], "I don't like what he is up to. He is taking too many pictures." As the thing progressed, this doctor was to make this presentation, and I said, "Mike, don't you dare go up there and make your presentation until you find out what this guy is up to." I went up to him and I said, "Who are you with? Where are your press credentials?" He said, "I don't have to show them to you." And I went right over to Arnold. I said "Who is he with? What is he taking all these pictures for?" Arnold said, "It is for our flyers, for our publicity flyers and things like that." I went to Mike and said, "Do not make your presentation until you demand and make a scene about this photographer. I want his film from both of his cameras." So Mike went up. He went up to the big tape recorder, and he unplugs it. He said, "Now this man with the camera, this is what he is doing with the camera." Arnold was speaking from the back, and no one could make any sense of him. But everyone got riled up over this. Arnold comes up to the microphone, but he is not successful with his explanation. Linda and I were saying, "Take the film out of the camera." Here we are—two homemakers! Sure enough, other people were saying the same thing. Arnold now appears so frustrated. They take the film out of the camera. People are now cheering. Then we started the meeting again.

Would you believe, a short time later we have the meeting at Goldsboro. Here is this man again! Someone said, "Here is that same man with the camera." The whole meeting he was observing me. I really believe they keep an eye on me. I am getting mad and more mad. He is getting all nervous standing back there. I want to know who he is and what he is up to. All of a sudden, he is gone. [Harold] Collins [Nuclear Regulatory Commission Assistant Director for Emergency Preparedness, Office of State Programs] all of a sudden stands up and says, "He is with me." The average person does not know that this goes on. Someone else said that she swears that this was the same guy who took the pictures [at the Newberry meeting]. Now remember, Arnold said this guy was from Met Ed. Now he is with the NRC. Linda got her film developed. She had taken his picture over at Middletown. Others said it was the same person. Here again, somebody lied to us. And they are trying to get their credibility back? We know damn well they were taking pictures of us.

Community mobilization efforts in Newberry and in the Three Mile Island area as a whole did not succeed. As time went by, more and more decisions went against the community. These included approval for the Krypton-85 releases and the electric rate increases, the continuation of the restart hearings despite the unresolved integrity issue, and finally the restart approval itself.

The legal attempt to prevent the restart of Unit 1 by forcing consideration of its psychological impact on nearby residents was dashed on 19 April 1983. The Steering Committee and others who protested the restart had experienced what would be a temporary victory on 7 January 1982 when the U.S. Court of Appeals for the District of Columbia ruled that, on the basis of the National Environmental Protection Act (NEPA), the Nuclear Regulatory Commission had to consider the psychological impact of the restart. However, on 19 April 1983, the Supreme Court ruled that the Nuclear Regulatory Commission did not have to consider possible psychological harm to nearby residents in deciding whether to reopen Unit 1. The decision was unanimous, and the Court held that such an interpretation of the NEPA went beyond the intent of Congress. In the view of the Court, NEPA covered only consequences that might affect human health by causing changes in water, air, or land.[2]

Perhaps mobilization efforts failed because there was too little community participation. Only 14 percent of the people we surveyed said that they were more politically involved in the period between 1979 and 1986 than before the accident. Sixteen percent said they were less involved. On the other hand, 20 percent of our sample said they attended meetings and rallies to stop the restart after its approval, 23 percent reported that they used political influence to stop it, and 38 percent said they wrote letters and signed petitions. Moreover, in the first several years after the accident people were very vocal. An interview in April 1980 with a Goldsboro Borough Council official indicates the general level of participation and involvement in the first year after the accident.

[Harold] Collins, shortly after he came to the area from the NRC, called me and asked if he could attend the council meeting. And I said yes, but that we had a large agenda and his time would be limited. And we invited the public, and we had nearly all the TV companies with their cameras recording everything. For the first time, I realized how some people really felt about TMI, with the expressions of their questions. They asked, . . . they were unmannerly [in] their method. But I sympathized with them because I am on edge. I can't say that I am completely at ease about TMI. I am on edge about it.

Since the accident, anybody connected with NRC, Met Ed, the EPA [Environmental Protection Agency], DOE [Department of Energy] have no credibility. They have lost their credibility in spite of the fact that we had all those agencies involved in a second meeting, a full house, standing room only. I think the majority who attended both meetings came from Newberry Township and most of the questions asked were by people from the area. Now the first meeting was more or less controlled because it was a council meeting. The second was not as closely controlled, and people were there with banners, armbands. By the tone of the questions, there was deep-felt resentment toward everything that was said by the officials who were speaking—Met Ed, EPA, NRC, all of them. NRC came under criticism. Collins was there. He took a lot of abuse. So did Gerusky [director of the Pennsylvania

Bureau of Radiation Protection at the time of the accident]. So did the vice president of Met Ed [actually General Public Utilities Vice President for Generation Arnold]. There was a young guy there from Syracuse University. I thought he was from the press but he was a major in journalism. He took several pictures, and the crowd resented that so much [that] one of the gentlemen jumped up and wanted to know the name of this fellow—Who was taking pictures? Was he from Met Ed or from NRC?—and implied they [community members] were under surveillance because of their views. So that caused quite a stir. I can sympathize with the people who are so tense, so very much afraid of the situation.

Steering Committee chair Pat Smith also spoke about the involvement of the community. She felt that the people were there when they were needed.

I think they [residents of Newberry] are letting it up to a few local people. I think they have faith in us. They just want to go on living because it has been really difficult. My life has never been the same. They want their life to return to normal, like it used to be. So they are going to get to that as close as possible. Most times, when we call upon them for financial assistance or help with the phones, they're there.

However, the failure of the legal effort to force consideration of the psychological impact of the restart was the real undoing of mobilization. The Supreme Court decision left the community with no real alternative but civil disobedience, an unacceptable course of action for most residents of this conservative community. The letters of protest, the petitions, the appearances at hearings and meetings had gotten them nowhere. Decisions were made against them regardless of these actions. The legal attempt to prevent reopening by forcing the Nuclear Regulatory Commission to consider the community's psychological well-being had appeared to be their best hope. With that hope gone, mobilization had nowhere to go.

## POWERLESSNESS AND RESIGNATION

Their failure left the residents of Newberry feeling powerless. As our surveys and interviews reflected, most resigned themselves to a fate decided by the people they mistrusted. Residents believed strongly that they had a right to a voice in the decisions that they believed affected their health and safety. However, they did not expect officials to listen to them. This was apparent at the time of our interviews in April 1980. With the passing of time and decisions against them, their expectations were confirmed. As the restart neared, our investigation indicates that most people took no action against it. For example, the most common response to the question, "At the time of the restart, what did you do?" was "Worry but go about my business." Seventy percent of the people we surveyed answered in this way.

In 1982 (see fig. 14), 58 percent of Newberry residents believed that community groups opposed to reopening Unit 1, the undamaged reactor, had little chance to win, and 36 percent believed that there was some chance. Only 6 percent believed there was a good chance that community groups could keep Unit 1 closed. The portion of residents who thought that Unit 2 could be kept closed was 16 percent, a bit greater than the number of people who thought that there was a good chance to keep Unit 1 closed but still quite a small proportion. Forty-four percent believed there was little or no chance for success and 40 percent that there was some chance. In 1986 (see fig. 15), after the restart of Unit 1, the portion of residents who believed that Unit 2 could be kept closed dropped to 3 percent. At that time, 73 percent believed that people in the community opposed to the restart of Unit 2 could not win.

During personal interviews, many people expressed the view that the community was powerless to affect the decision-making process. We

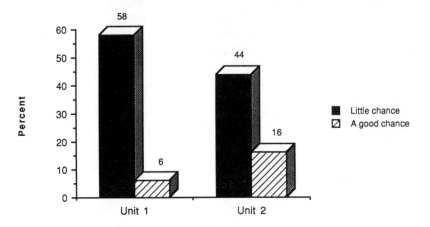

Fig. 14. Perceived chance of community groups to keep TMI closed, 1982

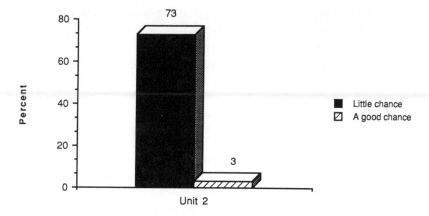

Fig. 15. Perceived chance of community groups to keep TMI–Unit 2 closed, 1986

asked people if they thought residents of the community would have a say in the reopening decision.

> Mrs. Brown: I don't think about it a whole lot, and I'm not in-volved. Sometimes I'm ashamed at my lack of involvement. Again, I'm not one for demonstrating and stuff. And I think, "Well, I should be if I don't want it open. I should be involved." And then I get to the other part of me saying, "What good will it do anyway?

> Another resident said: No, I don't think so. I think they're going to do what they want to do. When people expressed their feelings about releasing this Krypton gas, they didn't stop to consider, did they? They did what they wanted. And I think that's what they'll do. If they want to open that, they'll open it. And there's no way that people can stop them.

> Mrs. Caspar: So I can't say. I hope it will influence what they do, even if it's nothing more than to see that they get qualified people in there and to see that the people are informed, . . . let you know how bad it really is instead of, you know, well, they don't tell anybody [anything] until, like, later. . . . I think you have the right to know what is going on and how serious it is.

In the end, most people in Newberry shared the attitude of these two residents who determined to get on with life as well as possible.

Well, I don't think it does any good to worry about it. They're going to do what they want so I think we just have to continue on with our lives.

And Mrs. Caspar: Every so often when things come up down there I think about it. I think about it in depth for a period of time and wonder whether it's really the smart thing to do to stay here. Then, of course, I keep weighing the odds and say, "Well, maybe it will work out all right." You know, people are very optimisitic, I think, about things like this. They have to be. . . . They have jokes at work about [TMI], . . . and we laugh and everything, and people say, you know, "That's really wonderful that you can still laugh, that you can still make a joke of it when you live that close." And I say, "Well, what are you going to do? You're not going to sit around and bawl and be in a blue funk until it's over with!" God, that could be years. You could be depressed for five years!

In 1986 a resident expressed the same worry-but-go-about-my-business-attitude in a comment added to a questionnaire.

I generally try not to think about Three Mile Island. I know it bothers me, however, because when I hear a siren I hold my breath until I know it's not about Three Mile Island. Also, I tend to keep away from reading articles about Three Mile Island in the newspapers. Most of us go about our daily routine but deep inside wonder if each day could be our last. If an accident happens again will we have a chance? I guess we take it one day at a time. I just hope my kids live to lead a full life.

By and large, the mental health effects of the accident did not affect functioning. Our study indicates more anxiety, more depression, and more psychophysiologic symptoms of distress than in similar communities, a finding confirmed by other research. However, the distress that residents experienced did not indicate mental illness or impairment. People in Newberry carried on, focusing on what was really important to them. They were family people, and their families and friends were at the center of their lives. The irony is that the importance of family and friends was also the reason for their great concern about Three Mile Island. The tragedy is that their external calm concealed their hopelessness about affecting a decision they believed was vital to their own health and safety and that of their families and friends.

## ANGER, CYNICISM, AND LOSS OF FAITH IN THE DEMOCRATIC PROCESS

It was with much bitterness, however, that the residents of Newberry resigned themselves to their fate. Their failure to achieve representation in the decisions regarding decontamination of Unit 2 and the restart of Unit 1 provoked anger and cynicism toward Metropolitan Edison, the nuclear power industry in general, and the federal government. It even affected their basic faith in the democratic process in the United States. Their situation angered many residents of Newberry.

Mrs. Caspar: But then afterwards, to find out—if it was true then, I don't know—that they were actually a half hour away from a meltdown, and, . . . I didn't leave because I figured, "Well, okay, so Wednesday morning it leaked. If I didn't get it then, I'm not going to get it," because I figured the leak was all over. There was no danger. And all this time to realize [that Metropolitan Edison officials knew it was not over] I was mad!

There was also great anger and resentment over the rate increases that the utility obtained in order to remain solvent.

Mrs. Caspar: It just doesn't make sense that you should pay for somebody else's stupidity. You pay for your own mistakes. That's fine. I can accept that. But to pay for somebody else's! It's just not right! You've been exposed to it. Who knows what you're going to get that you'll have to pay for later on. Plus now you have to pay for their dumb mistakes. I just can't accept that!

Another resident expressed her anger in these words:

I'm disappointed that they've continued to let out the gas in spite of the different people telling there's other ways. But they've done it the cheapest way. What angers me is they've tacked this on my light bill. Now that upsets me. I cut back and cut back and cut back and my light bill is almost double—not the electricity we use, but the surcharge and the tax almost doubles my electric bill. And then they're [Metropolitan Edison] going to sue the company that made this and then they're asking the government for money so they're getting rich out of it. . . . Really, when you stop and consider all the people they're going to collect money from because of their stupid accident, we're all paying for it. That angers me.

Newberry residents came to take a cynical view toward Metropolitan Edison as motivated purely by self-interest and greed. Mrs. Kelsey expressed the view of many when she said:

> [Metropolitan Edison officials are] concerned about their money, and I think that's where the key lies. They want to get that thing back in operation, and that seems to be all they're concerned about—the money for money's sake. I really don't think that people's concerns matter to them much. Now, I don't know if the Nuclear Regulatory Commission—if that matters to them or not. I just think Met Ed is money hungry, and they just want to get it open for their livelihood.

Furthermore, the accident led many residents to question the basic assumptions of the nuclear power industry. Mrs. Hemingway was not a fan of nuclear energy prior to the accident, but she had been lulled by the assurances of the industry. The accident caused her previously negative views to crystallize.

> I think they [the nuclear industry] were taking it so much for granted. They had all these technological goodies, and it was just going to keep this safe, and the backup systems were going to work. So don't worry about it. Just push the buttons. That's it. But it just doesn't seem to be working that way. I really feel that sooner or later, maybe not necessarily at TMI, but someplace in the world, there's really going to be a bad, bad accident.

She also questioned the necessity for nuclear energy:

> It just seems to me that there are so many alternatives we could explore, you know, that I don't really think we have to go the nuclear route.

> Mrs. Brown: I don't know if we really need it [nuclear energy] or not, and I don't know if anyone knows if we really need nuclear power, if it's worth the risk. I don't know if it is. [In] my opinion, if it means—if shutting them down means that we'll have to go without the luxuries we've become used to like television and air conditioning and et cetera, then I think we're going to have to

learn to live without our luxuries. But if it actually means the
difference between freezing in the winter and not freezing, then
we're going to have to accept the risk. That's the way I feel. . . .
But I don't think it's as great a need as they're trying to make you
think it is. . . . If anything, we have to have it to run our television and the air conditioning—which is something we can learn
to get along without.

Mrs. Kelsey: I think there's other sources of energy that we can
use in Pennsylvania, especially coal. I think it [Three Mile Island]
should be turned into coal if used at all for energy.

About 40 percent of Newberry residents favored a ban on all nuclear
power plants although there was a slight drop to 36 percent in 1985. The
portion who were uncertain rose from 19 percent in 1979 to 31 percent in
1982 and remained there through 1985 (fig. 16).

Nor did government escape the cynicism of the people of Newberry. In
their view, federal and state governments were conspirators with the
utility company and the nuclear power industry.

Mrs. Hemingway: They [the state and federal governments] are
willing to just let it take its own course, let the utility do whatever it wants. . . . They let you say your piece. They make a big
deal about letting you say your piece. But then when push comes

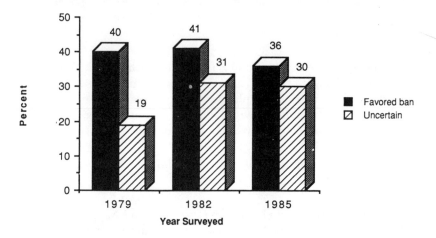

Fig. 16. Percent who favored a ban on all nuclear power plants

to shove, it's back to the same old thing of letting Met Ed do pretty much what the hell they want over there.

Mrs. Kelsey: I thought at least they [government authorities] would be concerned about the people's health. It seems like money is always where people are most concerned and human life is second. They worry about that second.

Attitudes had not softened by 1986, as the following comments, added to questionnaires, illustrate:

"After seven years it appears big business is more important to the government than the people. I now believe the 'Three Mile Island' protection is a political cover-up. Thank you for your efforts and concern."

"I feel many government and industrial decisions are economically based instead of based on the health and welfare of citizens."

"Money means more to government and Three Mile Island people than life or even safety. The Russians know exactly what I think I'll wake to some morning [referring to the Chernobyl nuclear power plant accident]. I have a monitor everywhere."

"It's a shame money, economics is always the major force behind decisions that are made in government, at all levels, instead of personal safety."

"Living with Three Mile Island is like living with cancer. You don't talk about it because you don't want to stir up those feelings of hopelessness and helplessness. U.S. officials like the Russian officials at Chernobyl will not admit that nuclear power is unsafe as long as someone with power is making money from it."

"We little people are only little things. Who cares when there is money to be made."

"My opinions have not changed in regard to Three Mile Island. Money has spoken, and we the people do not matter at all. We can be replaced. But our land in Pennsylvania counts. Shut down Three Mile Island!"

"Big business, big money, and the Republican Party can do almost anything regardless of the opinions of the common person. I feel this is how Three Mile Island was able to restart."

The statements of Newberry residents regarding powerlessness and cynicism indicate the blow that Three Mile Island dealt to these citizens' convictions concerning the opportunity of ordinary Americans to influence policy that affects their lives. They were not optimistic about their chances to participate in the decision-making process regarding Three Mile Island. The surprise to them was that government did not take their part but the part of the utility company.

Not surprisingly, observations about the role of the government in the Three Mile Island accident affected residents' perceptions of government and the democratic process. Only 4 percent of the residents we surveyed in 1986 were more satisfied with government than before the accident while 48 percent were less satisfied with government. Of the 48 percent who were less satisfied, 90 percent attributed their dissatisfaction to Three Mile Island (fig. 17).

The most dramatic finding presented in this graph is the response concerning faith in the democratic process of decision making. Over half the community had less faith in the democratic process and 91 percent of these attributed this, at least in part, to the Three Mile Island situation. Residents questioned how it was possible for nearly everyone in their

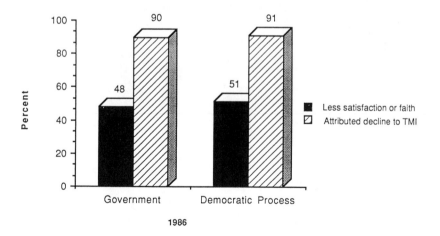

Fig. 17. Satisfaction with government and faith in democratic process compared to before TMI

community (and at the state governor's level, as well) to oppose the operation of Three Mile Island and yet for the decision, properly arrived at in a legal sense, to go against them. What happened to their rights? Is this not a land where the government responds to the will of the people, especially in areas where there is a perception of risk to health and safety?

Many people in Newberry came to believe as Walsh did when he wrote about the restart decision. "What arguments can the U.S. government use to persuade local citizens of the legitimacy of the restart decision? The Reagan Administration has frequently advocated the autonomy of the states and local communities. . . . Area residents have voted overwhelmingly against it. How can a Unit 1 restart decision be reconciled with democratic theory?"[3]

Neither mistrust nor its symptoms—fear for health and safety and distress—were successfully addressed. Mistrust of Metropolitan Edison, Nuclear Regulatory Commission, and other government officials associated with the accident remained high at least through 1986 and, as a consequence, so did the uneasiness of the residents of Newberry. Hopelessness and resignation prevailed in the face of defeat, their inability to restore their sense of safety. The result of failure to address mistrust or its symptoms was anger, cynicism about the utility company, nuclear power proponents, and government regulators, and loss of faith in the democratic process. Newberry had turned from an ordinary community into a fearful, angry, and cynical one as a result of the accident at Three Mile Island.

# SEVEN

## TRUST AND
## THE SOCIAL CONTRACT

FEAR AND DISTRESS among the people of Newberry were symptoms of their mistrust. Bitterness, anger, and cynicism were the result of their power-lessness to obtain relief from mistrust and its symptoms. But why should mistrust of Three Mile Island authorities lead to the profound bitterness and cynicism that we found among Newberrians? These reactions can be understood in terms of the concept of social contract, although a social contract that differs in some respects from the theory as developed by classical and modern contractarians.

### THE SOCIAL CONTRACT

The concept of social contract has a history that extends from at least the Middle Ages to the present day. Tracing its development in Western thought, Michael Lessnoff writes:

> Manegold (of Lautenbach in Alsace in about the year 1080), appar-ently, was the first man (or the first since ancient times) to offer a general contractual theory of political authority. The word "the-ory" is important: for Manegold is not alluding to any particular contract, but is rather claiming that a contract is the inherent

foundation of every people's relation to its ruler, setting the conditions and limits of the latter's authority and former's obligation.[1]

In the seventeenth and eighteenth centuries, Hobbes, Locke, Rousseau, and Kant developed theories about the social contract that have influenced our thinking ever since. Their assumptions concerned the primacy of the law of nature, the natural liberty and equality of man, and the dependence of political authority on social contract. Each of them except Hobbes applied contract theory to restrict the state's authority.

Lessnoff discusses an important issue in classical contract theory—whether a contract is hypothetical or ideal.

> The distinction between a hypothetical and an ideal social contract is an important one, and in one respect the former seems to be much the more valid concept of the two. . . . To invoke an ideal contract is to appeal to what individuals, ideally, ought to agree to, or what they would agree to if they were ideally moral beings. . . . The case of a hypothetical contract is different, and is indeed available as a possible way of reformulating the whole social contract tradition up to Locke (and perhaps Rousseau also). Thus interpreted, social contract theorists are understood to assert that, in certain circumstances considered to be relevant to determining political obligation, individuals or peoples would agree to government according to certain terms (or perhaps better, would be willing to agree). The typical circumstance of this hypothetical agreement, in contract theory, is, of course, the state of nature, that is, a condition where men lack centralized government. On the present interpretation, the state of nature too could be considered to be a purely imaginable or hypothetical state of affairs, or as a possible one, or even as perhaps once actual.[2]

Another important feature of social contract theories is their emphasis on the individual and individual rights. The social contract is seen to be made between the state and an individual or a collection of individuals because it is in these individuals' self-interest to make such a contract.

> One important strand of contract theory, which may well be held to be the most important and the most typical, is a highly individualistic theory, grounding legitimate political authority on its acceptance by individuals. . . . Is it plausible to suppose that there

can be such a consensus of individual wills as to provide a viable foundation for authority? . . . If the individual wills are not wilful but rational, it is postulated, consensus can be reached.[3]

The concept of the social contract useful for understanding the situation in Newberry relative to the accident at Three Mile Island is, first, a communitarian one. That is, the people of Newberry believed themselves to be part of a community, and that entity, the community, was one of the contracting partners. Second, the contract was considered actual by the people of the community, rather than hypothetical or ideal. Third, the contract dealt not only with political authority but also with the industries in their midst.

None of these notions is incompatible with the idea of the legal contract from which the social contract is derived. The basic notion of any contract is that it is founded on a promise that is enforceable.

Roughly speaking, a legal contract is constituted by a promise, but not by a promise alone, for also required is agreement between the parties that the promise be legally enforceable. . . . The social contract, too, is not constituted by a promise alone, for even if legal enforcement is irrelevant, enforcement as such is not, and the understanding that the contract is enforceable is part of its essence.[4]

Trust links the concept of social contract with community reactions to the accident at Three Mile Island. In its most general sense, trust of others—including institutions and organizations—is the expectation that an agreement or contract will be honored. Fiduciary responsibility and competence are what we usually expect,[5] but because they are promised by agreement, by contract. Therefore, the central notion of trust concerns obligation. Because of the agreement, the trustee is obligated to the one who trusts. Concomitantly, the one who trusts has the right to expect the promised outcome of the agreement from the trustee. Mistrust, then, is the expectation that another will renege on an obligation.

The agreement may be explicit, as with written contracts or oral promises, or implicit, as with social contracts based on group, institutional, or societal values. Since societies are ordered according to their members' values, trusting that implicit contracts will be fulfilled is equivalent to believing that the behavior of another will conform to societal norms and reflect societal values. It is, therefore, the expectation that another will play by the rules.

Trust is the evidence that people believe social contracts exist. People trust others because they believe that others feel obligated to fulfill a promise, usually to act competently in a role or to act with fiduciary responsibility but also to abide by society's other norms and behave according to other values.

The agreement that the people of Newberry believed was in effect in the Three Mile Island area prior to the accident is an example of an implied or social contract, for "while business firms are not expected to act altruistically, they are supposed to be responsible—to seek reasonable profits but not to put profit ahead of their social responsibility to the country."[6] Newberrians believed that Metropolitan Edison had promised the community fiduciary responsibility and competence with respect to the health and safety of its members. The utility's assurances prior to building the Three Mile Island plant and afterward were taken as a promise: nuclear energy is safe, and this plant is safe; community members have nothing to fear.

That the community trusted Metropolitan Edison regarding the safety of the Three Mile Island plant is evidenced by the unconcern with which the community generally responded to the construction of the nuclear power plant and its subsequent operation. Another indication is community response to the statement, "Before the accident at Three Mile Island, Met Ed/GPU assured people around here that Three Mile Island was safe, and I believed them." Seventy-five percent agreed with that statement. Therefore, to the extent that the accident was perceived as endangering health and safety, it was also viewed as a violation or betrayal of an unwritten agreement.

The accident was evidence to the community that the contract between itself and Metropolitan Edison had been violated. The utility had promised safety when it proposed to build a nuclear power plant at Three Mile Island but it had not fulfilled its promise. Regardless of Metropolitan Edison's assurances about the safety of nuclear energy and the impossibility of a severe accident, the events of March 1979 indicated that the utility would not or could not honor this promise. Moreover, utility company officials had concealed the seriousness of the accident from residents of the community immediately after it began. In the years that followed, utility company and NRC officials' efforts to restore public trust were feeble. It appeared to the community that Metropolitan Edison officials and those of the Nuclear Regulatory Commission were incompetent, irresponsible, or both with respect to the promise of community safety.

We, as a society, believe that contracts should and will be enforced. This is the other essential element of any contract, including the social contract. If contracts are violated, there should and will be means to force compliance with the original agreement or restitution for its violation. This is one conception of justice. Thus we feel an injustice has occurred if contracts are violated and not enforced, and this provokes anger, bitterness, and cynicism about a social system that does not honor its own rules.

In the United States, for example, an unwritten component of the social contract between society and its members guarantees that medical treatment will be provided to the sick. Even the poorest among us believe they deserve treatment for their illnesses. However, the medically uninsured and underinsured who are unable to obtain medical care for illness are surely bitter and cynical about the health care system and even the society that has reneged on its commitment to them. Moreover, it is cause for discomfort in all of us when we learn that some of our citizens cannot obtain medical care for their health problems precisely because it seems that a promise was made but not kept.

So, too, in Newberry, people believed they deserved "treatment"— either restoration of their trust in Three Mile Island officials or relief from the symptoms of their mistrust. Irrespective of the means, treatment meant reinstatement of the contract that assured them of safety in their community. However, because of the failure of officials to restore trust, reinstatement of the contract regarding community safety became synonymous with keeping Three Mile Island closed. Moreover, before the Three Mile Island accident, we believe that most residents of Newberry thought that, in America, social contract violations would be rectified, especially if they involved community health and safety.

However, if Metropolitan Edison was seen to have violated the contract, who should have enforced it? Even before the accident, the people of Newberry recognized their own powerlessness with respect to big businesses such as Metropolitan Edison and the nuclear power industry. Based on statements they made after the accident, it would seem they had little faith that the community alone could force "one of the big guys" to comply with a contract. Mr. Hayward's words probably expressed a widely held view. "When you fight a big outfit, as a rule, you don't win. That's what I feel, and Met Ed's pretty big."

Moreover, these were not unrealistic views that the people of Newberry held. The loss of community control has been recognized since the early sixties. Arthur Vidich and his coauthor J. Bensman state in their 1960 book, *Small Town in Mass Society*, that the community is a finite universe within which one can examine some of the major issues of our time, among them "the specific character of the relationship between the rural community and the dynamics of modern, mass, industrial society." They propose "to explore the foundations of social life in a community which lacks the power to control the institutions that regulate and determine its existence," and in the process he demonstrates how little autonomy the local community has in modern American society, a fact that often goes unrecognized in the community. Vidich and Bensman claim that "dependence on the institutions and dynamics of urban and mass society" is central to rural life. "The belief and illusion of local independence and self-determination prevent a recognition of the central place of national and state institutions in local affairs. The reality of outside institutional dominance to which the town must respond is given only subliminal, pragmatic recognition."[7]

In *Social Change and Human Purpose: Toward Understanding and Action*, R. L. Warren speaks to the subject of community and societal change. "Local communities are, in a sense, the end of the line, the place where the impact of structures and processes in the national society gets felt by people in their daily lives. No community is an island, and the more one becomes involved in purposive change at the local level, the more likely one is to become aware of the genesis of many local problems in the larger society." The shift from local community unit relations to extra community dominance Warren names the "great change" in community living, which includes "the increasing orientation of local community units toward extra community systems of which they are a part, with a corresponding decline in community cohesion and autonomy. As the relation of community units to state and national systems becomes strengthened, the locus of decision-making with regard to them often shifts to places outside the community."[8]

Mrs. Boswell probably expressed what, before the accident, the people of Newberry would have expected to happen given their restricted power over their community.

> "The little guy just does have no say. I've never seen the little
> guy win yet when you come up against a big organization. Now,
> if you have a big guy behind a little guy, then that helps."

Recognizing their powerlessness, after the accident the people of Newberry expected more powerful others to help, an ally with clout to even the sides. The logical ally was the federal government since it has reserved for itself absolute authority in matters pertaining to nuclear energy. The state government was also a potential supporter. The state and federal governments were powerful enough to counterbalance the might of Metropolitan Edison and the nuclear power industry.

Moreover, residents of Newberry believed that government should care about the health of the community, especially the public health sector of government. That was their contract with government. Herbert Gans, describing Middle Americans, suggests that "honesty is the principal value which people 'test' in their dealings with organizations, but when it comes to government and private enterprise they also want something more. Political leaders are expected to be representative, to represent the interests and values of the ordinary people who provide most of the votes that elect them."[9] Middle Americans may believe that government decisions do not often benefit the common person materially; that is, business is likely to receive more benefits. Unlike the poor, however, Middle Americans expect government to assure community health and safety.

Very early on, many Newberrians may have believed that within the federal government the Nuclear Regulatory Commission might be the agency to right their situation. However, if they thought that this agency was a regulatory body responsive to public concerns, this perception was quickly dispelled by Nuclear Regulatory Commission support of Metropolitan Edison's plan to reopen Three Mile Island despite widespread community opposition.

At one time, residents probably also believed that the Department of Health or the Environmental Protection Agency might side with the community, but no state or federal agency or department committed itself to their cause. Rather, government departments and agencies that became involved appeared to use all of their powers to convince or coerce the community to accept Metropolitan Edison's decisions regarding the cleanup of Unit 2 and the reopening of Unit 1 at Three Mile Island.

> Mrs. Kelsey: They [authorities] keep saying we need this nuclear. They keep pounding that into our heads with the news and everything. We need it. We need it. We can't do without it.

For the most part, local community concerns were ignored or ridiculed by those who might have helped. Locally elected officials who publicly supported the community seemed unable to achieve the desired results in the face of federal intransigence.

> Mrs. Boswell: But I don't see nothing in the future for that [help for the community]. I don't see anybody that is really interested in trying to keep it closed down . . . except us. So I don't know what's going to become of us or it.

In their effort to keep the Three Mile Island plant closed through legal intervention, the community of Newberry was essentially on its own. Although there were other intervenors, none had more power than they. They were all pleading a case, arguing that the psychological health of nearby residents would be harmed by the restart of Unit 1. This tactic, this strategy for working within the system, was the only one available to them. But there were no "big guys" behind them.

The mistrust of Newberrians was tantamount to their believing that a contract had been violated. When plans to reopen the plant were pursued by Metropolitan Edison, supported by the federal Nuclear Regulatory Commission, and unopposed by other government officials or agencies, the people of the community felt not only that a contract had been violated, but that their right to expect enforcement of the contract had been transgressed. A sense that justice had not prevailed arose among Newberry residents when their attempts to force compliance with the contract failed. Bitterness and cynicism resulted. They perceived themselves as victims. One resident said about the petitions circulated in Newberry to oppose the restart:

> "Probably when those petitions came through, everybody signed. Well, I would just bet those names didn't mean a thing. They just went into somebody's wastebasket because we are just people who pay the bills."

And Mrs. Boswell, reflecting on who would decide about the reopening, said:

> "We don't want to be guinea pigs. . . . I still think that we should have a say, too, in what goes on. I really do, because we're the victims."

They believed Metropolitan Edison placed money before people; the contract was a sham perpetrated in order to build the plant and increase company profits.

> Mrs. Caspar: We could still be sitting here on a time bomb and still not know it. But I think you have the right to know what is going on and how serious it is. But they didn't want to panic everybody. Would they rather have everybody dead? I mean, which would they rather have?! Of course, dead people don't sue.

> Mr. Crown: So I believe that American business is what runs this country, the almighty dollar, whatever way you want to put it,

and that financial considerations are going to dictate the TMI outcome.

Mrs. Brown: The company just wants [to reopen the plant for] the money. Everyone is out to make money. . . . They [Metropolitan Edison officials] care [about community opposition] from, I think, from a public relations point of view, the picture of the company.

Mrs. Carman: No, they're going to do what they want. . . . No, I don't think it [community feelings] would bother them at all. Because I feel they have one aim in mind and that is to raise money, to earn money. And I don't think they have any feelings as far as other people go—I don't think it bothers them. It makes me wonder if they have a conscience, because I know if I was in that position I would be very upset.

The government was seen as a conspirator of those who cared nothing about the people. Its officials were not abiding by their pledge to protect the health and safety of citizens, to act as guardians of the public trust.

Mrs. Hemingway: I feel very angry about it really, because I just feel that there was so much incompetence on the part of the utility, on the part of the NRC, on the part of the local governments—even, although they don't have that much say in it—by the fact that they aren't concerned about it at all and are willing to just let it take its own course, let the utility do whatever it wants. I think that they are not living up to their responsibilities as government bodies.

A Newberry Township official: The people at the governmental level should be representing their constituents, and when they make decisions in opposition to the wishes of the majority of the people, then this is not a good thing.

## THE FAILURE OF GATEKEEPERS

Our example of medical treatment for the sick as a social obligation and denial of such treatment as unsettling is an oversimplification of reality. Access to medical care is regulated by gatekeepers, that is, by physicians, who "are of critical importance in this process, and the practice of medicine may be viewed within the sociological perspective, as a system of rules for making symptoms into illness and for transforming persons into patients."[10]

A physician can decide that an individual is not ill, perhaps even a malingerer or a hypochondriac and, therefore, is not entitled to health care. The physician can conclude that an individual is demanding treatment that is inappropriate for his or her health condition and withhold the requested medical care. Even among the uninsured or underinsured, the physician is obligated to provide only what he or she considers necessary but minimum treatment. The uninsured or underinsured cannot be denied treatment, but they need not receive the maximum appropriate care to which others are entitled by virtue of their ability to pay. If a physician decides that treatment is unnecessary or inappropriate for an individual seeking it, medical care can be denied, and we are untroubled. We accept the decisions of physicians regarding access to medical care; they are the experts, and they have been trained to make these decisions.

A similar rationale operated at Three Mile Island to deny the people of Newberry their wish to keep the plant closed. Essentially, it was a matter of legitimacy. If one wants to continue a policy, it is best to dismiss those who want to change it by denying the legitimacy of their claims. Just as in the realm of medical care where potential patients must be seen by physicians who determine if their health claims are valid, the people of Newberry were studied by gatekeepers who decided whether they had legitimate claims to the outcome they sought.

## Mental Health Professionals

One group of legitimizers was mental health professionals—psychologists, psychiatrists, and psychiatric epidemiologists who studied the people living near Three Mile Island to determine if the accident had an adverse psychological effect on them. Presumably, the thinking was that nearby residents would be entitled to some kind of treatment if the accident had this consequence; it would validate their demand to have their concerns considered in some way. The kind of treatment to be prescribed was not specified. Although Newberry residents and those of neighboring communities believed that the finding of adverse mental health effects would justify keeping the plant closed, this was not a given.

In any event, many of the earliest published social scientific works dealing with the effects of the accident focused on its psychological effects. The President's Commission on the Accident at Three Mile Island was the first to publish a detailed analysis of the impact of the accident on the surrounding communities. The Behavioral Effects Task Group of the President's Commission, which studied the mental stress experienced at the time of the accident, found that "the most serious health effect of the accident was severe mental stress, which was short-lived. The highest levels of distress were found among those living within five miles of Three Mile Island and in families with preschool children."[11]

Many researchers have studied the mental health effects of the accident since then.[12] While some evidence of lingering effects was found, it appeared that these were not severe enough to be considered pathological. In "Three Mile Island: Psychology and Environmental Policy at a Crossroads," Hartsough and Savitsky summarized the conclusions of several major studies of the long-term mental health effects of the accident on the people living near Three Mile Island:

(1) Stress levels in the neighboring area to Three Mile Island increased sharply as a result of the accident.
(2) There were differential effects. The mothers of young children, for example, were identified as an at-risk group in the governor's evacuation advisory, and they apparently suffered the highest levels of psychological distress.
(3) Although significantly higher than normal according to statistical findings, the stress levels resulting from the TMI incident did not reach the intensity associated with either severe trauma situations or mental illness.
(4) The evidence for TMI-induced chronic stress is equivocal. Most studies show a drop in reported effects over time, and even those investigators reporting long-term effects fail to demonstrate their behavioral and clinical significance.[13]

In summary, the evidence of psychologists, psychiatrists, and psychiatric epidemiologists indicated that the accident did not produce pathological mental health effects. Anxiety, depression, and psychophysiologic symptoms may have been higher than in other communities but they were not high enough to indicate that people were ill. Mental health experts could not label most people in the Three Mile Island area as "cases," that is, people in need of treatment.

The issue of the mental health impact of restarting Three Mile Island was never considered by the Nuclear Regulatory Commission because the Supreme Court ruled that the commission did not have to consider the psychological impact of the accident on nearby residents. However, we believe that if it had been considered, the issue would have been decided against the community on the basis of the studies of the mental health experts and the conclusions that their research instruments and definitions of mental health forced them to reach. Most Newberrians were not sick by their standards.

## Social Scientists

Nor did the social scientists who study disasters legitimize the community's claim to attention. As we have previously said, traditionally, American sociology of disaster has taken the structural-functional approach to understanding how communities are affected by disasters. The structural elements of a community achieve balance or equilibrium over time in a context of general value consensus. When disasters occur, this balance is temporarily upset while disaster response mechanisms strive to restore the equilibrium. The magnitude and intensity of these responses may even bring the community closer than it was before the disaster. In any event, the balance is eventually restored with few, if any, long-term effects of the disaster remaining in evidence. These sociologists have been particularly adamant about the absence of long-term psychological trauma following a disaster.

Probably the best representative of the sociology of disaster approach is E. L. Quarantelli. In "The Consequences of Disasters for Mental Health: Conflicting Views," Quarantelli makes clear the distinction between what he terms the "individual trauma approach" and the "social fabric approach" to the study of the community impact of disaster. The individual trauma, which would tend to be used by psychologists, "holds that disasters constitute highly stressful and traumatic life events. These events are seen as producing very pervasive and deeply internalized psychological reactions among the victims. The victims are viewed primarily as attempting to cope with the meaning of the trauma of the disaster impact." The social fabric approach, which tends to be held by sociologists of disaster, "holds that disasters have differential rather than across the board effects. Some of the effects are positive as well as negative; many of them are relatively surface and short in duration. The varying problems of victims are more closely related to the post-impact response than they are to the disaster impact itself."[14]

Quarantelli argues that, while the social fabric position does acknowledge that many disaster victims exhibit a variety of transient symptoms that reflect emotional disturbance, little evidence exists of severe psychopathology, either short- or long-term, after a disaster. What does tend to cause long-term difficulties for the victims, he points out, are difficulties in obtaining human services after the disaster.[15]

While Quarantelli's work is representative of the more sociological approach to disasters in general, he has little to say about Three Mile Island specifically. *Impacts of Hazardous Technology: The Psycho-Social Effects of Restarting TMI-1* by J. Sorenson et al. is probably the most comprehensive attempt to incorporate the sociological perspective into the study of the impact of the accident on nearby residents. The authors concluded that while the accident itself had "a definite and measurable impact on the social and psychological well-being of people and social groups in the Three Mile Island vicinity, studies which examined the impacts suggest that the levels have decayed . . . over time."[16]

In other words, evidence suggested that not just the psychological variables but the sociological variables were returning to normal, which is precisely what sociologists of disaster would predict. The people of Newberry returned to work, school, and the business of raising families, running households, and participating in family and community activities. Disaster sociologists therefore could see no difference between this and other disasters that had only transitory disruptive impacts.

Nor did the authors expect the restart to be any different, projecting that reopening Unit 1 would have little effect on the community. Specifically, they projected that some concern would be expressed on the individual level, that a few individuals would feel anxious, but that there would be no somatic effect or clinical impairment. On the family level, they predicted that there would be some increase in tension in isolated cases, but that increases in conflict or decreases in cohesion would be unlikely. They envisioned no increase in family breakup attributable to the restart. Finally, they expected no long-term population change and no economic disruption in the community. They concluded that "the overwhelming evidence suggests that the restart issue will have no or at least no detectable effect on the communities and people in the vicinity of Three Mile Island."[17]

Sorensen has qualified this statement somewhat. He believes that return to normalcy has been slower than might have been predicted, and a new normalcy may replace the old one.[18] But the central argument of the book coincides with the sociology of disaster view that, after a disaster, sooner or later things will get back to normal. The authors argued that the restart would not affect this normalization process, and by their standards it would not. They attached importance to indicators of community functioning, and by these measures, the effect of the accident on Newberry was just as they had predicted: transitory.

## Physicians

Had physicians found residents physically injured by the accident, their findings would have validated the community's demand for attention. Again, however, we do not know what kind of attention would have been warranted besides actual medical care for diagnosed physical illnesses. Would they have warranted keeping the plant closed? This we do not know because the studies conducted by physicians and epidemiologists found no evidence of physical harm—no increased rates of cancer, miscarriages, birth defects, or other health problems associated with radiation exposure. It was another potential legitimizing issue for the people of the community that when scrutinized was found invalid.

Unfortunately, these studies were conducted under the auspices of the Pennsylvania Department of Health, whose findings were not accepted by the community because of the department's pre-investigatory view that the accident had no health effects and because the department would not allow independent inspection of the data. However, the community's perception of the legitimacy of these studies did not affect authorities' views about their legitimacy.

### Risk Assessment Authorities

According to current usage by risk assessment experts, risk is the potential for harm or the "potential for harm and/or for safety."[19] Risk assessment authorities comprise another group that has denied the legitimacy of the people of Newberry and those in similar situations by branding them Luddists—people who are against technological change and the risks it involves. This is a perspective that many business and government leaders have taken in an attempt to discredit groups opposed to business and industrial projects in their communities. It is an appealing argument if you are the Metropolitan Edison Company or the Nuclear Regulatory Commission; you would like to believe that the individuals who oppose your projects have made a perceptual error. They essentially want what is impossible—a risk-free environment. They are risk aversive; they do not want to live with risks of any magnitude, and therefore, they oppose all technological development.

This approach allows industry and government to dismiss community demands easily, because risks are an integral part of life and may even be necessary to achieve safety, if it is assumed that "safety results from a process of discovery. Attempting to short-circuit this competitive, evolutionary, trial and error process by wishing the end—safety—without providing the means—decentralized search—is bound to be self-defeating. Conceiving of safety without risk is like seeking love without courting the danger of rejection."[20]

Another, related, argument used to discredit the people in Newberry and communities like it is that the general public has not evaluated environmental risks appropriately. Perhaps an individual is not totally averse to risk, the argument goes, but he or she does not know how to properly assess it. People's fears are unfounded in that their risks are not as great as they perceive them to be.

This perspective is illustrated in the following passage concerning cancer risk. "In the past, cancer phobia, or excessive fear of cancer, was a problem in clinical medicine. A great accomplishment of the American Cancer Society in the 1960s was to reduce such fear by bringing the facts before the public. But during the last decade, a new form of mass cancer phobia has become widespread in the United States. This fear relates to the possible development of cancer because of community exposure to carcinogens in low doses from a wide variety of sources such as hazardous waste deposits, air pollutants and food additives. Such fear can lead to psychosomatic illness and ill health. At a time when life expectancy has never been higher and when the quality of life in old age is considerably improved, it may be asked whether this generalized fear of cancer is either good or justifiable. Nevertheless, people appear to make cancer paramount and to forget that there are many other illnesses as well. . . . In my opinion, this fear is not based on an accurate appreciation of the causes of human cancer either now or in the future; there is thus a large gap between the reality and public perception. This gap is widened by a distrust of public officials and by poorly balanced articles in the media. From a medical point of view, it is unethical to make people afraid unless a benefit can be demonstrated at the individual level."[21]

Another example concerns the risk of nuclear energy "Perceptronics [a firm of consulting psychologists] surveyed three groups: college students, members of the League of Women Voters, and business and professional members of the Active Club, a service organization. The three groups were asked to rank 30 activities including nuclear power generation, in order of risk. A fourth sample group, professional experts in risk assessment, used their special knowledge to rank the same 30 activities. Survey results dramatically demonstrate the difference between the risk perceived by experts and laymen. . . . The greatest divergence of perception concerned nuclear energy. Two samples of laymen rated it the most dangerous activity on the list of 30, and the third group (the Active Club) rated it eighth. The experts ranked nuclear energy 20th."[22]

Browne suggests that lay risk assessment cannot be ignored by policymakers. However, most authors making this kind of point rail against the constraints of lay risk assessment and decry its use as a basis of business or public policy or advocate public education about the "actual" probabilities associated with risky behavior. They discuss how to bring lay and expert risk assessment into line. When people suggest that perceived risk should be taken into account, it means something that looks like public relations.[23]

The legitimizers did not validate Newberry residents' demand to keep Three Mile Island closed. Medical and mental health professionals did not find residents of Newberry physically injured or psychologically impaired. Disaster specialists found them returned or returning to normal—perhaps a slightly different normality than before—but normal just the same; it was a community of socially functioning individuals. Risk assessment experts found them to perceive wrongly that the Three Mile Island nuclear power plant was a severe risk.

Essentially, physicians and risk assessment experts upheld the nuclear industry's view that the contract between Newberrians and Metropolitan Edison regarding health and safety had not been violated; the community was not physically endangered by the accident. Mental health professionals and disaster sociologists found that, even looking beyond the contract dealing with physical safety, the community had not been harmed by the accident; people were functioning, and they were not psychologically impaired by the accident.

# EIGHT

## NIMBY, THE NEW PARADIGM, AND COMMUNITY JUSTICE

DESPITE THE EXPERTS' assessment that Three Mile Island was not an instance in which industry failed to keep its promise regarding community health and safety, in 1991 it is almost impossible to imagine a community that would be unconcerned about the siting of a nuclear power plant within one-half mile of its border. It is difficult to envision a community that would not resist such a plant. We might even think that the people of Newberry were naive prior to March 1979. Moreover, current community concern extends to the siting of other hazardous technologies as well.

It is this point that justifies our theme of transformation. Mistrust of industry and government with regard to their commitment to community health and safety has permeated our society. And was not the accident at Three Mile Island one of several events that caused the spread of mistrust? Love Canal, Times Beach, and Three Mile Island— they shattered the view that industry was pledged to community health and safety and that government would ensure that industry kept this pledge. These events expanded the boundaries of beliefs regarding industries, government, communities, and health.

However, for this new perception to take root in the public mind required other events to support the shift. Unfortunately, the intervening years have been replete with cases that have led citizens to believe that many industries have endangered and continue to endanger communities, as at Three Mile Island, through knowing or unknowing incompetence or lack of fiduciary responsibility. The first example we cite indicates deception on the part of a research laboratory.

> Fraud in Toxicology Studies Charged to Big Laboratory
> Chicago, April 12 [1983]—Jury selection is under way here in the Federal trial of a research laboratory accused of misrepresenting data used by manufacturers to obtain Government approval for insecticides and herbicides. . . . The research concern, Industrial BioTest Laboratory of Northbrook, Ill., established in 1953, is one of the largest of 200 independent laboratories conducting safety tests on such items as cosmetics, drugs, pesticides, and food additives.[1]

The next story indicates the magnitude of the problem of toxic emissions from factories in the U.S.:

> Plant owners admit to release of toxins
> Washington, June 20 [1989]—Owners of 30 U.S. plants acknowledge releasing annually at least 1 million pounds each of chemicals suspected of causing cancer, according to federal figures disclosed Monday by a private group. . . . [David] Doniger [an attorney for the Natural Resources Defense Council] criticized the EPA for not having moved more swiftly to regulate such chemical releases.[2]

The following quote illustrates an industry's attempt to thwart or limit regulation:

> Chemical Industry Is Seeking to Defeat Toxic-Emissions
> Reporting Requirement
> Washington, December 9 [1985]—Supporters of the chemical industry hope to reverse this week a House vote to require extensive annual reports of potentially harmful chemical emissions to communities.
>     Yet it is becoming clear that Congress is going to impose some kind of new emissions-reporting requirement on handlers of toxic chemicals as a response to the accident that killed about 1,750 people in Bhopal, India, a year ago.[3]

Furthermore, the government has not always been the vigilant guardian of community safety. Another set of stories illustrates the kinds of failures that have involved government. The first portrays government as industry's protector:

E.P.A. Said to Bar Tests at Dow in '81

Chicago, March 24 [1983]—Officials at the Washington headquarters of the Environmental Protection Agency intervened in behalf of the Dow Chemical Company in 1981 to prevent agency investigators from testing waste water inside the grounds of the company's plant in Midland, Mich., according to present and former officials of the agency's regional office here.

Thwarted, the investigators had to resort to testing the waters outside the plant after discharge, a procedure they considered much less satisfactory since any pollutants would be diluted by river water and more difficult to detect. The testing was made in an effort to obtain information that the company had refused to provide voluntarily.[4]

Next is a General Accounting Office report published in 1988 about long-standing hazardous waste pollution of the environment by the Department of Energy—the government as polluter:

The information we compiled on the three additional installations confirms the findings we reported to you in our earlier report, namely, that the waste disposal practices used by DOE [Department of Energy] and its predecessor agencies over the past 40 years have released hazardous radioactive and chemical substances into the environment. For example, each of the three installations have reported soil contamination resulting from their inactive waste sites—sometimes at levels hundreds to thousands of times those of background levels. Further, inactive waste sites at FMPC [Feed Materials Production Center] and the Pantex Plant are suspected sources of some of the groundwater contamination detected at these installations, and are under investigation by DOE.[5]

Another report, also from the General Accounting Office, criticized the Environmental Protection Agency for its implementation of a polychlorinated biphenyl (PCB) control program—the government as inadequate regulator.

In 1976 the Congress required that the Environmental Protection Agency control the widely used chemicals, polychlorinated biphenyls (PCBs). Slow in implementing the mandate, however, EPA can offer only limited assurance that its control measures are being followed. Its enforcement program lacks overall direction and does not encourage quick compliance. Additionally, disposal facilities have developed slowly, meeting with considerable public opposition.[6]

The Department of Energy has also been found negligent in this respect. In 1988, the General Accounting Office found DOE's management and funding of environment, safety, and health programs insufficient at the DOE's nuclear defense facilities.[7]

Finally, the government, like industry, often cannot assess risk because of lack of information and is therefore unable to inform communities of their true risk.

> Government Cites Waterways Polluted by Toxic Chemicals
> Washington, June 13 [1989]—Agency officials said they could not assess the risks to public health presented by the contaminated lakes and streams. But they said that the new information confirms that much more needs to be done to meet the Government's goal of restoring the nation's waters to a state amenable to fishing and swimming.[8]

The history of hazardous waste disposal illustrates almost all the problems that lead people to mistrust industry and government concerning community health and safety. It contains examples of industry deceit and disregard for community health and safety, uncertain scientific knowledge, and inadequate government regulation and effort to assure safety in communities hosting dangerous technologies or their by-products.

In 1976, Congress mandated a hazardous waste monitoring system to go into effect in 1980. The law created a manifest system that would be used to follow toxic substances from their point of manufacture, through their use in industry, to their eventual disposal by approved toxic waste handlers. The public was assured that after the law went into effect toxic wastes would be properly disposed of, mostly in "leak-proof" landfills.

In the intervening years, industry good faith was brought into question. Several days before the law was to go into effect, it was reported that businesses were, and had been for some time, rushing to dispose illegally of their toxic wastes in order to avoid the expense of the new system or possible lawsuits in the future.

Toxic Wastes Hurriedly Dumped
Before New Law Goes Into Effect
Boston, November 15 [1980]—Thousands of tons of hazardous and toxic wastes are being hurriedly dumped into city sewer systems, spilled from moving trucks onto busy interstate highways and abandoned in shopping center parking lots around the country in a last-minute rush to dispose of the chemicals before a Federal "cradle-to-grave" waste monitoring system begins next week. . . . The wastes have polluted the water supply of hundreds of communities with dangerous and cancer-causing chemicals in recent years. In Massachusetts alone, for example, environmental officials say that 26 public water sources have been shut down because of chemical contamination in the last 18 months.[9]

In 1981, the U.S. General Accounting Office issued a report indicating that even though the law was in effect, the problems of hazardous waste disposal were far from over. It pointed out problems in a number of waste sites, difficulties associated with risk assessment, obstacles within the legal system to achieving settlement for claims, and inadequacies in the Superfund legislation.

Not much is known about the possible adverse health and environmental effects associated with the thousands of hazardous waste disposal sites now being discovered throughout the United States.
The Environmental Protection Agency is finding it difficult to carry out its mandate to protect human health and the environment from hazardous wastes because:
   • New waste sites are being discovered faster than they can be investigated and evaluated.
   • There is no strong scientific basis for determining risks.
   • Legal action seeking correction of hazardous waste problems is pursued for only a few sites.
Individuals seeking relief within the courts to satisfy hazardous waste compensation claims face great difficulties.
New "Superfund" legislation will provide some help, but it is too early to tell whether it will solve all of the problems presented by uncontrolled hazardous waste sites.[10]

An even bigger blow to communities concerned about the safety of hazardous waste disposal sites was the finding that there probably was no such thing as a "leak-proof" landfill.

Experts Showing Concern on Safety of Burying Toxic Waste in
Landfills

Washington, March 15 [1983]—Burying hazardous wastes on land,
by far the most common method of disposal in this country, may be
the least safe practice in the long run, according to an emerging
consensus of expert opinion.

This judgment applies not only to past practices, which virtually
everyone agrees were sloppy and dangerous, but also to some of the
most advanced techniques required under the tougher laws of recent years. . . . "They're not really secure," [Samuel S. Epstein, a
professor of environmental medicine at the University of Illinois
Medical Center in Chicago] said. "In fact, they're impractical and
unsafe unless you're prepared to spend overwhelming amounts of
money to produce hermetically sealed underground caskets with
linings that will resist degradation for as long as the chemicals
last."

The chief reason for the popularity of landfills is their low immediate cost in relation to incineration and many other alternative
disposal methods.[11]

Furthermore, the manifest system was found inadequate to detect
illegal waste disposal. In 1985, the General Accounting Office issued a
report concluding that the extent of illegal waste disposal was unknown,
identifying all generators and their waste products was difficult, and the
manifest system may have deterred but had not detected illegal disposal
by document forgery because generator or transporter inspections were
not designed to detect illegal storage or disposal.[12]

Moreover, the government effort to monitor hazardous waste sites was
found to be insufficient, according to a report issued by the General
Accounting Office in 1987.

Hazardous Waste: Facility Inspections
Are Not Thorough and Complete

RCRA [Resource Conservation and Recovery Act] hazardous waste
handler inspections are not as thorough and complete as they
should be. State, EPA regional, and EPA contract inspectors are not
detecting a substantial number of regulatory violations during inspections—many of which are considered by EPA to warrant immediate attention because of the severe environmental threats they
pose. In addition, inspectors are not covering all waste handler
activities in their inspections nor fully documenting deficiencies
they find.[13]

Finally, in 1987 another General Accounting Office report found that many waste handlers were uninsured so that if they were to harm individuals in a community, little compensation for the injured would be available.

> Pollution liability insurance continued to be generally unavailable [to companies that handle toxic substances]. Although more than 100,000 companies generate, handle, or dispose of hazardous substances, few of them have insurance for pollution risks.[14]

The preceding are examples of the kinds of events and processes which have confirmed the public's mistrust of industry and government regarding community health and safety. Three Mile Island, Love Canal, and Times Beach breached the belief that industry was not endangering communities; the years which followed brought much evidence to suggest that repair of the breach was not possible.

## NOT IN MY BACKYARD

In this book we have described the symptoms of mistrust only among the people of Newberry, their distress and their sense that the health and safety of their community are threatened after the accident. In most American communities, however, the evidence of mistrust is rather the zealous vigilance with which members protect their environment from new development that might affect their health and safety. The result of mistrust, the NIMBY (Not In My Backyard) movement is collective action aimed at avoiding what happened in Newberry and places like it. By stopping threats before they begin, communities are attempting to ensure that their members never experience the powerlessness or feel the fear, distress, anger, and bitterness of victims of technological accidents.

The phenomenon is described in a 1988 *New York Times* article.

> Tod Crumrine's battle started when he heard about the huge garbage incinerator a company wants to build 1,000 feet from his grain field in rural Nova, Ohio.
>
> For Phyllis Sterling, it began when a neighbor told her about a chemical-waste hauling company's plan to put a truck terminal across the road from the store she runs in Fannett, Tex.
>
> Anne Marie Mueser grew angry when she saw a thin black line on a map that meant utility executives were planning to run a gas pipeline through the middle of her orchard in Clinton Corners, N.Y.
>
> These people, in their own ways, recently said the same thing:

"Not in my backyard," and they meant it in the way people mean things only rarely, when they are angry enough or scared enough to fight.

"I fathered two children and I'll protect them," Mr. Crumrine said. "I'll do everything in my power to keep that incinerator from coming in here. And if it does get in here, we're leaving. But it will not get in here."

For Mr. Crumrine, Ms. Sterling and Ms. Mueser, activism is a new experience. But business executives know the protest pattern so well that they have a mocking nickname for it: N-i-m-b-y, for "not in my backyard." What they mean by Nimby is usually trouble.[15]

Unfortunately, but not surprisingly, NIMBY is a pejorative term. The term is applied to anyone who attempts to restrict business and government activity of any kind, individuals who oppose projects as diverse as restaurant construction and hazardous waste dump siting. The *Times* article goes on.

This is the age of NIMBY. Developers of everything from airport extensions to soup kitchens and McDonald restaurants have met the NIMBY squads.[16]

NIMBYs are denigrated by descriptions of what they do. In the eyes of industry, NIMBYs cripple business, halt progress, paralyze corporate response to the marketplace. They stall, stop, or shrink projects. They win thousands of battles as they interfere with the necessary functioning of society.

And academics and executives say NIMBY is growing dramatically as one citizen group after another uses the political system to cripple corporate projects. "What we see in many, many cases is that controversy need only reach a certain decibel level and progress on that project will often grind to a halt." . . . The NIMBY syndrome has introduced a paralysis in effective corporate response to marketplace incentives. . . . The question that business experts are just beginning to wrestle with is whether thousands of separate NIMBY victories will leave any backyards anywhere for the power plants, pipelines, factories, waste disposal sites, incinerators, high rise buildings, highways, half-way houses, and scores of other projects that the economy and society as a whole needs to

keep going. . . . NIMBYs, many industry analysts say, have become
a new force in American business life that could push the country
toward an unprecedented paralysis. . . . NIMBYs are people who
live near enough to corporate or government projects—and are
upset enough about them—to work to stop, stall, or shrink them.[17]

Aspersions are cast on NIMBYs by describing their methods.

NIMBYs organize, march, sue, and petition to block the developers
they think are threatening them. They twist the arms of politicians
and they learn how to influence regulators. They fight fiercely and
then, win or lose, they vanish. . . . NIMBYs are noisy. NIMBYs are
powerful.[8]

In fact, they behave in a most nonpassive way. The implied question is,
"Why don't they just lie down and submit like they are supposed to?"
   Business leaders feel besieged, and they are not sure how they came to
be in this war.

There have always been people who fought development. But until
recently, executives say, they were mostly bulldozer-blocking zeal-
ots, not the clear-eyed school teachers, suburban professionals, and
well-informed storekeepers who are appearing at zoning boards
and community meetings all over the country. . . . NIMBYs are
everywhere.[19]

Industry would like to believe, and have others believe, that the
NIMBY syndrome is the irrational reaction of the knee-jerk liberals of the
post-Watergate era. William Ruckelshaus, former head of the Environmental Protection Agency and an environmental consultant to industry
at the time of this publication, has suggested this connection.

Mr. Ruckelshaus is one of several commentators who traces the
roots of the NIMBY syndrome to the distrust of government that
grew out of the Vietnam War and the Watergate scandal.[20]

Such suggestions keep NIMBY a pejorative term, associating it with
society's often negative images of Vietnam era antiwar protesters and
Watergate era "nitpickers." Perhaps a NIMBY is someone who is part of
the "militant social movement" that rejects modern American society,
probably "anti-free enterprise," "anti-growth," and "anti-business," per-

haps part of the New Left.[21] Linking NIMBY with people who are said to harp on the country's faults denies the legitimacy and authenticity of their arguments.

In addition, the NIMBY claim that communities are endangered by industrial projects is challenged. As with nuclear energy, industry uses risk assessment experts to further discredit NIMBYs in such business-oriented publications as *Forbes*.

> One after another of the major "hazards" of the 1970's turns out to have been a false alarm or a severe exaggeration . . . the pursuit of zero risk, encouraged by some government officials and fed by legislators nervous of incurring the wrath of the self-styled "environmental community," threatens the health of our economy without doing much for the health of our citizens. . . . So here we are on the edge of spending tens or perhaps hundreds of billions of dollars on programs of doubtful benefit, acting not on proven facts but on hysteria and questionable statistical models. But who is there to see the big picture when a minority of activists have the politicians buffaloed and the media largely snowed?[22]

All these strategies challenge the legitimacy of NIMBYs and their issues, just as the legitimacy of Newberrians who wished to keep Three Mile Island closed was contested.

Yet the shift in public beliefs regarding industry and government's commitment to community health and safety represented by NIMBY has been brought about by the actions of industry and government themselves. The widespread perception that industries will jeopardize community health and safety either through negligence, incompetence, disregard, or the optimistic appraisal of risk began with Three Mile Island, Love Canal, and Times Beach. These events caused people to question their assumptions that industry would not impose serious health risks on communities and that government would act as the guardian of public health. Since then, too many events have provided support for the perceptual shift. NIMBYs are a reaction to the behavior of industry: their perceptions have a basis in fact.

We prefer to separate NIMBY groups concerned about health and safety issues from others. A more apt name for the syndrome of challenging and opposing perceived industrial development or projects that have health and safety implications is CAIHR, Communities Against Imposed Health Risks. When a business organization proposes to locate a new facility in a community, CAIHR asks, "How can we believe your promises of safety in the face of evidence that any one of the following scenarios could just as well be true? (1) your organization is deceiving us about the risks of this facility; (2) your organization has taken an overly optimistic view about the risks of this facility; or (3) your organization does not really know the true risks of this facility for the people of this community."

CAIHR asks, "How can we feel secure when government promises to regulate this hazardous technology when we know that: (1) government officials have been involved in industry cover-ups of health and safety threats to communities; (2) government regulatory effort is often insufficient for the job; and (3) government authorities may not know the true risks of this technology?"

Mistrust is the origin of CAIHR, and mistrust is the result of industry and government behavior. The case of Bhopal did not go unnoticed by the public. Although people were thankful that it did not occur in their community, Bhopal and its aftermath taught them a lesson the media did not invent. The Bhopal gas leak clearly illustrated the case of industry seeking to minimize its responsibility to communities.

On 3 December 1984, a Union Carbide plant in Bhopal, India, leaked methyl isocyanate, a pesticide, into the environment. At least 3,500 people died and 200,000 were injured as a result.[23] According to medical experts, the survivors of Bhopal are likely to suffer serious health problems throughout their lives. Many are likely to be permanently disabled and vulnerable to respiratory diseases as well.[24] Since that time, Union Carbide's commitment to public safety and social responsibility have been questioned. Questions arose about notification of the public regarding the leak.

> The Associated Press quoted Union Carbide's managing director in India, Y. P. Gokhale, as saying the gas leaked for 40 minutes before being shut off. The AP said United News of India reported that the factory siren didn't alert area residents until two hours after the leak began and that rescue workers didn't arrive until four hours after that. . . .
>
> Although Union Carbide said yesterday's accident was the first problem with the plant, United Press International quoted Indian officials as saying six people died at the same plant in 1977 after they were exposed to phosgene gas.[25]

Questions arose about whether Union Carbide knew about the danger of the plant prior to the accident and could have prevented it.

Jackson B. Browning, Union Carbide's vice president of health, safety and environmental affairs, said the government findings [of significant danger and long term effect] were, in some cases, similar to results seen in company tests run as early as 1980. Mr. Browning said the company reported those tests to both the U.S. government and the company unit that operated the Bhopal facility, but couldn't immediately say if the company had pointed out at the time that high-level methyl isocyanate exposures posed a risk of persistent lung damage.[26]

Questions arose about Union Carbide's motivation for seeking a trial in India.

There remain pressures working against a negotiated settlement. One is a possible move by Union Carbide to challenge the jurisdiction of the American courts, under the legal doctrine that foreign cases shouldn't be tried in the U.S. if courts in the foreign country can satisfactorily dispose of the matter. If Union Carbide does press this issue and succeeds in moving the litigation to India (where company officials have said it belongs), the level of compensation might be considerably lower.[27]

The Indian government spent $70 million for relief and rehabilitation. India sought $3.3 billion on behalf of the 500,000 claimants charging poor maintenance and design flaws. However, Union Carbide succeeded in obtaining a much smaller settlement.[28] Most experts agreed that they should have paid at least $1 billion to the claimants. Some have argued for as much as $4 billion for "compensation for direct and ancillary losses, not only to date but as far into the future as the impact of the disaster will continue to affect the victims."[29] To the shame of the United States, the amount was only $470 million.

To residents of communities in the United States, the Bhopal disaster illustrated the kind of corporate behavior that had become all too common. Perhaps Union Carbide stockholders applauded the settlement, but the Indian people and Middle Americans reading these accounts did not. To social scientists, it demonstrated "that enforceable international standards are clearly and urgently needed for hazardous activities, especially those operating in developing countries. Such standards would eliminate, or at least narrow, the gap between standards prevailing in the developed countries and those in the third world."[30]

Communities wonder how they can trust the courts or other government protectors when so much money is at stake. The behavior of Union

Carbide and other corporations demonstrates to them that an industry may claim that an accident was the result of sabotage or that people are using the incident to gain economic advantage. The wealth of the corporation may be used to minimize its financial responsibility for accidents. The Bhopal tragedy helped to shape these attitudes. It contributed to the mistrust with which people respond to the promises of business and government that toxins from the dump site will not leak into their drinking water, that the smoke from the new factory will not contain particles which will adversely affect health, or that the amount of carcinogens in emissions from the plant is so small that it poses no health threat.

Despite the view of industry to the contrary, however, CAIHRs (or NIMBYs) do not always win their battles. The story of community opposition to the Shoreham nuclear power plant on Long Island, New York, is a pertinent example.

Could the community deny the Long Island Lighting Company its plan to build and operate a nuclear power plant on the north shore of Long Island? Nuclear plant siting was exempt from state and local participation until the Three Mile Island accident. After that, states were required to be involved in formulating evacuation plans. The local Suffolk County legislature determined that since a workable evacuation plan was impossible, the utility should be denied permission to operate the Shoreham plant.

However, powerful interests wanted to see the Shoreham plant open. One indication of this was that the centralist newspaper, the *New York Times*, has called for its opening in many editorials.[31] In 1983, the governor of New York, Mario Cuomo, became involved. At first, hopeful that an evacuation plan could emerge, he established a fact-finding panel "to study various issues including the safety of the plant, whether it is possible to develop a workable emergency plan, and what effect the failure to open the plant would have on the economy of Long Island." By November, the governor's panel had confirmed the community's conclusion that a workable evacuation plan was not possible, legitimizing, according to the *Times*, "the most extreme positions taken by opponents of the nuclear power plant: that its location makes emergency planning impossible, that its economic value is near zero and the large cost overruns are far from over." The community continued expressing its strong opposition to opening the Shoreham plant. "Debra Shecher, President of the People's Action Committee, was the first of more than 125 registered speakers. 'Shoreham must not be opened. . . . Shoreham is a mistake . . . that can only be corrected by abandoning it.' "[32]

By 1989, the governor was desperately seeking a way out of this no-win situation and requested that the state legislature approve a settlement to close the Shoreham nuclear power plant. The legislators agreed to a plan in which the Long Island utility would sell the plant to the state for one dollar in exchange for an annual customer rate increase to Long Island Lighting Company of five percent and other financial measures meant to ensure the financial stability of the company. After the sale, New York would decommission Shoreham, and Long Island Lighting would write off the loss on its federal taxes.[33]

Although it appeared that the affluent Long Island communities had won, this was not the end of the story. The Nuclear Regulatory Commission was not going to concede defeat that easily. Even with the agreement between the state and the utility company essentially accepted, the Nuclear Regulatory Commission granted a full license for Shoreham's operation. Although it was the intent of the state to keep the plant closed, it would soon be apparent that the federal gesture was not symbolic. "Asserting that the Shoreham power plant has become a symbol of the country's commitment to nuclear energy, a top Federal energy official told Long Island business leaders today that the Bush Administration would do everything in its power to prevent the plant from being dismantled."[34]

When residents come up against a hazard in their community that they cannot get rid of or treat in some way, the same cynicism develops as did at Newberry. A paper by Celene Krauss entitled "Community Struggles and the Shaping of Democratic Consciousness," which describes the story of one resident's attempt to clean up a toxic dump site in New Jersey, could have been written by a member of the Newberry community. The loss of faith in democratic processes and the cynicism that developed at Three Mile Island are both present.

> In 1975, when [this respondent] began to suspect that his well water was polluted, his first action was to turn to the . . . Department of Health. As [he] describes this, "I believed that all I really had to do was pick up a phone and call the Department of Health and they would carry the ball from there, because it's their job to protect the integrity of the water supply, certainly the health of my children, my wife and myself, certainly the health of the community. So all I had to do is report it, you know. I blow the whistle and hey, here come the cops. I believed that it was government's job to inform and protect my family.
>
> "I had an abstract image of my country and my nation as an entity which could be trusted . . . if one sings 'My country 'tis of thee, sweet land of liberty . . . ' you're not thinking about congressmen and senators and mayors and town councilmen. You're think-

ing about an abstraction: my country, my nation. I trusted my government. I had a childlike, naive view that government was there to serve me.

"What they really said was to hell with [me], [my] wife, and [my] kids, to hell with the community. We have to worry about an industrial landfill, which is a draw for industrial corporations. Hey, what kind of faith are you going to have in your local government after that? They didn't give a damn about my kids. They worried about hurting industry, about hurting the growth of the town.

"I believed there was justice in the American courts. This is what I always taught my children. When we went to parades I told them to salute the American flag. Now I tell them there is no equity in our courtroom unless you have enough money to pay for it, that the laws are made for the rich and the powerful, and the richest and most powerful are the industrial giants and corporations."[35]

The major difference between this account and the story of Newberry is that the New Jersey residents won their fight after six years and the Newberry community lost. But both groups became soured on basic democratic processes, a much deeper problem than losing confidence in leaders who can be changed. This cynicism questions the legitimacy of making decisions in a democratic society. Pat Smith, who chaired the Newberry Township–Three Mile Island Steering Committee, put it this way.

I intervened with the PUC [Public Utilities Commission]. I was observing what was going on right after the accident regarding a rate hearing, and I did not like the way I was being represented by the consumer advocate staff. They are all a bunch of attorneys. None of them lived in our community, and they are representing me? Bullshit! So I thought, next rate case I would see what I could do. I was very surprised to learn that I could intervene like any attorney. I had all the rights. I could put witnesses on the stand. I said, "Listen to me. I represent the average person, ratepayer."

I wanted to prove to the local person that you do have a voice in government. You have some control. Previously, I had faith in the elected officials. They had a job to do, and they were going to do it. I got involved to have input, and to make it right. And then the decision came down to save Met Ed's life [by granting the rate increase]. Four months of my life. I don't think they heard me. It was like I was pushed aside. What I had to say did not make a dilly damn. Very disillusioning. Very much so. They appreciated Met Ed's problems more than those of the community.

I felt I was going to prove something to the average person—that you do have some control over what happens in your community. You not only pay for Met Ed but you pay for the commissioners' salaries. Now I want people to rethink. It is not as rosy as you think. I want them to start questioning. They have said to me, "What are you? Anti-American?" I am still the type who gets tears in my eyes when they play "America the Beautiful." But things have gotten out of hand. And I can't foresee an elected official straightening it out. I think it takes the average citizen. They better start listening to the average citizen like me.

Are the claims of CAIHRs, Newberrians, and others like them legitimate? Let us return to the example of Three Mile Island and the Newberry community. The gatekeepers found that the contract between Newberrians and Metropolitan Edison had not been violated; that is, the community's claims were not legitimate. On the basis of the findings of the gatekeepers at Newberry, one might conclude that the only illness that residents living near Three Mile Island had was radiation phobia, and, indeed, someone did conclude this. In 1984, Robert Dupont, president of the Phobia Society of America, "convinced the government that fear of a nuclear accident could be a psychiatric disorder" and was granted $85,000 by the Department of Energy to determine if these fears could be overcome with phobia treatment. Dupont claimed that "this fear is widespread, irrational and aggressively exploited by the political opposition to nuclear electricity," and he compared opposition to nuclear power to phobias such as the fear of flying.[36]

More kindly people have said that residents of communities near Three Mile Island perceived themselves to be at risk and this "perceived" risk was "real" to them and therefore must be addressed. However, the implication of these statements is that perceived risk is not real but subjective, whereas the risk assessment of experts is objective and real.[37]

The intent of this book is not to criticize the gatekeepers, who observed the situation in the Three Mile Island area and characterized it as they were trained to. If you have been educated to distinguish a horse and a pig, you cannot say that you have seen a horse when it was a pig that crossed your path. The researchers—psychiatrists, psychologists, epidemiologists, sociologists, political scientists, risk assessment experts—who came to Three Mile Island brought with them the tools of their professions—their instruments, their paradigms, their languages, and their methods of investigation. Contributing to the characterization of the accident as "the most studied nuclear accident in history,"[38] the researchers carefully and thoughtfully applied these tools and found what they had been trained to find. What they found did not entitle the community's concerns to legitimacy.

The issue is not that what these researchers found was wrong, but that what they did not investigate and therefore did not find was unimportant. That cow that crossed their paths was just as real and important as the pig they observed and studied. We maintain that Newberrians' perceptions and concerns were just as legitimate as those that legitimizers would have said merited treatment. We do not subscribe to the view that the people of Newberry were sick with radiation phobia or something of that sort, nor do we support the wrong-perception paradigm that holds that residents should have been reeducated, their thinking revised, reformulated, revamped, and otherwise made correct. In our view, their perceptions were valid and their concerns legitimate.

We are not traditional gatekeepers. Our weakness in comparison to standard legitimizers, however, was our strength in terms of the community. We had no vested interest in medicine, in traditional disaster sociology, in psychology and psychiatry, in risk assessment. We arrived in Newberry as social scientists with a general concern for Middle American communities and their quality of life. We tried to understand what they saw, how they viewed their situation.

## THE LEGITIMACY OF NEWBERRY'S CLAIMS

The issue turns on risk, and the issue of risk has two parts: risk assessment and risk taking, that is, the decision to take a risk. Both risk assessment and risk taking have subjective bases.

Expert risk assessment does not consider a number of factors that would considerably alter calculations of risk. "Some common ways in which experts may overlook or misjudge pathways to disaster include the following:

- Failure to consider the ways in which human errors can affect technological systems.
- Overconfidence in current scientific knowledge.
- Insensitivity to how technological systems function as a whole.
- Slowness in detecting chronic, cumulative environmental effects.
- Failure to anticipate human response to safety measures.
- Failure to anticipate 'common-mode failures.' "[39]

Risk determination is especially uncertain with regard to long-term exposure to low doses of potential carcinogens from dumps, factories, and power plants, the kinds of exposures that arouse public outcry and opposition. While the probability of dying in a train crash or an automobile accident may be reasonably determined, the risks of death from long-term, low level exposure to toxins are much less certain.

Moreover, scientists prefer to err on the side of caution. "Put simply, for the scientist a Type I error is 'an error of rashness,' when one concludes that an effect occurred when in fact it did not. Conversely, a Type II error is 'an error of caution,' when one disregards a real effect because of insufficient proof. . . . The norms of science attempt to guard against spurious conclusions that erroneously support theory; a theory that is truly predictive will be able to survive a stringent test. Accordingly, scientists strongly bias their work in favor of committing Type II errors and avoiding Type I errors. In the context of toxic exposure, a conservative judgment for a government or industry expert means caution in concluding that a place is unsafe."[40]

These observations lend support to Newberrians' view that they could not trust experts' risk assessments and should not be forced to accept decisions based on such imperfect evaluations of risk. Risk assessment is a process that disregards or de-emphasizes some factors that contribute to increased health risks and emphasizes factors which decrease risk.

Less often considered than risk assessment is risk taking, the second aspect of the risk issue that bears upon the validity of the community's claim to have its members' perceptions considered. Even if the probability of an untoward event were well known, decisions to take risks are not based on probabilities alone. Neither communities nor industries want to take every small risk and reject every large risk. Other factors enter into these decisions, including the benefits to be gained by taking that risk and considerations related to social values. Even the assignment of the term *benefit* to an outcome or object is a value judgment. Accepting the notion that a business must maximize profit assumes that profit is valued, that turning a profit is a beneficial consequence of some action. Moreover, even among valued outcomes, some are more valued than others. Accepting the notion that business must maximize profit under certain constraints assumes that some objects or outcomes are more valued than profits. Just as risk assessment is subjective, so is the decision to take risk.

The discrepancies between expert and lay risk assessment often relate not to differences in the perceived probabilities of risk but to differences in what is valued. Dread and potential for catastrophic loss of life are associated with lay risk assessment.[41] Yet finding one event more dreadful than another is a value judgment interjected into the appraisal of risk; deploring catastrophes that destroy communities more than accidents that take single lives is an evaluation based on values. Both indicate that people judge certain kinds of events and conditions as more undesirable than others. It is not simply a matter of assessing the probability of an event's occurrence that determines if a risk is worth taking. Is the desire to avoid events with catastrophic or dreadful consequences, however, inherently less worthy than, say, the desire to avoid losing money?

What view is more myopic than that which maintains that all we need to know in order to decide whether or not to undertake a certain activity (or permit our neighbor to undertake it) is the probability that a negative event will occur? The important decisions are related to how and whether an activity is defined as a risk or a benefit and making rules to decide how to rank those risks and benefits in the order of their desirability or undesirability. These kinds of issues will determine whether a risk is acceptable to either a community or industry. However, when risk assessment experts are called upon to testify to the minimal risks to communities of an industrial decision, they have already accepted, among other things, the industry's value judgments regarding the definitions of risks and benefits and the priorities (i.e., value judgments) that were used to rank them.

These issues enter into communities' decisions about risk taking as well. People in communities do not reject risk out of hand but they ask different questions than industry, and they reach different conclusions because very often they value different outcomes or have different priorities.

In Newberry, people found the risk of a functioning Three Mile Island nuclear power plant unacceptable. What were the values that went into their decision? First, they valued the community, both of the present—the community to which they were physically linked—and of the future—the community to which they were linked in time through their children and grandchildren. They found the idea that their area of Pennsylvania could be made uninhabitable by an accident at Three Mile Island "dreadful." It has a communitarian basis. They feared losing everything in the community, the destruction of their social and physical world. One resident of Newberry expressed a view that we believe most Newberrians held about the physical world in their area:

"I live in the second district of Newberry Township. I've lived there all my life. I am a native. We had a homecoming in our hometown after World War II, and the fellow who spoke at the dinner meeting we had stated that he had travelled the world wide. When it came time to come to retire—he was a colonel— and settle down, he said he would like to settle anywhere between Carlisle [Pennsylvania, near Newberry] and Philadelphia. This whole area of Pennsylvania is so beautiful.

Mrs. Boswell: Maybe we would never be able to come back here. That's a terrible feeling because you don't know what to take, and you have to leave everything here that you bought in a lifetime, things you cherish. You get to take so much, and that's it . . . and you wouldn't get the same as what you had here, and you'd know it was here, and you couldn't come back to it. . . . If there was a meltdown, things would have been much worse. All our families are connected, we are very close. It is good to be home.

Mrs. Hemingway: But then you're thinking, 'What if it really does melt down, and what if you have to leave your home and family and an area that you were born and raised in?' I lived in York [Pennsylvania, nearby] all my life. So my roots are really here. My friends are here.

Mr. Crown: In fact this entire area could be a radioactive wasteland. That bothers me at times. You know how the Carlisle Pike is really packed? Well, we were just sitting at a light, and all of a sudden I said, "Could you imagine what this would be like if TMI melted down? There would be no cars, just be empty." It was just a strange thought at a strange time. But thoughts like that come to my mind.

The residents of Newberry felt a kinship with the community of the future through children and grandchildren, and they considered the effect of an accident on the well-being of that community as well. They found equally dreadful the thought that children, the community of the future, could be harmed on a grand scale, either because of environmental destruction or their inability to live and have healthy children themselves.

Mrs. Willis: I get scared when I think of my grandson and the future. What are we leaving for them? Not very damn much in plain words because we're not leaving them any confidence in their forebears because what we're leaving them is a mess. How can they even survive?

Mrs. Willis's story about her husband's anger during the evacuation illustrates how unacceptable was an accident which threatens a parent's hopes and dreams for their children's future.

> He [her husband] said, "I don't care if we lose everything. He's
> [their son] got to have his things." He said, "It's not right." . . .
> And he came back in and picked that [bowl] up, and I had a cou-
> ple of etched glass dishes, and he picked them up, and he said,
> "Here, pack these. At least we'll have something to give the
> kids."

Newberrians valued equity. They asked, What are the benefits to me, my family, my community, and my society? They asked, Who is taking the risk and who is receiving the benefits? Is there a fair distribution of risk? They decided that there was not, and they were the guinea pigs, the victims.

They valued honesty. They felt as if they had been tricked into accepting Three Mile Island and then lied to about the seriousness of the accident of March 1979. Another resident of the community said:

> "I think I've just got my eyes open. I, maybe I see things a little
> better now because I guess I just couldn't believe that if the fed-
> eral government could say the governor should do this or say this
> or lean this way that they would do it. I figure, well, I like hon-
> esty. I like people to be honest no matter what, and I guess I get
> very disappointed when people, rather than tell the truth, they'll
> tell a half truth or assign to somebody else . . . what they really
> feel. So I guess this is a disappointment to me because I think this
> is the way the world is now. No matter what, they say what they
> feel they should say for somebody else's sake, not what is right."

Newberrians valued all of these—community, honesty, and equity—over profits. Mr. Crown found the risk of the accident more unacceptable because it was the result of putting profits before concern for his family's well-being. Recall his reflection on his stay at home when his wife and children had evacuated during the crisis and a meltdown was still feared.

> "I probably would have slept right through the siren or anything
> if there were any problems. The fact that my children would
> have been deprived of a father, husband, whatever, just because

of someone's profiteering—as far as I am concerned—that doesn't sit very well with me."

Because they perceived the consequences of a nuclear power plant accident as they did, they would have chosen other courses of action had they been making the decisions. They would have investigated other technologies. They would have asked if other courses of action could not result in a better risk/benefit/equity profile.

Mrs. Hemingway: It just seems to me that there are so many alternatives we could explore, you know, that I don't really think we have to go the nuclear route. We obviously need alternate energy sources, but solar could provide heating for houses and water. There's no reason we can't really get into gasohol and alcohol for vehicles. We certainly have plenty of room to grow corn and sugarcane.

They would have preferred other courses of action even if it meant giving up certain conveniences. They would have prioritized risks and benefits differently.

Mrs. Caspar: I don't really mind conserving that much. If people can conserve gas [for cars], why can't they conserve energy? Now I don't mean that I'd like to go back to the scrubboard and all that other kind of stuff. But I don't dry my clothes in the dryer. I hang them downstairs on the line. I'd like an outside line, but that's a sore subject [with my husband]. Anyway, so I hang them downstairs, and I do try to conserve as far as that goes. And look how they conserve gas. So if it's a threat to your life, which gas, if you want to pay the price, it's there. If they can conserve gas for that reason, why can't they conserve energy?

What Newberrians said is that an acceptable risk is not just one with a low probability of occurring but one that has been explained honestly, one that is equitably distributed, one that will not destroy communities of space or time, and one that has not been selected solely on the basis of profit.

In cases of hazardous technologies such as nuclear energy, the choice of whether a community or industry makes better risk-taking decisions is most often a choice between different values and priorities. To argue that one is preferable to the other on some objective level is nonsense. Neither risk appraisal is objective, neither more real than the other. The assessment of risk made by the people of Newberry was as real as that of the risk assessment experts.

## CHANGING PARADIGMS

Three Mile Island said to communities, "Johns Manville, the asbestos manufacturing company, may not be an anomaly." Subsequent events like it said, "Johns Manville is *not* an anomaly." By the mid-1980s, the social paradigm accepted by communities regarding their relationship to industry had changed. The old paradigm said that science and technology in the hands of industry with minimal regulation from government will lead to a better life for everyone. It was based on the belief that industry and people in communities had the same values and priorities, and promises about health and safety therefore meant the same to both.

Communities believed they need not be involved in decision making. By and large, they accepted the decisions of industry with regard to the development and use of new technologies because of their convictions about shared values. Furthermore, communities accepted this passive role because their residents believed technology had become too complex for them to understand and because they accepted the private property axiom that business had the right to make their own decisions unfettered by outsiders. Government would take care of the outliers, it was believed.

Events such as Three Mile Island have demonstrated to people in communities that they do not share the same values with industry and government and would not make the same decisions. Government would place defense interests above the health of the community living near the Hanford, Washington, nuclear weapons plant. Rather than seek more costly alternatives, industries that produce toxic by-products would dispose of toxic waste in rivers, streams, and landfills where they would contaminate local water supplies. The nuclear power industry would risk creating a toxic waste product of which it could not dispose in order to generate electricity profitably. In general, industry would choose short-term profit over consideration of long-term effects to the environment and community health, while government would choose to support industry or its own global agenda.

The paradigms of industry and government and communities thus were actually quite different, although communities were not generally aware of this until the events of which we write; their trust was unfounded. That industry and government were cognizant of the discrepancy is apparent when corporations or government attempt to conceal decisions that reveal their values and priorities. An example is the concealment of information about exposure of nearby residents to radiation from the Hanford nuclear weapons factory. Only through the Freedom of Information Act is it now known that federal officials deceived the public regarding their radiation exposure from the plant:

> Since 1944, when Hanford and nuclear weapons plants in Oak Ridge, Tenn., and Los Alamos, N.M., began to produce materials for atomic weapons and expose civilians to radiation, weapons-industry leaders have taken unusual measures to assure the public that the industry, which has operated in more than 30 states, was entirely safe. But documents made public since 1988, and the Energy Department's own admissions, have made clear that the Government was not always telling the truth.
>
> The worst accidents, mishaps and releases of radiation were kept secret. In instances in which the Government experts knew the public would be exposed to large amounts of radiation, such as fallout from the atmospheric testing of atomic bombs in Nevada during the 1950's, the industry's scientists prepared flawed studies that they asserted "proved" that the public had not been harmed.[42]

The differences in the values and priorities of industry and community is also revealed when industry takes optimistic views of risk that support their business plans or takes risks without knowledge about their consequences.

The new paradigm accepted by communities states that science and technology will accord communities a better life if people interject their values into the risk assessment and decision-making process. The advances of science and technology have social costs. Consequently, the impact of such advances must be weighed in advance by the people who will feel their adverse consequences. People must take an active role in protecting their communities since industry and government have priorities which are inconsistent with those of the community.

Furthermore, communities realize that science in the form of risk and environmental assessment can be used to support the agendas of industry and government and to stall community action. Communities are now aware of the difficulty of "proving" health effects and environmental damage; however, they will act upon imperfect knowledge because the past behavior of industry and government in these realms has begotten mistrust. For example, physician Michael Silverstein, formerly of the United Auto Workers, now writes "Scientific Solutions" for a new journal called *New Solutions*. He intends "to publish articles which are unembarrassed about urging strong action on the basis of less-than-definitive science, but which also explicitly acknowledge gaps, uncertainties and disputes about the knowledge base."[43]

Similarly, Lenita Andrewjeski who lives near the Hanford nuclear weapons plant constructed a "death map" that showed that twenty out of perhaps fifty men along a four-mile stretch of road near the plant had either died of heart attacks or undergone cardiac surgery before reaching their fiftieth birthdays. Although her investigation would not be considered a "sound epidemiological study," she and others who learned of it were activated by its results. Ms. Andrewjeski felt it was "just too many heart attacks for men who lead healthy outdoor lives and [were] still relatively young." Her map was the basis for releasing information about radiation exposure from Hanford and admissions by government officials about years of cover-up.[44]

This use of science is seen as necessary for at least two reasons. First, even other scientists are discredited by proindustry scientists when they challenge findings favorable to industry. For example, Ethel S. Gilbert, a biostatistician who has evaluated the radiation exposure records of workers at Hanford for the Department of Energy discussed Alice M. Stewart, chief researcher for the Three Mile Island Public Health Fund, who will also be studying these records now that they have been released. Dr. Gilbert "said that if Dr. Stewart evaluated the data according to methods accepted in scientific circles, it was unlikely that increases in cancer deaths caused by radiation would be found among the Hanford workers. But Dr. Gilbert said she was concerned that Dr. Stewart, an avowed opponent of the nuclear weapons industry, would evaluate the data in such a way that increases might appear falsely. . . . 'I don't think their methods are particularly appropriate.' "[45]

A second reason for using science in this way is that studies projecting death rates in the future and those attempting to reconstruct population exposures over a long period of time are often inconclusive. For instance, it is difficult to determine an individual worker's radiation dose from a worksite of many years when so many other factors could have influenced his or her health in the years preceding or following employment, or even during the years of employment. Even more difficult is determining doses for individuals living in communities where exposure was less focused and controlled than in the plant. Anthony M. Robbins, a professor of public health at Boston University, said about the worker and community health studies that will be conducted at Hanford, "Conducting these studies is a nice way to look good and be cooperative. None are likely to be conclusive."[46]

## POWER AND PREVENTION

In Newberry, we found people living with a risk that they found unacceptable. Although we maintain that they had a valid way of viewing their risk, no "legitimate" authority wants to grant this perception legitimacy. A community cannot simply decide that it does not want to live with a risk that risk assessment experts have decided is negligible, that doctors have decided has had no effect on their physical health, that disaster researchers have decided has had no impact on community functioning, and that psychologists and psychiatrists have decided has had no significant effect on their psychological well-being. Case closed.

Thus, the issue is not only whether Newberrians' claims were legitimate but also whether the community could legitimately decide whether or not to take the risk. It was a political struggle in which Newberrians were seeking to establish themselves as legitimate decision makers.

The difference between communities like Newberry and industries in disputes over risk taking is that in most cases the industry decides what risks the community will take; the only decision residents make, if they find out about the risks at all, is whether or not they consider them acceptable. Finding a risk unacceptable does not mean ridding the community of it. But this is the situation in which members of communities most often find themselves with respect to hazardous technologies: their risks have been decided for them and there is little latitude for change.[47]

We believe that as Newberrians were the risk takers, they were entitled to decide. The Three Mile Island plant may have been the property of Metropolitan Edison, but the risk of nuclear accident was the burden of the people who lived nearby; they would bear the effects of Metropolitan Edison's actions regarding that property. They were entitled to decide if the risk they had to live with was acceptable or unacceptable.

However, Newberrians' failure to win is more a matter of how they fought for their cause than the justice of their position. Using scientific results as their weapon and believing that ideology played no role in this dispute proved fatal. The community should not have attempted to "psychologize" their cause. Investigations into the extent of the problem were appropriate; however, using the results of the studies, no matter how conclusive, to obtain their ends was a doomed strategy. This was a public policy issue, not a scientific one, and it needed to be fought on those terms. The debate was contained by allowing the battle lines to be drawn by the legal system and the experts. The community needed to frame their cause in terms that would allow them to set the agenda and garner public support. They did not mobilize the general population outside of the Three Mile Island area because their issue had no appeal. The fight needed to be fought in political language in order to obtain general public mobilization. The fight had to be framed within the context of American politics; by psychologizing it, they were on their own and they could not win.

## A New Contract

First, we must recognize that communities cannot go back. The mistrust that spawned CAIHR is based on observation of events like Three Mile Island. These will not be forgotten. Industry and even government have to a large extent lost the good will of communities. Industry deplores this fact, wishing that by simply educating the public they could restore the former era of complacency. However, we believe industry must be educated to the concerns of communities and that the community's perspective must be included in the business plan. The community needs a new contract, one with the teeth of a young lion rather than an old man.

The old contract between industry and communities was rather like the traditional informed consent regarding medical treatment. The relationship between doctor and patient was not simply unequal in terms of the distribution of power but patriarchal. Informed consent was therefore a formality. The physician had already decided the preferable course of action and the patient's role was to ratify it. So with industry, its leaders expected residents of communities simply to accept without question their decisions about hazardous technologies. "We know what's best," they said.

Just as the doctor-patient relationship has changed much since the early 1970s, the relationship between industries and communities must change. The emerging doctor-patient relationship is based on mutual participation. More and more the patient is actively involved in providing information and setting treatment goals. Today, many patients are much more informed by physicians about their conditions, about the potential hazards and benefits of treatments, and about treatment alternatives. Consumerism has entered the old asymmetrical relationship. People seek second opinions and are willing to change doctors if they are not satisfied with the treatment they are receiving. People who are sick want decision-making power, and the patriarchal relationship is being replaced by partnership.

Similarly, the relationship between communities and industries must change. The old contract appeared to be one-sided but it was really reciprocal. Communities promised complacency and noninvolvement in return for economic development. Business decided the risks and whether they were acceptable. Now the contribution to an industry of the host community must be made explicit. People must have informed consent, in the new sense, with regard to hazardous projects near their homes.

## Informed Community Consent

Today the idea that residents should be informed about the risks of industrial projects in their communities would be met with general agreement. But informed is not enough; the emphasis must be on consent. There must be recognition that risk taking is based on more than calculations of the "potential for harm or safety." It is a subjective process, and the people who are taking the risks have a right to impose their own values on the decision to take risks. We advocate the involvement of the community members in such decisions. It is their right to decide since it is their health and safety that are at stake. People should not have to bargain for health. They will always be in a weak position compared to the corporate-scientific complex. They should be entitled and empowered.

There should be democratic participation in the decision-making process regarding environmental risks. More than monitoring, it should be real participation, not phantom democracy. In modern society, outcomes are determined by multinational corporations using complex technological systems beyond the reach of government and public discussion. Instead of people becoming less participative, it is time for them to become more so. Technological decisions must be incorporated into the democratic process. The future shock that we are facing is the result of government and industry failure to make the structural changes that this new order calls for. In the past, social scientists have focused only on the unwillingness of the individual to adapt to these social changes. We believe that it is these institutions that have not responded to the social changes.

Situations like the Three Mile Island accident do not have to end as they did in Newberry. Contracts can be renegotiated. Their renegotiation in the past led to the current state of community dependence with regard to industry decision making. But they can be renegotiated in the other direction as well. We believe Three Mile Island has demonstrated the end result of accepting loss of community power and implicit bargains between communities and their industries. It is not a good result for a democratic society: bitterly resigned citizens, many lacking faith in the democratic decision-making process.

CAIHR (or NIMBY) is a sign that communities are rethinking their relationships with government and the industries in their midst. It is a signal that communities insist that their perceptions and concerns be considered. However, CAIHR is only the beginning. The case of the Shoreham nuclear power plant tells us that if enough power lurks behind an industry project, ways may still be found to overcome the opposition of even the most privileged communities. Middle American and poor communities will have even less chance to influence risk taking.

Some CAIHRs have been more successful than were the Newberrians, yet a political movement beyond CAIHR is needed. A sense of the larger community must be developed in order to aid communities too politically weak or too poor to fight the prevailing business mode. CAIHRs' success will be limited unless many communities join to support each other and a general platform of beliefs about community health and the natural environment. They must become a general political force. Otherwise, business will move to take advantage of poverty and joblessness by increasing the incentives to communities to accept hazardous technologies that may injure their health and environment. Browning-Ferris, one of the nation's largest waste-disposal companies, seeking a new site in New York State, "said it was willing to negotiate a benefits package with any community in the state that was willing to accept a landfill. . . . Besides jobs and an increased tax base, the benefits could include host fees, property value protection and the cleanup of an old landfill."[48]

The Bush administration plan to allow the trading of "pollution rights" is another example of the ways in which a community's ability to determine its risks can be constrained in the absence of a general community movement. Under this plan, businesses will be able to buy and sell the right to pollute without any community input. The plan represents the complete removal of community participation and control from the issue of risk assessment.

## Reordered Industry Priorities

What would happen if industries had to obtain the consent of community residents before imposing health and safety risks on them? You might say industry and government have democracy phobia; they are afraid of real community power. But what would be the result? A restructuring of society, a reordering of priorities? Would that change be for the worse? If such a change were to occur, the strategic plans of industry would have to address community values. Risks would have to be acceptable to the people who would be taking them. Consequences for future generations would have to be considered—their environment, their health, and their ability to reproduce and survive. Risks would have to be more equitably distributed. Risk taking could not be decided on the basis of profit alone. If an industry's risks were unacceptable to communities, that industry would have to change its production methods. If there was no place left to "dump" the hazardous technologies and wastes of production as they are currently designed, production would have to be redesigned to obviate the need for dumping. Such a change would require a new type of economy, one based on alternative development policies, not on the assumption that industry can dump its garbage somewhere in the world or on some future generation.

In order that one company would not be disadvantaged relative to others, industries that misrepresented risks or disregarded community decisions would have to suffer severe consequences affecting their ability to conduct business. Conducting business should be not a right but a privilege that could be revoked if abused. Community values regarding health and safety risks would be included in the strategic plan of every business. Just as now a firm may fail for misunderstanding market-driven forces, it might fail for noncompliance with its social responsibility to communities. The advantage of applying such laws universally is that no one firm would be at a financial disadvantage for incorporating community values into its business plan. All businesses would be on an equal footing in this respect.

Furthermore, to assure that U.S. firms could compete with their world competitors, the federal government would have to enact laws that ensured that the manufacture of imported products complied with these standards. Equally important, U.S. corporations could not be effectively encouraged through tax advantages to move their plants to less restrictive environments.

Transformations already underway are forcing us to reinterpret the distinctive features of private property. In the past, private property had distinguishable attributes—what you earned and what you used were yours. Now, because of the way property is obtained, kept, and intertwined with subsidized technologies, it is hard to call it private because of the great potentialities for public disasters and social costs that are more far-reaching than at any time in history. These can wipe out populations or strikingly alter major ecosystems and social systems. We would be foolish as a nation to maintain our present view of private property in light of the complex technological systems that dominate our societies.

No doubt business leaders believe that community involvement would make conducting business overly difficult. "Will there be any place to put the 'necessary' but hazardous projects?" they ask. Although it might appear to be simpler to achieve their goals without community participation, in the long run this course would not benefit even business. Once an organization is perceived as untrustworthy it cannot pursue "business as usual" and expect mistrust to evaporate. It will take special efforts to reassure citizens that untrustworthy behavior has been addressed and corrected. Business is perhaps more hampered by public mistrust than by community involvement. Endemic mistrust leads to the scrutiny of every action and the disbelief of every industry statement regarding health and safety. When the public mistrusts a business, and that business proceeds as if nothing has happened, almost nothing that industry can say or do will reassure a community about its intentions and actions. From this perspective, the Three Mile Island accident is a laboratory for the study of how a business can create and foster public mistrust and the consequences of that mistrust for the industry. The mistrust did not affect only Newberrians but the nuclear industry as well. It destroyed the social relationships between the community, Metropolitan Edison, the Nuclear Regulatory Commission, and other proponents of nuclear energy.

Moreover, why should not industries consider the values which the community prizes? It appears at first that the community and industry have irreconcilable goals: maximization of profits versus what we might call maximization of quality of life, including health and safety. But the community, in the sense of places like Newberry, is only one level of a larger community that includes geopolitical entities such as Newberry as well as industry. We are all interdependent in the communitarian sense. Price wrote about the possibility of realizing ourselves to be members of wider and wider communities: "As our human sympathies and sense of mutual responsibility encompass segments of society (and, indeed, the national and world communities) far transcending the proximate community, the possibility is raised that communitarian values will lead us to policies of widened scope."[49]

Ideally, this widened scope will include industry and communities of physically proximate individuals. As much as people in communities like Newberry need industry, industry needs the Newberrians of society and their perspective—and not in the old sense that they passively accept business decisions. Industry with its science and technology holds the key to a future to which we can all look forward—an inheritance we will be proud to pass on to our children and grandchildren—but only if the goals of the community to maximize quality of life are incorporated into the business plan. Would we be worse off if industry leaders accepted this notion? We do not think so. We are all interdependent. It should not be industry versus community. It is the community of man, and this grows more apparent as technologies become more powerful and complex.

We observed not antitechnology or antiprogress sentiments in New-berry but great faith in technology, perhaps more than industry itself has. Newberrians believe that technology can solve the problems of declining quality of life. However, they believe that instead of trying to solve these problems, business has been trying to maximize profits at the expense of the quality of life of a significant and growing portion of the population and of future generations. This situation makes the risks of technology unacceptable to them. But risks in the name of creating a more just, a more safe, a more promising world for generations to come are acceptable, are worth taking.

Government needs to foster communality and change the vision of industry leaders regarding community concerns for quality of life. At the same time, government must bring into line corporations that now oper-ate beyond the control of the community and of the U.S. government.

The reflective views of the residents of Newberry tell us about life in this community. In many ways this was an ordinary community with ordinary people, a kind of haven for Middle Americans, decent folks. Perhaps the reader has a better job, reads more, and has a better educa-tion. But we believe the values of the people of Newberry can be recog-nized by most Americans. Both individualism and a sense of community were strong in Newberry, as in the United States in general. The people were concerned not only for themselves but for their families and others in the community. Newberrians, like other Middle Americans, may have known they were powerless, but the enclave in which they lived pro-vided them substance that they did not wish to lose. They were not unencumbered selves but situated ones in the communitarian sense, and they wanted to preserve their situation.[50]

The tragedies of the accident at Three Mile Island and similar events have transformed American communities. The old paradigm has been replaced by the new, at least for Middle Americans who are asked to allow potentially dangerous technologies into their communities. The new paradigm requires a community to examine the "shadow costs" to quality of life and forces it to reexamine its understanding of private property. This is the proper meaning of communality and the new para-digm.

The United States was a beacon along with other Western countries for the democratization of Eastern Europe, and we all stand to gain. Similarly, we will all benefit if communities are seen as a beacon for the democratization of technological risk assessment and risk taking. The Three Mile Island accident occurred more than eleven years ago. Less than ten years from now, the twenty-first century will be upon us. We can enter this century with promise—forward thinking with shared governance—or with institutional lag. Unfortunately, many of our industries and their government regulators operate within the old paradigm. Communities can help them to become progressive and to join the move toward an optimal quality of life in the new century.

The move to community involvement should not be looked upon as a threat to society but as a great democratic movement similar to the emergent grass-roots democratization of Eastern Europe. It has the potential to redemocratize the U.S. citizenry, leading to greater participation, more scrutiny, more consensus building, and more community responsibility. Moreover, it can provide scientists with goals and objectives more suited to a long-term view of life on earth.

Newberrians' perceptions are just as valid as those of the people who put a nuclear power plant in their community and insisted that it stay despite their protests after the accident. We advocate a new contract between industry and communities in which communities hold the power to advise and consent. We advocate this because we think it is just that the people taking the risks should decide what risks are acceptable and because we believe in the values that communities want to interject into the risk-taking decisions: concern for community health, present and future, equity, and quality of life before profits. The reader may not agree with our analysis and conclusions, but at least we have stated them openly. And perhaps, we will provoke a thoughtful consideration of what the reader values and what policies regarding environment and communities are consistent with those values.

# APPENDIX

## STUDY METHODS

OUR FIRST SURVEY was conducted at the request of the Newberry Township Health Committee that had been formed by a community group, the Newberry Township–Three Mile Island Steering Committee. The purpose of the study was to investigate the attitudes of community members about the accident at Three Mile Island and the accident's impact on them.

In October 1979, we drew a probability sample from community per capita tax rolls, which contained the names of every adult member (eighteen years and over) in every household in Newberry Township and Goldsboro. From this list, we contacted 523 people by telephone. Of those contacted, 391 responded, for a response rate of 75 percent. The interviews lasted between forty-five and ninety minutes. All interviews took place between 8 October 1979 and 18 November 1979. The questionnaire was similar to that used by the Behavioral Effects Task Group of the President's Commission on the Accident at Three Mile Island.

Neither the Steering Committee nor the Health Committee had the funds to pay for this undertaking. Therefore, Raymond Goldsteen trained volunteers from the community to conduct the interviews. Because the interviewers were volunteers, he took considerable care to instruct them in the necessity for and method of unbiased interviewing. Training sessions with the interviewers led him to believe that interviewer bias would not be a problem. However, he conducted verification calls to respondents and analyses of the responses by interviewer to assure that the interviewers had not influenced the outcome of the survey. Furthermore, comparison of our results with those of other researchers in the area show our findings to be similar.[1]

We prepared a final report for the Health Committee in 1980. Our results and the events surrounding the decontamination and restart efforts convinced us, however, that we needed to continue our work until the plant was reopened, closed forever, or resolved in some other way. After the first survey in 1979, all studies were conducted independently of the Health Committee.

We endeavored to follow the group of 391 over the next four years. In September 1980 we randomly selected 180 subjects from the original 391 and mailed a questionnaire to each of them. Of this group, 146 responded, for a completion rate of 81 percent. In April 1980, twenty residents and twenty community leaders were contacted for face-to-face interviews.

We attempted to reinterview the entire sample through mail surveys in 1982, 1985, and 1986. The completion rates were 66, 54, and 58 percent, respectively. The final completion rate of 58 percent is conservative, however, since we know that 14 members of the panel died between 1979 and 1986 and that 73 moved, leaving no forwarding address. Thus, it appears that of the original panel, only 304 were still in the community when our 1986 survey was sent. If the completion rate were calculated using this figure, it would be 74 percent. Even if one assumes that no one moved from the original group of 523 except those in our panel (i.e., the 87), the completion rate calculated from the time of first contact in 1979 to 1986 would have been 52 percent. We believe that no matter how one calculates noncompletion, our figures are well within acceptable ranges for longitudinal panel studies spanning seven years.

In spite of these relatively good completion rates, we also studied how the sample had been affected by nonresponse and attrition. The factors that must be considered are how those who moved differed from those who remained in the area and how those who did not respond to the later surveys differed from those who remained in the sample.

When people who moved from Newberry were compared to those who stayed, we found no statistically significant difference on any variable except that the "movers" lived 3.8 miles on the average from the reactor and the "stayers" 3.3. Also, the "movers" had lived in Newberry an average of 11 years versus 16 years for the "stayers." Statistically speaking, the two groups were alike in their attitudes toward nuclear power and were similarly affected by the accident.

We found no differences between nonrespondents and respondents within the panel of 391 except that the nonrespondents lived *closer* to the reactor than the respondents (2.8 and 3.4 miles, respectively). Also, more of them were more opposed to the Unit 2 restart than were the respondents (85 and 73 percent, respectively). At first, this finding puzzled us. Later analysis caused us to suspect that those who lived closest to the reactor wanted to avoid thinking about it. Our questionnaire may well have been an unwelcome reminder of an event that these people preferred to forget.

The last type of noncompletion we need to consider is that which took place in 1979 during the initial telephone interviews. We know that 391 adult residents of Newberry Township and Goldsboro responded from a sample of 523. Were there differences between the respondents and the nonrespondents? On all demographic variables our sample matches the 1980 census description of the community, with one notable exception. Our respondents were disproportionately female while the community was almost evenly divided. The analysis of trends presented in this book, therefore, was based on a weighted sample that adjusted for the sex difference in the initial response. We did this to ensure that our findings were unbiased because we found that women were more likely than men to be upset by the accident. They also differed on several of the other social-psychological variables. The net effect of weighting was to make the community impact of the accident reflect more accurately the less upset and more conservative male response.

The costs of the first study were borne by the Newberry Township–Three Mile Island Steering Committee. Our involvement in that survey, including questionnaire development, training and supervision of interviewers, analysis of data, and report writing, were without remuneration from any source including the committee. We paid most of the costs of later studies. Computer time was donated by the schools with which we have been affiliated, mostly Stetson University and the University of Illinois at Urbana-Champaign.

# NOTES

## CHAPTER ONE

1. D. E. Price, "Assessing Policy: Conceptual Points of Departure," p. 157.
2. M. Weber, *The Theory of Social and Economic Organization*, p. 136.

## CHAPTER TWO

1. Goldsboro Historical Association, *Life and Times of Goldsboro*, p. 8.
2. U.S. Department of Commerce, Bureau of the Census.
3. U.S. Department of Commerce, Bureau of the Census, *Statistical Abstract of the United States, 1986.*
4. U.S. Department of Commerce, Bureau of the Census, *York County, Pa.*
5. M. Rogovin and G. T. Frampton, Jr., *Three Mile Island: A Report to the Commissioners and to the Public*, vol. 1, p. 2.
6. Ibid.
7. Public's Right to Information Task Force, D. M. Rubin, Head, *Report of the Public's Right to Information Task Force to the President's Commission on the Accident at Three Mile Island*, pp. 34–36.
8. Ibid., pp. 36–39.
9. Ibid., pp. 41–45.
10. Ibid., pp. 46, 50.
11. S. M. Lipset, *The Confidence Gap.*

## CHAPTER THREE

1. President's Commission on the Accident at Three Mile Island, J. G. Kemeny, Head, *Report of the President's Commission on the Accident at Three Mile Island*, p. 141.

2. Ibid., p. 90.

3. Ibid.

4. Ibid., p. 91.

5. Ibid.

6. M. Rogovin and G. T. Framton, Jr., *Three Mile Island: A Report to the Commissioners and to the Public*, vol. 1, pp. 21, 23.

7. President's Commission, *Report of the President's Commission*, p. 112.

8. Ibid., p. 134.

9. Ibid., p. 138.

10. Ibid., p. 34.

11. Public's Right to Information Task Force, D. M. Rubin, Head, *Report of the Public's Right to Information Task Force to the President's Commission on the Accident at Three Mile Island*, p. 78.

12. Ibid., pp. 79, 80.

13. Ibid., pp. 79–103.

14. Ibid., p. 97.

15. Ibid.

16. Ibid., p. 103.

17. Ibid.

18. Rogovin and Frampton, *Three Mile Island*, p. 62.

19. Public's Right to Information Task Force, *Report of the Public's Right to Information Task Force*, p. 143.

20. Ibid., p. 145.

21. Ibid., p. 163.

## CHAPTER FIVE

1. E. L. Quarantelli and R. R. Dynes, "Community Conflict: Its Absence and Its Presence in Natural Disasters"; E. L. Quarantelli and R. R. Dynes, "Response to Social Crisis and Disaster"; E. L. Quarantelli, *Disasters: Theory and Research;* E. L. Quarantelli, "The Consequences of Disasters for Mental Health: Conflicting Views."

2. J. Mirowsky and C. E. Ross, "Social Patterns of Distress."

3. A. Baum, R. L. Gatchel, and M. A. Schaeffer, "Emotional, Behavioral, and Physiological Effects of Chronic Stress at Three Mile Island." See also M. A. Schaeffer and A. Baum, "Adrenal Cortical Response to Stress at Three Mile Island."

4. R. L. Goldsteen, J. K. Schorr, and K. Goldsteen, "Longitudinal Study of Appraisal at Three Mile Island: Implications for Life Event Research."

5. B. Barber, *The Logic and Limits of Trust*, pp. 14–15.

6. W. Robbins, "Symposium Marks 3 Mile Island Observance," *New York Times*, 29 March 1983, p. A17.

7. J. L. Wilson, "Appeals Court Reverses Dismissal of Bid for Injunction on TMI Water," *Evening News* (Harrisburg, Pa.), 19 March 1980, p. A3.

8. "What's Venting at TMI is Frustration and Fear . . . As Alternatives Are Ignored." *Philadelphia Inquirer*, 23 March 1980, p. 6L.

9. "Radiation Levels Normal Again: 2nd TMI Meeting Relatively Calm," *Evening News* (Harrisburg, Pa.), 21 March 1980, p. 1.

10. R. Winslow, "Nuclear Decision: Despite Opposition, Three Mile Island Plant Could Reopen Shortly," *Wall Street Journal*, 10 April 1985, p. 1.

11. General Public Utilities Corporation, *Three Mile Island One Year Later*, p. 15.

12. J. Lawrence, "Criticism of TMI Is Given to PUC," *Evening News* (Harrisburg, Pa.), 18 March 1980, sec. 3, p. 21.

13. B. Keisling, "TV Story Killed: River Dries Up by Three Mile Island," *The Guide* (Harrisburg, Pa.), 16 July 1980, p. 1.

14. R. Kapler, "TMI: It's a Paradise Island for the Saboteur," *The Guide* (Harrisburg, Pa.), 6 February 1980, p. 1.

15. R. D. Lyons, "Crews at Reactor Criticize Cleanup," *New York Times*, 28 March 1983, p. A1.

16. M. Rood, "NRC to Discuss TMI-1 Restart Again Feb. 13," *Evening News* (Harrisburg, Pa.), 1 February 1985, p. B3.

17. See note 10 above.

18. P. M. Boffey, "Radiation Risk May Be Higher Than Thought," *New York Times*, 26 July 1983, p. C1.

19. A. M. Weinberg, "The Nuclear Future," *New York Times*, 23 July 1979, p. A17.

20. B. Franke and D. Teufel, "Radiation Exposure Due to Venting TMI-2 Reactor Building Atmosphere," pp. 1–2.

21. E. P. Radford, "Ionizing Radiation," p. 726.

22. Ibid., p. 733.

23. "Met Ed Bills Much Higher," *York Dispatch* (York, Pa.), 27 June 1980, p. 2.

24. B. Keisling, *Project David*.

25. "Epidemiologist Skeptical of Connection: Medical Team Probes TMI-Thyroid Link," *Sunday Patriot News* (Harrisburg, Pa.), 23 March 1980, TMI insert, p. 11.

26. "State Reviewing Activists' Request for Raw TMI Data," *Evening News* (Harrisburg, Pa.), 29 January 1985, p. B1.

27. A. G. Levine, *Love Canal: Science, Politics, and People*, pp. 72, 76, 112.

## CHAPTER SIX

1. E. J. Walsh, "Local Community v. National Industry: The TMI and Santa Barbara Protests Compared."

2. J. H. Sorensen, J. Soderstrom, E. Copenhaver, S. Carnes, and R. Bolin, *Impacts of Hazardous Technology: The Psycho-Social Effects of Restarting TMI-1*, pp. 15–16.

3. E. J. Walsh, "Three Mile Island: Meltdown of Democracy?" p. 60.

## CHAPTER SEVEN

1. M. H. Lessnoff, *Social Contract*, p. 12.

2. Ibid., p. 94.

3. Ibid., p. 7.

4. Ibid., p. 3.

5. B. Barber, *The Logic and Limits of Trust*.

6. H. Gans, *Middle American Individualism: The Future of Liberal Democracy*, p. 40.

7. A. J. Vidich and J. Bensman, *Small Town in Mass Society*, pp. ix, x, 102, 292. See also R. L. Warren, *The Community in America* and *Social Change and Human Purpose: Toward Understanding and Action*.

8. Warren, *Social Change and Human Purpose: Toward Understanding and Action*, pp. 250, 53.

9. Gans, "Middle American Individualism," pp. 39–40.

10. E. G. Mishler, "Critical Perspectives on the Biomedical Model," p. 160.

11. President's Commission on the Accident at Three Mile Island, J. G. Kemeny, Head, *Report of the President's Commission on the Accident at Three Mile Island*, p. 13.

12. See E. J. Bromet, D. K. Parkinson, H. C. Schulberg, L. O. Dunn, and P. C. Gondek, *Three Mile Island: Mental Health Findings;* E. J. Bromet and L. O. Dunn, "Mental Health of Mothers Nine Months after the Three Mile Island Accident"; M. A. Dew, E. J. Bromet, H. C. Schulberg, L. O. Dunn, and D. K. Parkinson, "Mental Health Effects of the Three Mile Island Nuclear Reactor Restart"; P. S. Houts, R. W. Miller, G. Tokuhata, and K. Ham, "Health-Related Behavioral Impact of the Three Mile Island Nuclear Incident"; G. J. Warheit and J. Auth, "Disasters and Mental Health: A Model for Estimating the Psychological Impact of Restarting the Three Mile Island Unit 1 Reactor"; A. Baum, R. J. Gatchel, and M. A. Schaeffer, "Emotional, Behavioral, and Physiological Effects of Chronic Stress at Three Mile Island"; and L. M. Davidson and A. Baum, "Chronic Stress and Posttraumatic Stress Disorders."

13. D. M. Hartsough and J. C. Savitsky. "Three Mile Island: Psychology and Environmental Policy at a Crossroads," p. 1116.

14. E. L. Quarantelli, "The Consequences of Disasters for Mental Health: Conflicting Views," p. 14.

15. Ibid., pp. 17–18.

16. J. H. Sorensen, J. Soderstrom, E. Copenhaver, S. Carnes, and R. Bolin. *Impacts of Hazardous Technology: The Psycho-Social Effects of Restarting TMI-1*, p. 102.

17. Ibid., pp. 125–26, 171.

18. J. H. Sorensen, personal communication.

19. A. Wildavsky, *Searching for Safety*, p. 3.

20. Ibid., p. 228.

21. J. Higginson, "Etiological Factors in Human Cancer," p. 48.

22. M. W. Browne, "In the Human Equation, Risk Perceived Is Risk Endured," *New York Times*, 30 March 1980, p. D22.

23. M. Pavlova, "Education of the Public About Potential Health and Environmental Effects Associated with Hazardous Substances."

## CHAPTER EIGHT

1. N. Sheppard, Jr., "Fraud in Toxicology Studies Charged to Big Laboratory," *New York Times*, 13 April 1983, p. A18.

2. "Plant Owners Admit to Release of Toxins," *Daily Illini* (Champaign, Ill.), 20 June 1989, p. 1.

3. R. E. Taylor, "Chemical Industry Is Seeking to Defeat Toxic-Emissions Reporting Requirement," *Wall Street Journal*, 9 December 1985, p. 8.

4. R. Reinhold, "E.P.A. Said To Bar Tests At Dow In '81," *New York Times*, 25 March 1983, p. A16.

5. U.S. General Accounting Office, *Nuclear Waste: Supplementary Information on Problems at DOE's Inactive Waste Sites*, p. 1.

6. U.S. General Accounting Office, *EPA Slow in Controlling PCBs*, cover page.

7. U.S. General Accounting Office, *Nuclear Health and Safety: DOE's Management and Funding of Environment, Safety, and Health Programs*.

8. P. Shabecoff, "Government Cites Waterways Polluted by Toxic Chemicals," *New York Times* (national edition), 14 June 1989, p. 13.

9. M. Knight, "Toxic Wastes Hurriedly Dumped Before New Law Goes Into Effect," *New York Times*, 16 November 1980, p. A1.

10. U.S. General Accounting Office, *Hazardous Waste Sites Pose Investigation, Evaluation, Scientific, and Legal Problems*, cover page.

11. P. M. Boffey, "Experts Showing Concern on Safety of Burying Toxic Waste in Landfills," *New York Times* (national edition), 16 March 1983, p. A20.

12. U.S. General Accounting Office, *Illegal Disposal of Hazardous Waste: Difficult to Detect or Deter*.

13. U.S. General Accounting Office, *Hazardous Waste: Facility Inspections Are Not Thorough and Complete*, p. 2.

14. U.S. General Accounting Office, *Hazardous Waste: Issues Surrounding Insurance Availability*, p. 2.

15. W. Glaberson, "Coping in the Age of 'Nimby.'" *New York Times* (national edition), 19 June 1988, sec. 3, p. 1.

16. Ibid.

17. Ibid.

18. Ibid.

19. Ibid.

20. Ibid.

21. S. M. Lipset, *The Confidence Gap*, pp. 16, 17, 364, 295.

22. W. T. Brookes, "The Wasteful Pursuit of Zero Risk," *Forbes*, pp. 160–72.

23. S. Hazarika, "Bhopal Payments Set at $470 Million for Union Carbide," *New York Times* (national edition), 15 February 1989, p. 1.

24. B. Meier, "Bhopal Gas-Leak Victims Likely to Face Life-Long Health Problems, U.S. Finds," *Wall Street Journal*, 4 February 1986, p. 8.

25. "Poison Gas Leak at Union Carbide Plant In India Kills Hundreds, Injures 10,000," *Wall Street Journal*, 4 December 1984, p. 2.

26. Meier, "Bhopal Gas-Leak Victims."

27. R. Friedman, J. B. Stewart, B. Meier, and M. Miller, "Parties in Bhopal Case Want Fast Settlement, But Hurdles Are High," *Wall Street Journal*, 12 April 1985, p. 1.

28. Hazarika, "Bhopal Payments Set."

29. W. Morehouse and M. A. Subramaniam, *The Bhopal Tragedy*, p. 54.

30. Y. K. Tyagi and A. Rosencranz, "Some International Law Aspects of the Bhopal Disaster," p. 1110.

31. Editorial. "Open Shoreham." *New York Times*, 23 November 1983.

Editorial. "Yet Another Shoreham Failure." *New York Times*, 17 December 1983, p. 22.

Editorial. "The Pied Piper of Shoreham." *New York Times* (national edition), 24 January 1989, p. 26.

Editorial. "Bobbing and Weaving on Shoreham." *New York Times* (national edition), 17 February 1989, p. 22.

32. M. Oreskes, "N.R.C. Agrees to Take Part In Cuomo's Shoreham Study." *New York Times*, 11 May 1983, p. B4.

M. L. Wald, "Preliminary Shoreham Findings Give Support to Plant's Critics." *New York Times*, 22 November 1983, p. B2.

J. T. McQuiston, "Shoreham Plant Draws Criticism At L.I. Hearing." *New York Times*, 16 December 1983, p. B2.

33. C. D. May, "Nuclear Agency Backs Full License for Shoreham." *New York Times* (national edition), 18 April 1989, p. 32.

34. S. Lyall, "Federal Official Pledges Fight to Save Shoreham." *New York Times* (national edition), 16 June 1989, p. 28.

35. C. Krauss. 1989. "Community Struggles and the Shaping of Democratic Consciousness," pp. 234, 233, 235, 236.

36. H. Kurtz, "U.S. Probes Fear of Nuclear Power: DOE Hires Phobia Expert to Examine Public Concerns," *Washington Post*, 30 October 1984, p. A1.

37. Browne, "Human Equation, Risk Perceived Is Risk Endured."

38. U.S. General Accounting Office, *Three Mile Island: The Most Studied Nuclear Accident in History*, p. 1.

39. P. Slovic, B. Fischhoff, and S. Lichtenstein, "Facts and Fears: Understanding Perceived Risk," pp. 187–88.

40. M. R. Edelstein, *Contaminated Communities: The Social and Psychological Impacts of Residential Toxic Exposure*, p. 131.

41. Slovic, Fischhoff, and Lichtenstein, "Facts and Fears."

42. K. Schneider, "Now the U.S. Asks What Its Radiation Did in the Cold War," *New York Times* (national edition), 29 July 1990, sec. 4, p. 20.

43. Council on Occupational and Environmental Health, National Association for Public Health Policy, "'New Solutions' Will Address Problems of Science Policy," *NAPHP COEH Newsletter*, June 1990, p. 3.

44. J. Coates, "Victims Used 'Death Map' to Connect Cancers, Plant," *Chicago Tribune*, 23 July 1990, sec. 1, p. 4.

45. K. Schneider, "Radiation Records of 44,000 Released," *New York Times*, 18 July 1990, p. A19.

46. Schneider, "Now the U.S. Asks."

47. D. Nelkin and M. Pollack, 1980. "Problems and Procedures in the Regulation of Technological Risk."

48. A R. Gold, "Wanted, Land for Dumping; Benefits Offered," *New York Times* (national edition), 20 July 1990, p. A8.

49. D. E. Price, "Assessing Policy: Conceptual Points of Departure," p. 163.

50. M. J. Sandel, "The Political Theory of the Procedural Republic."

## APPENDIX

1. C. B. Flynn, "Three Mile Island Telephone Survey: Preliminary Report on Procedures and Findings."

# BIBLIOGRAPHY

Barber, B. 1983. *The Logic and Limits of Trust*. New Brunswick, N.J.: Rutgers University Press.

Baum, A., R. J. Gatchel, and M. A. Schaeffer. 1983. "Emotional, Behavioral, and Physiological Effects of Chronic Stress at Three Mile Island." *Journal of Consulting and Clinical Psychology* 51:565–72.

Bromet, E. J., and L. O. Dunn. 1981. "Mental Health of Mothers Nine Months after the Three Mile Island Accident." *Urban and Social Change Review* 14:12–15.

Bromet, E. J., D. K. Parkinson, H. C. Schulberg, L. O. Dunn, and P. C. Gondek. 1980. *Three Mile Island: Mental Health Findings*. Washington, D.C.: National Institute of Mental Health.

Brookes, W. T. "The Wasteful Pursuit of Zero Risk." *Forbes*, 30 April 1990, 145:160–72.

Davidson, L. M., and A. Baum. 1986. "Chronic Stress and Posttraumatic Stress Disorders." *Journal of Consulting and Clinical Psychology* 54:303–8.

Dew, M. A., E. J. Bromet, H. C. Schulberg, L. O. Dunn, and D. K. Parkinson. 1987. "Mental Health Effects of the Three Mile Island Nuclear Reactor Restart." *American Journal of Psychiatry* 144:1074–7.

Edelstein, M. R. 1988. *Contaminated Communities: The Social and Psychological Impacts of Residential Toxic Exposure*. Boulder, Col.: Westview Press.

Flynn, C. B. 1979. "Three Mile Island Telephone Survey: Preliminary Report on Procedures and Findings." NUREG/CR-1093. Washington, D.C.: U.S. Nuclear Regulatory Commission.

Franke, B., and D. Teufel. 12 June 1980. "Radiation Exposure Due to Venting

TMI-2 Reactor Building Atmosphere." Study prepared by the Institute for Energy and Environmental Research, Heidelberg, Federal Republic of Germany, for the Three Mile Island Legal Fund, Washington, D.C.

Gans, H. 1988. *Middle American Individualism: The Future of Liberal Democracy.* New York: Free Press.

General Public Utilities Corporation. 28 March 1980. *Three Mile Island One Year Later.* Parsippany, N.J.: General Public Utilities Corporation.

Goldsboro Historical Association. 1976. *The Life and Times of Goldsboro.* Goldsboro, Pa.: Goldsboro Historical Association.

Goldsteen, R. L., J. K. Schorr, and K. Goldsteen. 1989. "Longitudinal Study of Appraisal at Three Mile Island: Implications for Life Event Research." *Social Science and Medicine* 28:389–98.

Hartsough, D. M. and J. C. Savitsky. 1984. "Three Mile Island: Psychology and Environmental Policy at a Crossroads." *American Psychologist* 39:1113–22.

Higginson, J. 1983. "Etiological Factors in Human Cancer." In *Public Policy, Science, and Environmental Risk,* edited by S. Panem. Washington, D.C.: Brookings Institution.

Houts, P. S., R. W. Miller, G. Tokuhata, and K. Ham. 1980. "Health-Related Behavioral Impact of the Three Mile Island Nuclear Incident." Parts 1 and 2. Harrisburg, Pa.: Pennsylvania Department of Health.

Keisling, B. 1981. *Project David* (pamphlet).

Krauss, C. 1989. "Community Struggles and the Shaping of Democratic Consciousness." *Sociological Forum* 4:227–39.

Lessnoff, M. H. 1986. *Social Contract.* London: Macmillan Education Ltd.

Levine, A. G. 1982. *Love Canal: Science, Politics, and People.* Lexington, Mass.: D. C. Heath and Company.

Lipset, S. M. 1987. *The Confidence Gap.* Rev. ed. Baltimore, Md.: Johns Hopkins University Press.

Mirowsky, J., and C. E. Ross. 1986. "Social Patterns of Distress." *Annual Review of Sociology* 12:23–45.

Mishler, E. G. 1989. "Critical Perspectives on the Biomedical Model." In *Perspectives in Medical Sociology,* edited by P. Brown. Belmont, Calif.: Wadsworth Publishing Company.

Morehouse, W., and M. A. Subramaniam. 1986. *The Bhopal Tragedy.* New York: Council on International and Public Affairs.

Nelkin, D. 1974. *Jetport: The Boston Airport Controversy.* New Brunswick, N.J.: Transaction Books.

Nelkin, D., and M. Pollack. 1980. "Problems and Procedures in the Regulation of Technological Risk." In *Societal Risk Assessment: How Safe is Safe Enough?* edited by R. C. Schwing and W. A. Albers, Jr. New York: Plenum Press.

Pavlova, M. 1987. "Education of the Public About Potential Health and Environmental Effects Associated with Hazardous Substances." In *Risk Assessment and Management,* edited by L. B. Lave. New York: Plenum Press.

President's Commission on the Accident at Three Mile Island, J. G. Kemeny, Head. 1979. *Report of the President's Commission on the Accident at Three Mile Island.* 0-303-300. Washington, D.C.: U.S. Government Printing Office.

Price, D. E. 1981. "Assessing Policy: Conceptual Points of Departure." In *Public Duties: The Moral Obligations of Government Officials,* edited by J. L. Fleishman, L. Liebman, and M. H. Moore. Cambridge, Mass.: Harvard University Press.

Public's Right to Information Task Force, D. M. Rubin, Head. 1979. *Report of the*

*Public's Right to Information Task Force to the President's Commission on the Accident at Three Mile Island.* Washington, D.C.: U.S. Government Printing Office.

Quarantelli, E. L. 1979. "The Consequences of Disasters for Mental Health: Conflicting Views." Columbus: Ohio State University Disaster Research Center.

———, ed., 1978. *Disasters: Theory and Research.* Beverly Hills, Calif.: Sage.

Quarantelli, E. L. and R. D. Dynes. 1976. "Community Conflict: Its Absence and Its Presence in Natural Disasters." *Mass Emergencies* 1:139–152.

———. 1977. "Response to Social Crisis and Disaster." *Annual Review of Sociology* 3:23–49.

Radford, E. P. 1986. "Ionizing Radiation." In *Maxcy-Rosenau Public Health and Preventive Medicine*, 12th ed., edited by J. M. Last. Norwalk, Conn.: Appleton Century-Crofts.

Rogovin, M., and G. Frampton, Jr. 1980. *Three Mile Island: A Report to the Commissioners and to the Public.* NUREG/CR-1250, vol. 1. Washington, D.C.: U.S. Nuclear Regulatory Commission.

Sandel, M. J. 1988. "The Political Theory of the Procedural Republic." In *The Power of Public Ideas*, edited by R. B. Reich. Cambridge, Mass.: Ballinger.

Schaeffer, M. A., and A. Baum. 1984. "Adrenal Cortical Response to Stress at Three Mile Island." *Psychosomatic Medicine* 46:227–37.

Slovic, P., B. Fischhoff, and S. Lichtenstein. 1980. "Facts and Fears: Understanding Perceived Risk." In *Societal Risk Assessment: How Safe is Safe Enough?* edited by R. C. Schwing and W. A. Albers, Jr. New York: Plenum Press.

Sorensen, J. H. 1988. Personal communication.

Sorensen, J. H., J. Soderstrom, E. Copenhaver, S. Carnes, and R. Bolin. 1987. *Impacts of Hazardous Technology: The Psycho-Social Effects of Restarting TMI-1.* Albany, N.Y.: State University of New York Press.

Tyagi, Y. K., and A. Rosencranz. 1988. "Some International Law Aspects of the Bhopal Disaster." *Social Science and Medicine* 27:1105–12.

U.S. General Accounting Office. 1981. *EPA Slow in Controlling PCBs.* CED-82–21. Washington, D.C.: U.S. General Accounting Office.

———. 1987. *Hazardous Waste: Facility Inspections Are Not Thorough and Complete.* GAO/RCED-88-20. Washington, D.C.: U.S. General Accounting Office.

———. 1987. *Hazardous Waste: Issues Surrounding Insurance Availability.* GAO/RCED-88-2. Washington, D.C.: U.S. General Accounting Office.

———. 1981. *Hazardous Waste Sites Pose Investigation, Evaluation, Scientific, and Legal Problems.* CED-81-57. Washington, D.C.: U.S. General Accounting Office.

———. 1985. *Illegal Disposal of Hazardous Waste: Difficult to Detect or Deter.* GAO/RCED-85-2. Washington, D.C.: U.S. General Accounting Office.

———. 1988. *Nuclear Health and Safety: DOE's Management and Funding of Environment, Safety, and Health Programs.* GAO/RCED-88-227FS. Washington, D.C.: U.S. General Accounting Office.

———. 1988. *Nuclear Waste: Supplementary Information on Problems at DOE's Inactive Waste Sites.* GAO/RCED-88-229FS. Washington, D.C.: U.S. General Accounting Office.

———. 1980. Three Mile Island: *The Most Studied Nuclear Accident in History.* EMD-80-109. Washington, D.C.: U.S. General Accounting Office.

U.S. Department of Commerce, Bureau of the Census. 1981. *Pennsylvania.* Washington, D.C.: U.S. Government Printing Office.

———. 1985. *York County, PA.* Washington, D.C.: U.S. Government Printing Office.

———. 1987. *Statistical Abstract of the United States, 1986.* Washington, D.C.: U.S. Government Printing Office.

Vidich, A. J., and J. Bensman. 1960. *Small Town in Mass Society.* Garden City, N.Y.: Doubleday and Company.

Walsh, E. J. 1983. "Three Mile Island: Meltdown of Democracy?" *Bulletin of the Atomic Scientists* 39(3):57–60.

———. 1984. "Local Community v. National Industry: The TMI and Santa Barbara Protests Compared." *International Journal of Mass Emergencies and Disasters* 2:147–63.

Warheit, G. J., and J. Auth. 1983. "Disasters and Mental Health: A Model for Estimating the Psychological Impact of Restarting the Three Mile Island Unit 1 Reactor." Unpublished. (Available in the Disaster Research Center Library, University of Delaware.)

Warren, R. L. 1972. *The Community in America.* 2d ed. Chicago: Rand McNally & Company.

———. 1977. *Social Change and Human Purpose: Toward Understanding and Action.* Chicago: Rand McNally College Publishing Company.

Weber, M. 1964. *The Theory of Social and Economic Organization.* New York: Free Press.

Wildavsky, A. 1988. *Searching for Safety.* New Brunswick, N.J.: Transaction Books.

# INDEX

*Note: Interviews have not been indexed.*

Active Club, 189
Allegheny Mountains, 11
American Cancer Society, 189
Andrewjeski, Lenita, 215
Arnold, Robert C., 132, 139
Associated Press, 12, 201
Atomic Energy Act, 139
Atomic Energy Commission, 4
Atomic Safety Licensing Board, 139

Barber, Bernard, 130
Bechtel Corporation, 136–37
Bensman, J., 179–80
Bhopal gas leak, 192, 201–3
Brennan, William, Jr., 140–41
Brokaw, Tom, 142
Browne, M. W., 189
Browning, Jackson B., 202
Browning-Ferris, 219

Burke, Edmund, 3
Bush administration, 204, 219

CAIHR. *See* Communities Against Imposed Health Risks
Cancer: and Hanford nuclear weapons factory workers, 215; and Newberry residents, 121, 122 (fig. 4, fig. 5), 149–50, 153, 156, 188; and radiation exposure, 142, 143–44; and risk assessment, 189
Carter, Jimmy, 25, 135
Chernobyl nuclear accident, 1
Communities: and control, 179–80; definition of, 3–4; and disasters, 186–87; and informed consent, xvi, 218–23; interdependence of, 221; in Newberry, 3–4, 177; and public policy, 3; relations with industry and government, xvi–xvii, 2, 3, 213–15, 217–23; and risks, 2; and trust, xvi, 177–78

Communities Against Imposed Health
Risks (CAIHR), 200–201, 206, 217,
218–19; success of, 203, 219
"Community Struggles and the Shaping
of Democratic Consciousness"
(Krauss), 204–5
"Consequences of Disasters for Mental
Health: Conflicting Views" (Quaran-
telli), 186
Crumrine, Tod, 197–98
Cunningham, Jordan, 158
Cuomo, Mario, 203

Democracy: changing view of, xv; and
technological risk, xvi, xvii, 219–20,
222
Denton, Harold, 25, 26, 33, 151
Disasters, 117; and Newberry residents,
186–87, 190; psychological effects of,
186; sociology of, 186–87
DOE. See United States Department of
Energy
DOH. See Pennsylvania Department of
Health
Doniger, David, 192
Dow Chemical Company, 193
Dupont, Robert, 206

Eastern Europe, 222, 223
Environmental Protection Agency, 181,
199; and hazardous wastes, 195, 196;
inadequate regulation of, 192, 193–94
EPA. See Environmental Protection
Agency
Epicor II, 133
Epstein, Samuel S., 196

Fabian, Blaine, 22
Floyd, James, 139
Forbes, 200
FMPC (Feed Materials Production Cen-
ter), 193
Freedom of Information Act, 148, 214

Gamble, David, 140
Gans, Herbert, 181
General Public Utilities (GPU), 1, 11,
178; and decontamination of accident, 21; and incompetence of Metropolitan Edison, 135; rate increase of,

144–45, 163, 169; and restart of Three
Mile Island, 140; suit filed against, 133
—Nuclear Corporation (GPUN), 132,
136–37, 138, 139
—Service Corporation, 139
Gilbert, Ethel S., 215
Gokhale, V. P., 201
Goldfrank, Joan L., 135
Goldsboro, 2, 7, 8–9, 35. See also
Newberry
Government: and hazardous waste
monitoring, 196–97; as inadequate
regulator, 192–94; as industry's protec-
tor, 193; and informed community
consent, 219, 222; mistrust of, 191,
192, 194, 197, 200, 217; as polluter,
193; and risk assessment, 194; rela-
tions with communities, xvi–xvii, 2,
3, 213; values of, 213
GPU. See General Public Utilities
GPUN. See General Public Utilities Nu-
clear Corporation
Grimes, Brian, 25
Guide, The. See Harrisburg Guide

Hanford, Washington, nuclear weapons
plant, 213–14, 215
Harrisburg, 12, 131, 132; antinuclear
groups in, 13; characteristics of, 5–6;
distance from Three Mile Island, 10;
population growth in, 9; radiation lev-
els in, 23
Harrisburg Evening News, 133–34, 135,
139–40
Harrisburg Guide, 135–36
Hartsough, D. M., 185
Hegel, G. W. F., 3
Hendrie, Joseph A., 133
Herbein, John G., 22
High pressure injection pumps (HPI),
18–10
Hobbes, Thomas, 176
HPI. See High pressure injection pumps

Impacts of Hazardous Technology: The
Psycho-Social Effects of Restarting
TMI-I (Sorenson et al.), 186–87
Industrial BioTest Laboratory, 192
Industry: and informed community con-
sent, 218–23; mistrust of, 191–92, 194,

200, 217, 221; and NIMBY syndrome, 199; and private property, xvi, 220; relations with communities, xvi–xvii, 2, 3, 213, 217–23; values of, 208–9, 213
Institute for Energy Analysis, 142
Institute for Energy and Environmental Research, 142

Jersey Central Power and Light Company, 11, 144
Johns Manville, 213

Kant, Immanuel, 176
Kemeny, John, 135
Kemeny Commission, 135
King, Lawrence P., 136–37
Klucsik, David, 134
Kneale. See Stewart, Alice M.
Krauss, Celene, 204
Krypton-85, 133, 138, 142–43, 152, 163

Lancaster County, 11, 148
League of Women Voters, 189
Lessnoff, Michael, 175–76
Levine, Adeline, 150
LOCA. See Loss-of-coolant accident
Locke, John, 176
Long Island Lighting Company, 203–4
Loss-of-coolant accident (LOCA), 17, 20. See also Meltdown
Love Canal, 150, 191, 197, 200
Luddists, xvi, 188

Manegold (of Lautenbach), 175–76
Marx, Karl, 3
Maxcy-Rosenau Public Health and Preventive Medicine (Radford), 143
Mechanicsburg, 6
Medical professionals, 187–88, 190; and consumerism, 217
Meltdown, 17, 19, 20, 21, 25–26
Mental health professionals, 184–85, 190
Met Ed. See Metropolitan Edison
Metropolitan Edison (Met Ed), 1, 8, 180, 188; community attitudes toward (prior to accident), 15, 128–29, 178; community mistrust of, after accident, 16, 36, 127–53, 154, 156, 169, 174, 178, 179, 182, 221; decontamination of Three Mile Island, 132, 134,

138, 142, 143, 157, 181 (see also Three Mile Island Nuclear Power Plant accident, decontamination of); development of Three Mile Island, 4, 11, 15; falsification and destruction of records by, 139–40, 153; management of accident by, 20, 21, 22, 23, 26–27, 33, 34; management prior to accident, 134–35, 152–53; news releases by (prior to accident), 11–13; news releases by (after accident), 21, 22, 23, 24, 25–26, 33–34, 127; rate increase of, 145, 163, 169, 205–6; reopening of Three Mile Island, 138, 141, 157, 169, 181, 182 (see also Three Mile Island Nuclear Power Plant, reopening of); social contract with Newberry residents, 178, 179, 182, 190; support by Nuclear Regulatory Commission, 131–32, 138, 141, 151, 153, 181, 182; views on nuclear energy of, 12–13
—Communication Services Department, 11–12
Middle Americans, 181, 202, 207, 219; Newberrians as, 10, 36, 222
Middletown, 8, 13, 26
Middletown Press and Journal, 13
Mueser, Anne Marie, 197–98

Nagasaki, 142
National Environmental Protection Act (NEPA), 163–64
Natural Resources Defense Council, 192
NEPA. See National Environmental Protection Act
New Cumberland, 6
New Jersey Department of Health, 204
New Solutions, 214
New York State Department of Health, 150
New York Times, 136–37, 141–42, 197–98, 203
Newberry (see also Newberry Township): animals in, affected by accident, 146–47, 153; antinuclear action in (prior to accident), 11, 155–65; community in, 3–4, 177; electric rate increase in, 131, 145, 163, 169; physical environment of, 5–8, 14–15; population of, 8–9; residents of (see Newberry residents)

Newberry residents: and ban on nuclear power plants, 171 (fig. 16); and belief in safety of plant (after accident), 27–28; and belief in safety of plant (prior to accident), 128–29, 178; and cancer, after accident, 128, 149–50, 153, 156, 188; characteristics of, 8–10, 36, 116, 222; and disaster specialists, 186–87, 190; evacuation of, 21, 24–25, 26, 28, 117, 142; failure to prevent reopening, 216–17; faith in technology of, 222; fears for health and safety of, 36, 118, 121, 122 (figs. 4 and 5), 128, 146–51, 153, 154, 155, 174; and federal government, 169, 171, 173–74 (fig. 17), 180–81, 182, 183; feelings of powerlessness and resignation of, 36, 116, 165–67 (figs. 14 and 15), 168–69, 171 (fig. 16), 173 (fig. 17), 174, 175; hypothyroidism in infants of, 148; and mental health professionals' findings, 184–85, 190; mistrust of authorities associated with accident, 16, 23, 36, 116, 127–53 (figs. 8, 9, 10, and 11), 154, 156, 174, 175, 178, 179, 182, 221; opposition to re-opening by, xv, 156–58 (figs. 12 and 13), 163–65, 182; perceived danger by, 118, 119 (figs. 1 and 2), 120, 121 (fig. 3); perceived decline in quality of life of, 118, 126–27, 154; and physicians' findings, 187–88, 190; psychological distress of, 118, 125–26 (fig. 6), 127, 153, 154, 157, 168, 174, 175, 182, 184–85, 187; radiation exposure of, 34, 118, 127–28, 132, 133, 141–44, 156, 188; ratepayers' strike by, 145; reactions to accident by, 26–29, 34, 117; relocation of, 155; and risk assessment, 188–90, 209–12, 222; social contract with Metropolitan Edison, xvii, 178, 179, 182, 190; values of, 9–10, 15, 116, 168, 211
Newberry Township, 2, 7, 8–9, 35. See also Newberry
Newberry Township Health Committee, 157
Newberry Township–Three Mile Island Steering Committee, 157, 158, 162, 163, 205
NIMBY Syndrome. See Not in My Back Yard Syndrome

Not in My Back Yard (NIMBY) Syndrome, xv, xvi, 2–3, 203, 218–19 (see also Communities Against Imposed Health Risks); definition of, 197; methods of, 199; strategies to discredit, 198–200
NRC. See Nuclear Regulatory Commission
Nuclear energy, 12–13, 142
—industry, 1–2, 150, 169
Nuclear Regulatory Commission (NRC), 8, 188; community attitudes toward (prior to accident), 15; community mistrust of, after accident, 23, 36, 131–32, 137–41, 150–51, 153, 154, 174, 178, 221; and decontamination of Three Mile Island, 142; news releases by (after accident), 21, 22, 23–24, 25–26, 33–34, 117; restart hearings of, 138–40, 163–65, 185; role during Three Mile Island accident, 20, 21, 22–26, 33, 34; and Shoreham nuclear power plant, 204; support of Metropolitan Edison by, 131–32, 138, 141, 151, 153, 181, 182
—Special Inquiry Group, 11

PANE. See People Against Nuclear Energy
Pantex Plant, 193
PEMA. See Pennsylvania Emergency Management Association
Pennsylvania Department of Health (DOH), 148–50, 181, 188
—Division of Epidemiological Research, 148
Pennsylvania Electric Company, 11
Pennsylvania Emergency Management Association (PEMA), 24
Pennsylvania Power and Light Company, 145
People Against Nuclear Energy (PANE), 157
People's Action Committee, 203
Perceptronics, 189
Philadelphia Inquirer, 133
Phobia Society of America, 206
Pilot-operated relief valve (PORV), 18–19, 20, 139
PORV. See Pilot-operated relief valve
President's Commission on the Accident

at Three Mile Island, 17, 18, 20, 21, 22, 134, 184. *See also Report of the Public's Right to Information Task Force to the President's Commission on the Accident at Three Mile Island*
—Behavioral Effects Task Group, 184–85
Price, David E., 3, 221
Price-Anderson Act, 141
Project David, 145–46
PUC. *See* Public Utility Commission
Public Utility Commission, 134, 144, 147, 205–6
Public's Right to Information Task Force, 21, 24

Quarantelli, E. L., 186

Radford, Edward P., 143
Radiation, 142; debate over effects of, 141–44, 153; exposure of Hanford nuclear weapons factory workers to, 214, 215; exposure of Newberry residents to, 34, 118, 127–28, 132, 133, 141–44, 156, 188; exposure to, and cancer, 142, 143–44; levels of, in Harrisburg, 23; off-site levels of, 20, 21, 22–23, 25; release of contaminated water into Susquehanna, 20, 132–33; released during accident, 1, 20, 21, 24, 34, 142–43
Rambo, Sylvia H., 132–33
RCRA. *See* Resource Conservation and Recovery Act
Reagan Administration, 174
Reiber, Mike, 135
*Report of the Public's Right to Information Task Force to the President's Commission on the Accident at Three Mile Island*, 12–13. *See also* President's Commission on the Accident at Three Mile Island
Resource Conservation and Recovery Act, 196
Risk assessment, 2; and cancer, 189; democratization of, xvi, xvii, 219–20, 222; by government, 194; mistakes made by experts, 207; and Newberry residents, 188–89, 190, 209–12, 222; and nuclear energy, 189, 212; used to discredit NIMBYs, 200; and value judgments, 208–9, 212–13, 220; and

value judgments of Newberry residents, 209–12
Robbins, Anthony M., 215
Rood, Mick, 139
Rousseau, Jean-Jacques, 176
Rubin, D., 21
Ruckelshaus, William, 199

Savitsky, J. C., 185
"Scientific Solutions" (Silverstein), 214–15
Scranton, William, 23, 24–25
Shecher, Debra, 203
Shoreham nuclear power plant, 203–4, 219
Silverstein, Michael, 214–15
*Small Town in Mass Society* (Vidich and Bensman), 179–80
Smith, Ivan W., 140
Smith, Pat, 162, 165, 205
*Social Change and Human Purpose: Toward Understanding and Action* (Warren), 180
Social contracts, 175–77; medical treatment as, 179, 183–84, 217; and trust, xvi, 177–78; violation of, 178–79
Sorenson, J., 186–87
Sterling, Phyllis, 197–98
Sternglass, Dr. Ernest, 141
Stewart, Alice M., 142, 215
Susquehanna River, 5, 6, 7, 8, 10, 35, 135; release of radiation-contaminated water into, 20, 132–33
Susquehanna Valley Alliance (SVA), 132–33
SVA. *See* Susquehanna Valley Alliance

Thornburgh, Richard, 26, 28, 142
Three Mile Island, 10–11, 15
Three Mile Island-Alert (TMIA), 140, 157
Three Mile Island Nuclear Power Plant: accident at (*see* Three Mile Island Nuclear Power Plant accident); attempts to keep closed, xv; attitudes toward (prior to accident), 13–14, 15; news releases concerning (prior to accident), 11–13; proximity to nearby communities, 8; reopening of, 4, 126, 138–41, 152, 156–58 (figs. 12 and 13), 163–67 (figs. 14 and 15), 169, 174, 181,

T.M.I. Nuclear Power Plant (*cont.*)
182, 187; security of, 135–36; Unit 1—
4, 11, 125, 126, 131, 132, 138, 139, 140,
141, 156, 157, 163, 164, 166, 169, 174,
181, 182; Unit 2—1, 11, 16, 17, 18, 131,
132, 134, 135, 139, 142, 143, 153, 156,
157, 166, 169, 181
Three Mile Island Nuclear Power Plant
accident, 1, 16–21; community reactions to, 26–29; decontamination alternatives, 133, 143; decontamination
of, 17, 21, 26, 34, 131, 132–38, 142, 143,
153, 155–56, 157, 169, 181; effects on
animals, 146–47, 153; evacuation precipitated by, 21, 24–25, 26, 28, 117,
142; and equipment malfunction, 21,
24; and hydrogen bubble, 25–26, 34;
and off-site radiation levels, 20, 21,
22–23, 25; and operator error, 21, 23–
24; and possibility of meltdown, 17,
19, 20, 21, 25–26; radiation released
during, 1, 20, 21, 24, 34, 134, 142–43;
and subsequent population growth, 9;
as violation of social contract, xvi,
177–79
Three Mile Island Public Health Fund,
215
"Three Mile Island: Psychology and Environmental Policy at a Crossroads"
(Hartsough and Savitsky), 185
Times Beach, 191, 197, 200
Tocqueville, Alexis de, 3
Tokuhata, Dr. George, 148
TMIA. *See* Three Mile Island-Alert
Trust, 130–31; and social contract, xvi,
177–79

UCS. *See* Union of Concerned Scientists
Union Carbide, 201–3. *See also* Bhopal
gas leak
Union of Concerned Scientists (UCS),
140, 142, 143
United Auto Workers, 214
United News of India, 201
United Press International, 12, 201
United States:
—Congress, 24, 192, 193, 194
—Court of Appeals for the District of
Columbia, 163
—Department of Energy, 137, 193, 194,
206, 214, 215
—General Accounting Office, 193–94,
195, 196, 197
—Middle District Court, 132

Vidich, Arthur, 179–80
Vietnam War, 199

*Wall Street Journal*, 134, 140
Walsh, E. J., 157, 174
Warren, R. L., 180
Waste disposal (hazardous), 193–97
Watergate scandal, 199
Weber, Max, 3
Weinberg, Alvin M., 142
Weiss, Ellyn, 140
Wilson, Cher, 135
Winslow, Ron, 140

York county, 11
York *Dispatch*, 145